*f*P

DEATH OF A DISSIDENT

The Poisoning of Alexander Litvinenko
and the Return of the KGB

ALEX GOLDFARB WITH
MARINA LITVINENKO

FREE PRESS
New York   London   Toronto   Sydney

Free Press
A Division of Simon & Schuster, Inc.
1230 Avenue of the Americas
New York, NY 10020

First Free Press hardcover edition May 2007

FREE PRESS and colophon are trademarks of Simon & Schuster, Inc.

For information about special discounts for bulk purchases,
please contact Simon & Schuster Special Sales at 1-800-456-6798
or business@simonandschuster.com

Manufactured in the United States of America

1   3   5   7   9   10   8   6   4   2

Library of Congress Cataloging-in-Publication Data

Goldfarb, Alexander.
Death of a dissident: the poisoning of Alexander Litvinenko and the return
of the KBG / Alex Goldfarb; with Marina Litvinenko.
p. cm.
1. Litvinenko, Alexander, 1962–2006. 2. Dissenters—Russia (Federation)—Biography.
3. Federal'naia sluzhba bezopasnosti Rossii. 4. Political crimes and offenses—Russia
(Federation) 5. Russia (Federation)—Politics and government—1991– I. Litvinenko,
Marina, 1962– II. Title.
DK510. 766.L58G65 2007
327.12470092—dc22
[B]   2007012510

ISBN-13: 978-1-4165-5202-4
ISBN-10: 1-4165-5202-2

To Sasha

CONTENTS

CONTENTS

PART IV:
THE MAKING OF A PRESIDENT
(Russian-Style)

PART V:
THE RETURN OF THE KGB

CAST OF CHARACTERS

THE SPIES

Barsukov, Mikhail Ivanovich, director of the FSB (1995–1996)

Khokholkov, Evgeny Grigorievich, head of the FSB's Division of Operations against Criminal Organizations (URPO)

Kovalev, Nikolai Dmitrievich, director of the FSB (1996–1998)

Trofimov, Anatoly Vasilievich, Moscow FSB chief (1994–1997), assassinated in 2005

Volokh, Vyacheslav Ivanovich, head of the FSB's antiterrorism unit (ATC) (1993–1998)

THE WHISTLE-BLOWERS

Gusak, Alexander Ivanovich, Sasha's supervisor in URPO

Litvinenko, Alexander Valterovich (Sasha), poisoned in 2006

Ponkin, Andrei Valerievich, Sasha's second in command

Shebalin, Viktor Vasilievich, member of Sasha's URPO unit (possibly a mole)

THE OLIGARCHS

Abramovich, Roman Arkadievich (Roma), former partner of Berezovsky, co-owner of Sibneft

Berezovsky, Boris Abramovich, former controlling partner in ORT television, owner of LogoVAZ and co-owner of Sibneft, deputy secretary of National Security Council (1996–1997)

Gusinsky, Vladimir Alexandrovich (Goose, Volodya), former owner of NTV television and Most-Bank

Potanin, Vladimir Olegovich, head of Unexim Bank, first deputy prime minister (1996)

THE REFORMERS

Chernomyrdin, Viktor Stepanovich, prime minister (1992–1998)

Chubais, Anatoly Borisovich, first deputy prime minister (1994–1996)

Gaidar, Yegor Timurovich, prime minister (1991–1992)

Malashenko, Igor Evgenievich, founder and former president of NTV

Nemtsov, Boris Yefimovich, first deputy prime minister (1997–1998)

Rybkin, Ivan Petrovich, speaker of the Duma (1994–1996), secretary of National Security Council (1996–1998), presidential candidate (2004)

Soros, George, American philanthropist

Yeltsin, Boris Nikolaevich, president of the Russian Federation (1991–1999)

Yeltsin, Tatyana Borisovna (Tanya), daughter of Boris

Yumashev, Valentin Borisovich (Valya), journalist, Yeltsin's chief of staff, married Tatyana Yeltsin

THE AUTOCRATS

Korzhakov, Alexander Ivanovich, head of Yeltsin's security (FSO) (1991–1996)

Kulikov, Anatoly Sergeevich, minister of the interior (1995–1999)

Lebed, Alexander Ivanovich, chief of Yeltsin's National Security Council

Primakov, Evgeny Maksimovich (Primus), foreign minister (1996–1998); prime minister (1998–1999)

Skuratov, Yuri Ilyich, prosecutor general (1995–1999)

Voloshin, Alexander Stalievich, Putin's chief of staff (1999–2003)

CAST OF CHARACTERS

THE REBELS

Dudayev, Dzhokhar, first president of Chechnya (1991–1996), assassinated

Maskhadov, Aslan, third president of Chechnya (1997–2005), killed in a raid

Udugov, Movladi, Islamist leader, member of Dudayev and Maskhadov governments, in exile since 1999

Yandarbiyev, Zelimkhan, second president of Chechnya (1996–1997), assassinated

Zakayev, Akhmed, minister of culture, foreign minister, in exile since 2002

THE TERRORISTS

Barayev, Arbi, warlord, killed in 2001

Barayev, Movsar, leader of Moscow theater siege, killed in 2002

Basayev, Shamil, warlord, killed in 2006

Gochiyayev, Achemez, suspect in Moscow apartment bombings, denies involvement, now in hiding

Khattab, Amir, Jordanian-born warlord, leader of Wahhabi, killed in 2002

Raduyev, Salman, warlord, died in Russian custody in 2002

THE INVESTIGATORS

Felshtinsky, Yuri Georgievich, coauthor with Sasha, *Blowing Up Russia*

Kovalyov, Sergei Adamovich, human rights activist, Duma member

Morozova, Tatyana and Aliona, survivors of Moscow apartment bombings

Politkovskaya, Anna Stepanovna, journalist at *Novaya Gazeta*, assassinated in 2006

CAST OF CHARACTERS

Schekochihin, Yuri Petrovich, Duma member, journalist, poisoned in 2003

Tregubova, Elena Viktorovna, journalist and author of *Tales of a Kremlin Digger*

Trepashkin, Mikhail Ivanovich, maverick FSB officer, lawyer, arrested in 2003

Yushenkov, Sergei Nikolaevich, Duma member, leader of Liberal Russia, assassinated in 2003

THE SUSPECTS

Kovtun, Dmitry, businessman, former GRU officer

Lugovoy, Andrei, businessman, former FSB officer

Putin, Vladimir Vladimirovich (Volodya), FSB director (1998–1999), prime minister (1999), president (2000—present)

Sokolenko, Vladislav, former FSB officer

DEATH OF A
DISSIDENT

AUTHOR'S NOTE

This is a very personal story of one man's life and death, but it is also the story of historic events and the deeds and misdeeds of world leaders.

I have written the personal story with the benefit of firsthand knowledge. I have written the history with confidence that it conveys Sasha Litvinenko's beliefs and conclusions, and my own. I do not propose that I am a neutral observer. I do maintain that I am an honest one and one who, with Marina's assistance, can best speak for Sasha.

All quotations from conversations are based on my own recollections or on the recollections of direct participants in those conversations. Others may remember the conversations differently, and others have put forward different accounts of the historic events recounted here. The ultimate truth may be determined by history. My truth, and Sasha's, is here for the reader.

Part I

THE MAKING OF A DISSIDENT

CHAPTER 1

ASYLUM

New York. October 25, 2000

My cell phone rang before dawn.

"*Salut,*" a voice said. "Where are you?" It was Boris Berezovsky, who until a few months earlier had been one of Russia's richest and most powerful oligarchs. Now he was an expatriate. He was calling from his house in Cap d'Antibes in the south of France. He had fallen out with Russia's new president, Vladimir Putin—whom Boris himself had groomed for the job—and announced that he would not return to Russia from a vacation in France. Putin was busily purging Berezovsky's people, who were ubiquitous, from Russia's power structure. Boris was mindful of wiretapping, so he could not begin the conversation until I assured him I was not in Russia.

"Do you remember Sasha Litvinenko?" Boris asked.

I did. A member of the organized crime division of the Federal Security Bureau (FSB), the KGB's successor agency, Lt. Col. Alexander (Sasha) Litvinenko was one of Boris's men. Two years earlier, he had become a national celebrity after calling a press conference where, flanked by four masked officers who supported his allegations, he claimed that some rogue generals in the FSB had plotted to assassinate Berezovsky. This happened shortly after Boris Yeltsin replaced the previous FSB director, a seasoned three-star general, with Putin, who was then a low-level ex-spy and a dark horse from the Kremlin administration.

Going against *Kontora* (the Company) on prime-time TV did not sit well with the folks at Lubyanka HQ. Shortly afterward, Litvinenko was arrested on a charge concocted by Internal Affairs that he had beaten up a suspect some years earlier. He spent several months in Lefortovo, the infamous investigative prison of the old KGB. I had asked Boris to introduce me to Sasha at the time, because I was running a public health project under George Soros to contain an epidemic of TB in Russian prisons. I wanted to quiz Sasha about the medical services in Lefortovo. I had gained access to the regular prisons of the Justice Ministry, but Lefortovo, an FSB domain, was off-limits. Any occasion to meet a former inmate was a chance to begin to assess the state of that secret place.

"Yes, I remember Litvinenko," I said.

"Well, he's in Turkey," said Boris.

"You call at 5 a.m. to tell me that?"

"He's fled."

Sasha was hiding in a hotel on the Mediterranean coast with his wife and son, preparing to hand himself over to the Americans. Could I be of help, Boris inquired, as "an old dissident, and an American to boot? We believe you're the only one who can help him."

"Why is that?"

"Because you have the right connections."

———————

A few hours after Boris's call, and after I had spoken by phone with Sasha himself, I walked into the Old Executive Office Building in Washington, D.C., for a meeting with an old friend, a Russian specialist who worked on President Clinton's National Security Council.

A relaxed policeman briefly glanced at my ID. It was still almost a year before September 11. The U.S. presidential elections were just two weeks away and nobody in Washington cared all that much about Russia. I made it into the building in a few short seconds.

"I can give you ten minutes," my friend said. "So what's the urgent matter you can't discuss over the phone?"

I told him about Litvinenko and that I was planning to go to Turkey and bring him over to our embassy.

"As an official of the U.S. government, I have to tell you that we are not in the business of luring Russian agents into defections," he replied. "As your friend, I'll tell you: don't get involved. Such matters are for professionals, which you are not. There'll be unforeseen circumstances, trust me. It can become dangerous. Once you get into this, you will not be in control. One thing will lead to another, and there's no telling where you'll end up. So my advice to you: Go home and forget the whole thing."

"And what will happen to Litvinenko?" I asked, remembering Sasha's anxious voice on the phone.

"That's not your problem," he replied. "He's a big boy and he knew what he was doing."

"What would happen if he walked into our embassy on his own?"

"First of all, they won't let him in. They have serious security issues there. Ankara isn't Copenhagen. By the way, what kind of documents does he have?"

"I don't know."

"Second, even if he does get in, he'll be talking to consular officials whose job"—he smiled—"is to keep people out of America."

"But he's not an ordinary applicant for a tourist visa."

"Well, if he can prove that, then maybe"—he hesitated, picking the right word—"*other people* will talk to him. In theory, they could put in a word for him, but that would depend . . . "

"On what he can offer them?"

"You got it."

"I have no idea what he could offer them."

"There, you see, I told you: you're no professional." My friend smiled at me as I got up to leave.

———————

I had already decided not to take his advice. I had once been a dissident, a Jewish biologist in Moscow who agitated against the Soviet regime. I had gotten out in 1975. My father, also a scientist, was a well-known refusenik who could not get permission to leave for another decade after me. Helping people escape the clutches of Moscow was in my blood. I was soon on a plane to Turkey.

If you didn't know better, the Litvinenko family, staying in a small seaside hotel, looked like Russian tourists, typical of those who crowded the south coast of Turkey. The fit paterfamilias took his morning run on the beach, his pretty wife sported a week-old tan, and their mischievous six-year-old boy raised no suspicions among the locals, for whom tourists from the north are the main fuel of the economy.

But a closer inspection revealed the strain affecting the fugitives. It was in the way Sasha peered at every new person around, in Marina's tear-puffed eyes, and in little Tolik's need for constant attention from his parents.

Turkey is one of the few places where visitors from Russia can enter without a visa, or rather, by buying one for $30 at the border. Marina and Tolik had entered on ordinary Russian passports from Spain, where they had gone on a tour. Sasha's documents were false; he showed me a passport from one of the ex-Soviet republics, with his photograph but a different name.

"How did you get it?"

"Have you forgotten where I used to work? A hundred friends are worth more than a hundred rubles, as they say."

"But how do we prove that you're you?"

He showed me his driver's license and his FSB veteran card as Lieutenant Colonel Litvinenko.

"Tell me, have your watchers in Moscow discovered that you're gone?"

"Yes, they've been looking for me for the past week."

"How do you know?"

"We called my mother-in-law."

"If you called from here, then they know you're in Turkey."

"I used this," he said, showing me a Spanish calling card. "You go through an access number in Spain so the call can't be traced. They are thinking that we are in Spain."

"You shouldn't have called. I would not be surprised if they have already reported you to the Interpol for robbing a bank."

"Listen, I had to let our parents know we're all right. They didn't know we were leaving." Sasha's light gray eyes momentarily flashed with defiance. "Damn the bastards, they're chasing us like rabbits!"

Marina and I exchanged glances. This was his first emotional outburst over several hours of conversation, but I could see that staying calm was an effort for him.

The next day we rented a car and drove north to Ankara. We sped along the empty highway through a cloudless night in a rocky desert, and Sasha told me stories about the FSB to keep me awake at the wheel.

In Ankara's Sheraton hotel, we were met by Joseph, a small, punctilious American lawyer, a specialist on refugee matters whom I had contacted before leaving for Turkey. Boris Berezovsky was footing the bill, so Joseph kindly agreed to fly in for a few hours from Eastern Europe, where he was on business.

Joseph explained that to claim asylum Sasha should have entered the United States first. Outside America, he could apply only for a refugee visa, and there was an annual quota. He would have to wait for months, maybe years.

"In their day, Soviet refugees were allowed into America easily," I said.

"Well, that was the cold war," Joseph explained. "In theory, there is an expedient form of entry, which we call 'parole for reasons of public interest.' You need a top-level decision for that.

"In any case, I recommend that your friends apply formally for admission as refugees, so that the documents are in the system, and then have them wait in Turkey while you go to Washington and try to pull some strings."

"Joseph, after all, Sasha is a KGB officer and not some ordinary refugee."

"I can tell you a secret," the lawyer said. "The CIA keeps a stash of clean green cards. All they have to do is fill in the name. If they need the person, he ends up in Washington in a few hours, bypassing all the immigration procedures. But that's a deal you have to make. You give them goods, they give you protection. You have to decide: either you're fleeing from tyranny, or you're dealing in secrets. It's hard to combine the two."

I translated for Sasha.

"I have to review my portfolio," he said sarcastically.

Joseph gave Sasha one final warning before saying good-bye. "In any case, if it comes to horse trading, be firm: your visa comes first, then you give them whatever they want."

––––––––––

In the late afternoon of October 30, as the holder of an American passport, I led the Litvinenkos to the citizens' entrance of the American Embassy in Ankara, past the line of less fortunate humans stretching along the embassy fence under the supervision of two police cars.

I had given the embassy several hours' advance notice, so they were expecting us. A young man said, "Welcome to the United States Embassy. I am the consul. Please let me have your documents, Mr. Litvinenko." A marine took away our mobile phones and handed us guest passes on metal chains.

We were led through an empty courtyard. Our host entered a combination into the digital lock, the metal door screeched open, and yet another marine led us into a strange room without windows. In the middle was a table with chairs, with a ceiling fan rotating overhead. A video camera stared at us from the wall, with a monitor underneath. Sasha and I exchanged glances. This was "the bubble," the type of soundproof room that appears in countless spy novels. As soon as we sat down, the door opened and another American, around forty and wearing dark glasses, came in.

"This is Mark, my colleague from the political section," the consul said.

Just as my Washington friend had told me, I thought. People from the consulate and "other people."

"Well, Mr. Litvinenko," the consul said. "How can we help you?"

The rest followed our lawyer's scenario. Sasha told them his story and asked for asylum for himself and his family, and the consul replied that he understood their situation and he sympathized, but embassies don't grant asylum. As for a refugee visa, that process takes time, please fill out the form, we'll try to speed it up, but the decisions are made in Washington.

I said that I would try to get advanced parole for them in Washington.

"That makes sense," agreed the consul.

Despite the fan, it was hot in the bubble, and we were thirsty. Tolik grew quiet, sensing that something very important was happening. Fat tears rolled down Marina's cheeks.

"In view of Mr. Litvinenko's special circumstances," I said, "there are reasons to fear for their safety. Could they be settled in some secure place, perhaps where embassy personnel live, while their case is being considered?"

"Unfortunately, we cannot do that."

"Which hotel are you staying in?" Mark spoke for the first time.

"The Sheraton."

"I think you're exaggerating the danger. The Sheraton is an American site, and we are in a Muslim country. There is a threat of terrorism, so they have decent security at the Sheraton. I'd like to have a few words with Mr. Litvinenko alone." And before I could even ask the question, he added, "We won't need a translator."

Sasha nodded, and we left. The consul led us to the gate, returned our passports, and wished us luck. I took Marina and Tolik to the hotel. We walked in silence past the handrails for visa seekers; by now the lines were empty. The street was still blocked off. There was no traffic, and the air was still. I glanced at high-rise buildings visible over the tops of the trees. Behind one of those windows Russian agents must be lurking, aiming their binoculars, taking pictures of us. I hoped the Americans would at least have the sense to escort Sasha back to the hotel.

———

Mark called nearly four hours later, when it was already dark: "You may come and pick up your friend."

The hotel was within walking distance of the embassy, but Sasha wasn't ready to face his family yet. "Let us drive around a while," he said, climbing into a yellow Zhiguli cab. "I need some time to pull myself together."

"What took so long?" I could not wait to hear what happened.

"It took them a while to crack me," said Sasha.

"What do you mean, 'crack'?"

"Well, make me talk. There was a secure hookup with Washington. And the guy on the other side—by the way, he looked as if he was your twin brother—was quite a character. Spoke Russian without an accent. And he had a whole team standing by. First, he was checking me out. He'd ask a question and then wait for his friends to run and match it with what they had. And after they figured out what I could know, for three hours he tried to pull just one name out of me. Like 'You know, I really want to help you, but you have to give me something to show for you. I can't go upstairs empty-handed.' That's the usual technique."

"What did you do?"

"Well, I finally gave them something. I sat there and sat, and then I thought, what the hell. I have nothing to lose. He really jumped when I told him my tidbit—it was one name. 'Right, right, that's just what I need. Thank you very much. Write the name on a piece of paper, would you please?'"

"Have they promised you anything at all?"

"No, nothing. Go to the hotel and wait. Well, now whatever happens, let it happen." His indifference was a poor disguise for his tension. I tried to imagine how I'd feel in his place, at the mercy of my look-alike on the screen, with so much at stake and not knowing what to do. Tell all or keep my mouth shut? And what was the name that he gave them?

Our dinner that night was a pathetic sight. Tolik was cranky, Sasha was silent, mulling something over, and Marina and I tried to keep up the conversation. Sooner or later I had to go home. In fact, my return flight to New York was booked for the next morning, but I did not dare tell this to them.

10

Suddenly Sasha said, "They're here already. See the guy with a newspaper at the bar? He was in the lobby on our floor and then came down here. Let's check it out."

He left the table and went to the men's room. The man turned so that he could see the men's room door. Sasha came out and went to the lobby. The man shifted again, to keep an eye on him.

"Idiots. If I worked like that, I'd have been fired a long time ago," Sasha said, handing me the free English-language paper he had picked up in the lobby. "What's the news?"

I glanced at the front page of the *Turkish Times*. "Rounding Up Russians" was the headline. The article reported that there were two hundred thousand illegal Russians in Turkey who were involved with prostitution and transporting asylum seekers into Europe, and the authorities were rounding them up and deporting them to Russia. Not exactly the kind of story Sasha needed to hear. "You think he's alone?" I asked, changing the subject back to our tail.

"Yes, he is, otherwise he wouldn't have run after me from floor to floor. You don't need more than one—where would we go from the hotel at night? They probably caught up with us at the embassy. We have to get out of here."

We looked at each other and said at the same time, "Good thing we didn't return the car."

"Marina, take Alex's room key, unobtrusively," Sasha said. "Go upstairs, get packed, move everything up to Alex's room and wait for him. If that guy is alone he will stick with me."

Marina yawned, said, "See you tomorrow, boys," and dragged sleepy Tolik to the elevator. Half an hour later, Sasha and I got up. The man at the bar stayed put.

Our rooms were on different floors, theirs on the seventh, mine on the eighth. As the elevator stopped, our eyes met, and I sensed the panic in him: the distance to his door he would have to walk alone—an ideal target. He stepped out.

When I entered my room, Marina was watching TV. Tolik, dressed in his street clothes, was asleep on my bed.

It took us two trips to the underground garage and a quarter hour to get all the baggage, along with the sleepy Tolik, into the car. Finally, I called Sasha's room: "We are ready. Go."

Three minutes later, he jumped into the car, and we shot out of the hotel. It was 1:30 a.m. I kept peeking in the rearview mirror for pursuers, but Sasha told me not to bother: it's impossible to know if you are being followed in city traffic. Once we were out on the highway, we would see.

"If I only knew which way to go," I said. We didn't have a map of Ankara.

There were several yellow taxis at the corner. A group of cabbies stood around, discussing something heatedly. I pulled up.

"Which way to Istanbul?" I asked in English. "Istanbul, Istanbul!"

A long explanation in Turkish followed. I gestured to a driver that I would follow him until he got us on the road. A half hour later we were headed in the right direction.

"Stop the car," Sasha said after a sharp turn. "Wait ten minutes." No one followed, and we went on in silence.

"I won't go alive," Sasha suddenly said. "If the Turks turn me in, I'll kill myself."

I looked in the rearview mirror. Marina and Tolik were asleep.

A few minutes later he said, "I'll go turn myself in to the Russians. Plead guilty, do my time. That's still better than rotting in Turkey."

"Don't be stupid," Marina said without opening her eyes.

"So, what's your plan?" Sasha asked me.

"Get to Istanbul, check into a hotel, and get some sleep—it's the fourth night I have not slept well," I said. "And then think about a plan."

"Want me to drive?"

"No, I don't. If we're stopped, you have one name on your driver's license and another on your passport. We'll be sunk right away."

Night driving loosens lips. Especially if you've just burned your bridges, your wife and kid are asleep in the backseat, and your listener is the only friendly soul in the unknown new world. Within three hours I knew Sasha's whole story, except, perhaps, for the secret that had created such a furor at the CIA.

A heavy fog descended at daybreak. Judging from the odometer, we should have been approaching Istanbul, but all that lay ahead was a thick, milky wall. What if the cab driver had played a trick on us, sending us in the wrong direction? We were running out of gas. I drove on, thinking that my Washington pal had been right: I was heading into the mist toward the unforeseen. Who knows where we would be an hour from now if we ran out of gas on the empty highway and the police pulled up and checked our papers.

Suddenly, out of the fog, came a green sign: Kemal Ataturk Airport—Istanbul. Another fifty yards farther lay the long-wished-for gas station.

Using our new navigational method, we hired a cab to lead us to the Hilton Istanbul. Making full use of Berezovsky's expense account, we took a king's suite, with a view of the Bosporus. We crawled to our beds, leaving a Do Not Disturb sign on the door.

I woke up at 4 p.m. and turned on my mobile—it had been off ever since we left Ankara because I was afraid that we could be tracked somehow. A dozen new messages registered on the screen. Mark from the U.S. Embassy had called every half hour, and with every message his voice sounded more anxious: Where were we? Why did we disappear? He had important news for us.

"Sorry, Mark, we were catching some sleep," I said.

"Thank God," he said. "You were not in the hotel and we were worried. Good news, pal: we're taking them. Twenty minutes, we'll pick them up."

"The problem is we are in Istanbul."

"Istanbul? Why in the world did you go there?"

"Someone was watching at the hotel, so we ran."

"I see. Well, that's a complication. Is anyone watching you now?"

"I don't think so."

"Okay, keep your phone on. I'll get back to you."

When he called again his voice sounded different: "Bad news, pal, they've changed their mind. We are not taking them."

"What do you mean 'changed their mind'?" I did not grasp the full consequences at first. The dimensions of the catastrophe dawned on me only slowly, gradually burning a hole in the tranquil scene around me: a cozy hotel room, Sasha on the balcony observing the Bosporus, Tolik watching cartoons on TV, Marina unpacking. What would I do with them now?

"Don't you get it? They changed their mind at HQ," Mark repeated in a subdued voice. "You're on your own, we cannot help you."

"Is it because we went to Istanbul?" I said the first thing that came to mind, just to keep the line open.

"No, of course not. I can't tell you why . . . I am really sorry. Good luck," he said, and hung up.

That is why I could never work for the government. I could never communicate news like that. Being an avid reader of John le Carré, I harbored no illusions about the spy business, but this still took me by surprise. To drop a man after he's given them what they needed! I had to tell them what I thought of them.

I dialed Mark's number. A recording said something in Turkish, the only discernible words being "Türkish Telekom." Probably the account didn't exist anymore, now that the operation was aborted. There was no point in calling the embassy landline. Surely there was no Mark on the staff.

I went to the lobby and called Boris, away from Sasha's and Marina's hearing.

"Where the hell are you? I've been calling all day," he asked.

"There are complications, I will tell you later. In short, we were at the embassy, but the Americans are not taking them."

Boris never gives up. While we were driving through Turkey, he had already developed Plan B: a yacht had been chartered in Greece to pick us up and sail into neutral waters.

"And then what?" I asked. "Sail forever, like the Flying Dutchman? You can get lost in a big city, but you can't hide on a yacht. Sooner or later they'll have to come ashore and show their papers."

"But this will at least give us some time to put our thoughts together."

"I have a different plan," I said, "but I can't talk about it on the phone."

Sasha needed to be inside a country in order to claim asylum. Yet he could not board a flight bound for any desirable country without a visa, which was impossible to obtain with his passport. My plan was to purchase tickets back to Moscow, with a plane change in a Western European airport. He could ask for asylum during his layover. Flight connections did not require a visa as long as you stayed within the transit zone at the airport. I went online to check plane schedules.

"Where do you want to go? France, Germany, or England?" I asked.

"I don't care," Sasha said, "just as long as we get out of here as soon as possible."

"I don't care, either," said Tolik.

"I want to go to France," said Marina.

"I think that England would be better," I said. "At least I'll be able to explain over there who the heck you are."

The next morning, an odd group appeared at the registration counter of Turkish Airlines: a bearded American who spoke Russian, with no baggage but with a passport nearly filled up with Russian entry stamps; a beautiful Russian woman with a nervous child and five suitcases; and an athletic man claiming to be a citizen of an insignificant nation, who was wearing sunglasses despite the cloudy weather. The glasses allowed him to professionally scan the airport crowds. I caught the eye of a Turkish policeman observing us. He must have decided that Sasha was my bodyguard.

We checked in for a flight to London, with a change at Heathrow to an Aeroflot flight to Moscow. The registration went smoothly, but the border guard at passport control took an inordinate interest in Sasha's passport. The rest of us had passed through without incident, and we stood and watched while he turned Sasha's passport around, examining it from all sides, and looking at it under ultraviolet light, for a good few minutes. At last he stamped it and waved him on. Made it, I thought.

We had only a few minutes left and we raced through the nearly empty airport to the gate.

"Is that it? That's it?" Marina asked, glowing.

And then I saw them. Two Turks of a certain type were following us at a distance. It was impossible to miss them: they were the only ones moving at our speed, as if we were all one team.

"See them?" I asked.

Sasha nodded.

"They latched onto us at passport control."

"Yes, I noticed."

We ran up to the gate. The flight was closing; we were the last to board. Our escorts sat down at the gate and stared at us. A young woman in a Turkish Airlines uniform took our boarding cards and passports.

"You are all right," she said to me. Turning to Sasha and Marina, she said, "But you don't have a British visa." She looked at them inquiringly.

"We have a direct connection to Moscow," I said. "Here are the tickets."

"And where are the London–Moscow boarding passes?"

"We have to change airlines, we'll get them in London."

"Strange," she said. "Why are you going through London when there's a direct Istanbul–Moscow flight in an hour?"

"We always go through London, to shop duty-free at Heathrow," I said, pleased with my quick thinking.

"I need to get permission," she said, and spoke in Turkish into her radio. "My colleague will take their documents to the office for the boss to take a look. Don't worry, we'll hold the plane."

Sasha was as white as a sheet. One of our escorts followed the airline staffer. The other continued watching us, unperturbed. I took Tolik by the hand and went to buy him some candy at the nearest stand. Ten minutes or so went by. Two figures appeared at the end of the hallway: the young woman and our Turk.

16

"Everything's in order," she said, handing Sasha the documents. "Have a good flight!"

We ran into the Jetway. Before takeoff I managed to call a friend in London and asked him to find an asylum lawyer to meet us at Heathrow.

"Did you get what's happened?" Sasha asked.

"Yes, the Turks escorted us to the plane and made sure we got on."

"They had my false name in their computer. It means that the Americans tipped them off. No one else knew the name," he concluded.

For the five days I spent in Turkey I kept expecting fate to materialize in the form of a ferocious Turkish policeman. Instead, fate's messenger turned out to be a British immigration officer, whose marked politeness did not bode well.

"What you have done," he said to me, as he looked over Sasha's false passport, "bears stiff penalties in the United Kingdom. Do you understand that I can arrest you for illegally bringing in asylum seekers?"

I knew that they couldn't do anything to Sasha, whose new lawyer was waiting for us in arrivals with a copy of a fax sent to the home office; we had communicated with him by phone before presenting ourselves to the border control. As for me, my fate was in the hands of the immigration official. And he apparently did not share my romantic nostalgia for the days of heroic defections from behind the Iron Curtain.

"With due respect, sir," I said, "there are exceptional circumstances in this case. Mr. Litvinenko and his family were in danger. It was a question of life and death."

"Russia, as far as I know, has a democratic government," he parried. "Why didn't you take him to your own country? Your embassy refused to accept him and you decided to solve your problem at our expense, isn't that so? Were you paid by Litvinenko for this?"

"No, I did it out of humanitarian concern, knowing the British tradition of giving asylum to fugitives from tyranny."

"Out of humanitarian concern, I will not arrest you, but I am banning you from entry into the United Kingdom. We are releasing Litvinenko into his solicitor's custody, and you are taking the first flight back to Turkey."

He stamped my passport with the border control imprint, then crossed it out with relish and added a notation.

"But I don't need to go to Turkey," I protested. "I need to go to New York."

"You're being deported to Turkey! And a new passport won't help," he said, guessing my thought. "I'm entering you in the computer as a smuggler of asylum seekers. You'll have to apply to our embassy for advance clearance in case you want to come here. And I doubt that you will get it."

Sasha and Marina stared at me in disbelief when I explained what was happening. I had to use all my powers of persuasion to calm them: notwithstanding the official's apparent fury, I said, they were perfectly safe now. They were on British soil and they had nothing to fear.

The immigration official kept his word. From the British computer, his notation traveled into the American network and apparently will linger there forever. Even though the Brits removed the ban a few months later, I am still stopped occasionally by U.S. Border Control and asked to explain what happened in Heathrow on November 1, 2000. But that night, I could not care less about getting a permanent stain on my electronic reputation; it was well worth the satisfaction of seeing Sasha, Marina, and Tolik being led away by two solemn policemen into the safety of a brightly lit terminal.

When I got back to the States, I spent a long time trying to find out what had occurred during those few hours that the CIA had reversed their decision. None of my contacts wanted to even hear about it. "Be grateful that it all turned out fine and don't stir up trouble," everyone said. Finally, a retired spy, a veteran of the cold war who understood these things, told me what had likely happened.

"In this kind of situation, speed is of the essence," he said. "As soon as it becomes known that someone is about to cross to the other side, all the formal and informal channels turn on: 'We know our man is in Turkey, and we know that he is going over to you. If you take him, then we will step on your tail somewhere else, we'll expel somebody, we'll do this or that to you, so don't even think of taking him.' Then the Americans will start wondering whether this guy is worth the trouble. It's one thing when a defection occurs quietly and it becomes known much later, or never. A person disappears, and that's it. It's another thing when the bargaining begins. When you left for Istanbul, you lost time. In those few hours, the Russians figured out what the Americans were up to and blocked the transfer. That morning, you still had a chance, but by afternoon, Moscow pulled the strings and it was too late."

"So who do you think were watching us at the hotel, Russians or Americans?"

"Russians, of course. But they wouldn't have tried to do anything bad there: too complicated and noisy. They would wait it out and eventually get them back from the Turks."

"And the Turks in the airport?"

"I doubt they were tipped off by Americans. If the Russians spotted you at the embassy, they had enough time to give the Turks his photo. Or maybe his passport was not that good after all. You got really lucky. The Turks apparently decided to let them go so as not to get involved. Next time, move faster."

For me, there wouldn't be a next time. For Sasha, on the other hand, not even London would be safe from the long arm of the FSB.

CHAPTER 2

THE STRANGE MAJOR

On the road to Istanbul, October 31, 2000

It was before our airport dramas, probably just during the window of time that changed the CIA's mind about giving him refuge, that I first began to learn Sasha's secrets. Our long nighttime drive from Ankara to Istanbul was an eye-opener and my introduction to Sasha's past.

The woman in the backseat, asleep with her son, had been his only ally in all his travails. Everything he told me in the car—about gangsters and oligarchs, terrorists and politicians—he described as happening either Before Marina, or After Marina. The major reference point in his life was not his birth or graduation, not the day he joined the KGB, not even his flight from Russia. It was the summer day in 1993 when they first met. Whatever happened *before* was not really interesting to him. Meeting her was a touch of magic that transformed everything into the extraordinary. Marina stayed out of his affairs, and he avoided telling her many things that were dangerous to know. But she was always his polestar.

Before Marina, Sasha's personal life had been difficult. Born into a short-lived college marriage, from the age of three Sasha was brought up by his paternal grandfather in Nalchik, a small town in the northern Caucasus, while both his parents formed new families in other parts of the country. His grandfather took him to the zoo, and the movies on Sundays. "When I was five, my grandfather brought me to the regional history museum in Nalchik, showed me the banner of the Red Army regiment in which he fought the Nazis, and told me that all our family had defended Russia and I would, too," Sasha told me. He loved his grandfather, and owed him everything, but as he grew older he needed something more. In his last years at school, he became an avid athlete. He focused on the pentathlon to the point of obsession. His trainers, his teammates, and the thrill of competition became his whole life. Even more than his grandfather, they gave him a secure base, a sense of attachment and commitment that he'd lost when his parents left.

When he turned seventeen, his father, discharged from the army, returned to Nalchik with his new wife and children. They moved in, the grandfather's house grew overcrowded, and Sasha's whole routine collapsed. He tried to integrate into his father's family but could not. He loved them, but he felt sidelined. So he found a way to join the army nearly a year before the usual draft age of eighteen. He was right out of high school, following in his father's and grandfather's footsteps.

He took to it immediately. "Military service is somewhat like sport," he told me in the car, "only it's not a game anymore: you are part of a real team fighting a common enemy—and on the right side, so you think. When they asked me to join the KGB, it seemed perfectly in line, so I accepted enthusiastically, strange as that may seem to you."

My own background was just the opposite: I was a secure child with loving parents in Moscow. We considered the KGB to be evil incarnate, and I never did any sports. Being drafted into the army in my youth would have been a catastrophe. "If you don't study hard, they'll haul you into the army," my father, a professor of microbiology, used to say.

I asked Sasha what he had done in Kontora. He caught the tone of suspicion in my question.

"I was a young lieutenant when I joined the KGB," he said. "Hadn't seen anything in life except the army, and I thought I was going to be protecting people from harm. That the Agency had a dark past—the Gulag, you know, millions of victims—I didn't learn until the 1990s, when they started to write about it."

First Sasha served in the Division of Economic Security, and then in the Anti-Terrorist Center (ATC), always working on the same thing: organized crime, assassinations, kidnappings, and criminal links in the police. His career advanced, and he married his high school sweetheart and had two children. Unfortunately, just like his parents' brief attempt, it wasn't a happy marriage.

Sasha was an operative detective, an "oper" in the trade lingo. He kept secret files on mobsters, studying their personal affairs, their networks, their contacts with businessmen and politicians. What Sasha knew—and how he knew it—was rarely revealed in court. Yet to official investigators, his stuff was priceless. He solved crimes before charges were made. He worked behind the scenes. He eavesdropped. He recruited and ran agents.

"'KGB agent' sounds horrible to people. They think of snitches reporting on their friends or spies in America," Sasha continued. "But that's not true. And not fair. Most of our agents are undercover, working inside gangs, and they are real heroes. They know that if they're blown, they are as good as dead. My agents were my best friends, and they kept dealing with me and they helped my family when I was imprisoned. So there are agents and agents.

"Do you understand the difference between an oper and a formal investigator?" He was getting excited as he explained the intelligence business to me. Scenes from his career flew past. He did what he loved and apparently did it well. "The investigator follows the tracks of the crime. In his book, there are victims, suspects, witnesses, and so on. And he collects evidence, legally processed and packaged. But an oper like myself deals with a would-be criminal, my operational 'object,' and I want to know everything about him before he even commits a crime so that he can be stopped in time, or at least more easily caught. My stuff is not 'evidence,' it's 'operative information,' see?"

Most of the people who fell under his purview—murderers, bank robbers, kidnappers, drug dealers—were not pleasant folk, and he had no regrets about his work. There was one exception, though: at one point his object became the human rights activist Sergei Grigoryants, whom I also knew. It was his only political case prior to 1997, when he was told to target Boris Berezovsky.

It was during the first Chechen War. The famous "Fifth Line," the Fifth Chief Directorate of the KGB that had dealt with dissidents in the Soviet era, was long gone. People like Grigoryants ended up under the eye of the ATC, an example of how the war pushed Russia back into the old ways of the USSR.

Grigoryants was investigating reports of a massacre of civilians by federal troops in the Chechen village of Samashki on April 12, 1995. Toward the end of that year, he was supposed to travel abroad for a human rights conference. He was bringing videotaped evidence of Russian troops shooting civilians in Samashki. Sasha's unit was brought in for an unusual assignment: to plant some shotgun shells in Grigoryants's companion's bag at Moscow International Airport so that they would be stopped for a search. During the phony search, his videotapes would be confiscated and "accidentally" damaged.

"That's the only case I'm ashamed of," Sasha said.

"I hereby accept your repentance and forgive your sins. Amen," I joked. "By the way, if you were twenty years older, I could have been one of your objects."

I told him how, in the 1970s in Moscow, under the vigilant eye of the KGB, I passed information about political prisoners to Western correspondents. Sasha explained to me the nitty-gritty of how an oper would have kept tabs on me. The lecture would have been immensely useful twenty years ago, and was still amusing today. Notwithstanding different backgrounds, we had a lot in common.

Marina met Sasha on her thirty-first birthday, June 15, 1993. She had been divorced for four years, a free and self-confident woman, enjoying life, not seeking a serious relationship. She lived in her old room in an apartment with her parents, retired industrial engineers, in a huge residential complex just south of the center of Moscow. She had never met anyone from the "services" before. When her best friend, Lena, told her that she and her husband wanted to bring an agent along to her birthday party, Marina's eyes popped: "That's some strange present you have for me."

"He's not like a secret agent at all," Lena protested. "He's funny. He has a great sense of humor, you'll like him. Besides, he saved us." She explained how Sasha was helping her husband fight off racketeers who were extorting money from his business.

"All right, then, bring your KGB man," Marina said.

Sasha's interest in Marina was already piqued because Lena had told him that she was a dancer. In his line of work he met all kinds of people, but never women who danced for a living. Marina took up dancing while still in college, where she was studying oil engineering. After graduation she decided that the oil business was not for her and went into ballroom dancing full-time, even winning some competitions. By 1993, she was teaching dance and aerobics.

That night the guests stayed late. They talked about the final resolution of Lena's husband's problem, planning for Sasha to arrest the extortionists as money changed hands. Marina, who had loved crime stories from childhood, could not believe her eyes: could this fellow, "light somehow, radiant, and as emotional as a child," really handle the bandits who had recently beaten Lena's husband and threatened to break his legs if he did not pay up?

To Marina, despite his cheery confidence, Sasha seemed "uncared for, unanchored somehow." When the subject of divorce happened to come up, Sasha said that he was married and would never divorce because of the children. Marina had a rule against dating married men, yet the way he said it made her feel that not all was well in his family.

She saw him again in a week. Sasha was leaving on vacation after successfully arresting the gang who had terrorized her friends, and Lena called her to join them for a farewell party at the train station. To her surprise, Sasha was alone, no wife or children around.

"His wife kicked him out. Because of us," Lena whispered into her ear. "They were supposed to go away last week, but he stayed on to finish our case. So she made a scene, and when he came home that evening, all his things were piled up outside the door. He hasn't been home in a week. And this isn't the first time. If not for the kids, he would have left her ages ago."

"Well, so long, see you again," Sasha called from the window as his train departed.

Lena gave her a sly look. "Just remember that you can only be serious with this guy. He's incapable of quick affairs. So don't even think about it."

"I wasn't even considering it," Marina said.

Sasha showed up again about three weeks later. He had asked his wife, Natasha, for a divorce.

Slowly and shyly, he began courting Marina. "Suddenly he would show up at my door with flowers, then vanish for a few days, only to unexpectedly call and invite me to the movies." She wasn't sure why she put up with it, but she was as hesitant to reject as to encourage him. He too was in no hurry to rush the situation.

"Sasha knew how to wait, but he never gave up on what he wanted."

Once, when he asked her for a date, she told him she had already made plans with a girlfriend to go to a concert. Just before the intermission, when the applause had died out, she felt a light tap on her shoulder: Sasha sat right behind her, smiling, with a plastic bag full of bananas in his hands.

"I must go away for a while, so I wanted to leave you with a supply," he explained. On their first date, she had told him that she loved bananas.

Sasha had been transferred to the Anti-Terrorist Center and this was his first trip for the new job. With his boss, he was heading to the North Caucasus republic of Adygeya to hunt a major gangster, the local mob king, whose gang was responsible for several killings and kidnappings in Moscow.

"After the concert, he walked me home and said that he did not want to go. I knew that he meant because of me, and that made me feel good. I didn't want him to go either. Gradually I grew accustomed to him being around. He exuded reliability and comfort. I may not have been looking for that, but when he left, I realized that I missed him."

Sasha called from the airport when he got back. He spent that night at her place and never left. It was early August. Her parents were at their country dacha. Sasha and Marina had the apartment all to themselves. When her parents came back, he said that he would move into an apartment owned by the FSB, but Marina's mother insisted that he move in with them; she "had accepted him as a son from the start."

"When I think about why we were so happy, it's because we could be ourselves. No need to pretend, to worry about being attractive, there was nothing to conquer and nothing to prove. That was obvious to us from the first day, and it was so natural. Neither of us had ever thought this was possible, and we were amazed by it to our last day together."

In October, Marina announced that she was pregnant. It was one more miracle from Sasha: this was her very first pregnancy, after a previous marriage and medical advice that she needed fertility treatment. Sasha was thrilled by the news. "Now I can be sure that you won't leave me," he said.

"Usually you hear that kind of reasoning from women," Marina retorted, with a smile.

As she later explained, "The traditional roles in our family were often reversed: he allowed me to be the boss in most things, perhaps as compensation for his overly 'masculine' work."

But she could always sense that he had another side of him, very hard, which he tried not to show her and which, she said, "turned on in extraordinary situations, like the auxiliary shift in a four-wheel drive." He would leave to her all decisions about their apartment renovation, yet when he planned their escape from Russia, she did not have a hint of what was going on until the very last moment; he took it all upon himself, and when he finally told her about it there was no point in arguing, and no time to try.

The first time she saw the other side of him was when she went to a driving school not long after he had moved in. As the classes came to an end, the instructor announced that those who did not want to bother taking the actual driving test could bring in $200 and give it to him "for the cops," and then drop by the school to pick up their license soon thereafter. Marina was a pretty good driver and she decided to take the test. The traffic patrolman flunked her deliberately. He made it clear that she should pay up, or flunk continuously. As he put it, "The next test is in a week, lady. Now, it seems, we'll be driving around once a week."

In a panic, Marina ran to the school. The instructor, shaking his head sadly, said, "You're not in the group anymore, so it will be $300 now."

Sasha was infuriated. "Do you really think that I fight corruption day and night for you to pay bribes to those cops?"

He went with her to the next test, called the traffic patrolman aside, said a few quiet words to him, flashed his FSB card, and gave him a look that Marina had never seen before. The cop blanched and couldn't think of anything better than to offer to pass her without even bothering with the test. Sasha grew even angrier, snapping, "I'll stay in the car and we'll test her together. If she passes, she passes, if she doesn't, she'll be back."

After the test, Sasha instantly switched back to his normal, easygoing, boyish self, smiling and slapping the patrolman on the back. Marina never forgot that look. She was not afraid of it; she was glad to have it at her disposal, "just in case."

They were married in October 1994 at a registrar's office, when their son Tolik was already four months old. They had not wanted to make a big deal about it; after all, it was a second marriage for both. Besides, they thought, marriages are made in heaven and certainly not in gloomy bureaucratic settings. But when they went inside wearing their usual blue jeans, the registrar said, "You have a son, and when he grows up he'll want to see a photograph of your wedding. Think about how you want to look in it."

"Sasha had only one suit—light-colored. He went home to get it and he gave me some money to buy a dress, but of course I couldn't find a thing for that money. So even in our wedding we traded roles: the groom wore white and the bride was in black, the only formal suit I had."

Shortly afterward she met his colleagues. At first they seemed like nice guys, but she noticed that Sasha stood out somehow.

"It was three things. First, he didn't drink, while they couldn't relax any other way. Second, it was money. Sasha did not know how to handle money. I mean, we always had enough, but we did not live luxuriously. We finally did buy an apartment, but it was small, just a one-bedroom. Our car was an ordinary Zhiguli. When his friends began driving foreign cars and buying fancy apartments, it became obvious that Sasha did not know how to do what they were doing: make money."

Sasha explained to her that the money came from taking outside jobs, "selling enforcement services on the market," as he called it. At the time, the police and the FSB were permitted to take outside "consulting" contracts to compensate for the government's inability to pay decent salaries. "I'm no good at that," he explained.

Third, he was hesitant to use the power that came with the FSB badge. That little red card could open any door, in stores, at the theater, wherever, because people were still terrified of the KGB. But except for her driving test, he never used it. His pals mocked him. Yet "he didn't disapprove of them, at least not then. They were a good band. He was a team player."

At least, at first.

———————

To hear him tell it, Sasha was a team player who didn't always pass the ball. He began to wonder about some of his teammates within the first years of his new life with Marina. And he met the man who would eventually win his loyalty away from his team and his entire agency.

"When I first met Berezovsky, our service was no longer the KGB but not yet called the FSB. It was the FSK, the Federal Counterintelligence Service. This was the most decent period in our history: the repressions were over and corruption was only beginning. I was a major in the service, assigned to our antiterrorism and organized crime division. On that day there was an assassination attempt on Boris. He was already a big shot. The director sent a memo to all divisions: anyone with any information should investigate. I decided to talk to Boris, since I had some thoughts on who could have done it."

I remembered the attack on Berezovsky very well; it was the first time I had heard his name. A photo of a bombed car had appeared on the front page of *The New York Times*.

A remote-controlled bomb placed in a parked blue Opel exploded at 5:20 p.m. on June 7, 1994, as Berezovsky's gray Mercedes pulled out of the gates of The Club, his company's reception house in downtown Moscow. His driver was killed instantly, but somehow, miraculously, Berezovsky and his bodyguard suffered only minor burns. The blast blew out windows in an eight-story house across the street and wounded six pedestrians. It was one of the first big contract hits in the era of privatization. In those days commercial disputes and business conflicts were usually settled with the help of gangsters rather than in the courts. Law enforcement, like the other branches of government, stood helpless, shell-shocked by Russia's economic reforms.

"We never found out who was behind that attack," Sasha said, "but it definitely had to do with the auto business, since Boris wasn't doing much else in 1994—he sold Zhiguli and Mercedes automobiles." Boris was running the country's first capitalist car dealership, LogoVAZ (a name derived from *logic* in honor of his former life as a mathematician and the acronym *VAZ* for the Volga Automobile Factory). He founded LogoVAZ in 1989 and had not yet begun to branch out into the media, airlines, and oil industries. Sasha's original theory was that the hit was related to a turf war; at the time, LogoVAZ was buying up showrooms all over the city, which had been controlled by racketeers from a gang known as Solntsevo. But Sasha later came to believe that it was someone from VAZ, the producers of Zhigulis, one of the colossal state enterprises under the Soviets that produced about half of all cars driven in Russia. It was terribly bloated and inefficient, and Boris was trying to take that company private.

"He had a financial person, Nikolai Glushkov, who was doing due diligence on VAZ," Sasha explained. "Glushkov was poking into the management's ties with intermediary firms. So someone at VAZ put out a contract on Boris."

Sasha described the classic conflict of Russian privatization. Investors would invariably discover that profits were skimmed by third-party sales companies and that the core enterprise had been running at a loss, kept afloat by government subsidies. As a rule, the sales companies were owned by the enterprise director or his family or friends, usually all Soviet holdovers. In effect, they were bilking the state they represented. Privatization meant the end of this shell game, and their prosperity, as it broke up the sales structures.

"The VAZ contract on Boris was to be carried out by the Kurgans, not the Solntsevo guys," Sasha explained. These were two of the most famous organized crime groups in those days. "The Kurgans did not have their own business and specialized in contract killings. They'd knock off anyone. They had their own people in the Moscow police and even in the Agency."

When Sasha went to see Boris to talk through all this, they exchanged telephone numbers and agreed to stay in touch. In the ensuing months, they saw each other a few times, but the investigation did not go far: the Chechen War began in December, and it became a priority for the FSB. Ordinary crimes, including mob hits, took a backseat.

December 10, 1994: Three Russian divisions invade Chechnya, a mountainous, predominantly Muslim province in southern Russia. Grozny, the Chechen capital, is surrounded. Separatist president Dzhokhar Dudayev's regime is under siege. The Russian divisions are met with massive resistance and suffer severe losses—nearly two thousand dead—during a botched attempt to take Grozny on New Year's Eve.

By late 1994, Boris Berezovsky all but abandoned his automobile business—which did extremely well without his attention—and turned to a new endeavor, the mass media, which was intimately tied to the precarious world of Russian electoral politics.

Russia's market reforms were in their third year. Coming to power in 1991 when he engineered the dissolution of the USSR, Boris Yeltsin undertook reforms harshly and decisively: he did away with state price controls, dropped customs barriers, and embarked on a crash privatization program. In four years of "shock therapy" his chief adviser, Anatoly Chubais, the thirty-eight-year-old boy wonder of Russian economics, did the impossible: he auctioned off and privatized tens of thousands of enterprises, moved more than half the workforce into the private sector, and somehow kept the economy from sliding into uncontrolled inflation.

Yet these successes cost ordinary Russians dearly. The lack of purchasing power in the impoverished population and the reduction of state subsidies brought entire branches of the economy to a halt, primarily in the military-industrial complex and also among producers of consumer goods, who could not stand the competition from Western manufacturers who were flooding the country with everything that ordinary Russians had lacked, and craved, for so long. Western clothing, cars, and electronics were in great demand by anyone who could afford them.

Unfortunately, fewer and fewer had the money to buy them. Millions fell below the poverty line. Civil servants—teachers, doctors, officials, police—were not paid for months at a time. Taxes were not collected, since the tax service was still being created (there had been no taxes in the Soviet system). The intelligentsia in the universities and science labs lost faith in democracy. Crime rose. The army grumbled. Capitalism and the market lost their appeal. More and more Russians thought nostalgically about the good old days of the USSR.

On the other hand, freedom flourished. After seventy years of Communist dictatorship, journalists could write what they wanted, there were no more political prisoners, anyone could get a passport to travel abroad, voters could pick among a dozen political parties, and eighty-six regions and ethnic republics of the Russian Federation gained self-rule and could go about their business without interference from the Kremlin.

Yeltsin's main dilemma throughout his entire administration was just how far he was willing to violate democracy in order to save it. In fall 1993, the Supreme Soviet—the parliament, which was still full of ex-Soviet apparatchiks—had blocked his reforms and called on federal regions to rebel. Yeltsin disbanded the legislature and sent tanks to smoke out the deputies who barricaded themselves inside; 140 died in the melee. It was a tough choice, but the alternative had seemed worse: total economic collapse and political implosion.

The Communists did not quit. As Yeltsin's presidential term continued, he was opposed once again by a newly elected hostile parliament, the Duma, where the tone was set by Communists as well as the neo-fascist party of Vladimir Zhirinovsky, who openly advocated an authoritarian model of government. There was every reason to expect the coming presidential election to be a catastrophe: Gennady Zyuganov, the Communist candidate, was polling in the 30 percent range as Yeltsin's numbers plunged into single digits by the onset of the Chechen War.

Berezovsky had gained entrée into the Kremlin inner circle just a few months previously. He was forty-six years old. The journalist Valentin Yumashev, who had ghost-written the president's memoirs and subsequently married Yeltsin's daughter Tatyana, introduced Berezovsky to two of Yeltsin's entourage: his chief of staff, Viktor Ilyushin, a liberal, and Gen. Alexander Korzhakov, the chief of Kremlin security, called the Federal Service of Okhrana (FSO), the agency that supplied bodyguards to federal bureaucrats. Korzhakov's power, however, reached far beyond security; he was the de facto representative of all the secret services and the intelligence community in the Kremlin.

The pressing concern among all of Yeltsin's people was the presidential election in 1996. With every passing week Yeltsin's chances of winning a second term seemed worse.

After reviewing the situation, Boris Berezovsky came up with a fresh idea: use the senescent Soviet television—Channel One, broadcasting to 200 million people across ten time zones—to work for Yeltsin's reelection campaign. Thus was born ORT; the initials in Russian stand for Russian Public Television, a.k.a. Berezovsky's channel.

Before Boris, Channel One used to be Ostankino TV, a mosaic of studios and programs that the Duma Communists were trying to get their hands on, insisting that state TV should be subordinate to the legislative branch. At the time, the only private—and the best managed—network in the country was NTV, owned by Vladimir Gusinsky, which held roughly 15 percent of market share. But it was clear that whoever controlled Channel One would have access to the majority of Russia's viewers. Berezovsky convinced Ilyushin and Korzhakov that he was the man who could control the airwaves for the benefit of the reforms and the president.

But it was easier said than done. Ostankino was a colossal, clumsy structure, overgrown with innumerable useless auxiliary services and subdivisions, with a swollen staff and an astronomical deficit of $170 million a year. Advertising revenues were less than a fifth of that.

Ostankino was a black hole in the government's budget, a structure that simply could not be salvaged. It would be easier to shut it down and start from scratch. This was just what Berezovsky proposed to Yeltsin's advisers: to grant the license for Channel One to a new joint-stock company, in which 51 percent would belong to the state and 49 percent to private funders, controlled by Berezovsky, who would build a management structure that would run the network at a profit, or at least reduce losses to a manageable level.

The presidential decree dismantling Ostankino and creating ORT in its place in early December 1994 went almost unnoticed, as all eyes were then on the nascent conflict with the Chechen separatists. But three months later ORT dramatically announced its presence by calling a moratorium on advertising.

Berezovsky's goal was to cut all ties between the Ostankino studios and the shadow structures that sold advertising time. Sasha's description of the dilemma of privatization held true: the network lost hundreds of millions, while major graft was outsourced to third-party organizations that did its selling. Even by modest estimates advertisers paid five times as much as the network actually received from them. Most of the money was handed over in envelopes full of cash, and it remained in the pockets of producers, middlemen, and gangsters. The intention of Boris's new management was to use a hiatus of a few months to build an in-house sales department, cutting out all the middlemen.

The moratorium was announced on February 20, 1995. On March 1, Vlad Listyev, ORT's new director general, was gunned down by an assassin at the door of his Moscow home. Listyev was Russia's Larry King, its most popular TV host, the darling of the country. In mourning, every television station in the nation went off the air for twenty-four hours. The entire country was in shock.

The morning after the murder, an emergency meeting was convened in the office of the deputy director of the FSB. Sasha, a major, was the lowest-ranking officer in the room. He told the assembled generals that he believed Listyev's murder and the attempt on Berezovsky eight months earlier were the work of the same group, the Kurgan gang, which had penetrated Moscow's police department.

"Suddenly, I got a message on my pager from Berezovsky," Sasha told me, staring into the foggy Turkish night. " 'Call immediately.' I notified Trofimov and he said, 'Go call him.' "

"Who is Trofimov?"

Sasha looked at me as if I were a schoolboy. "Gen. Anatoly Trofimov, chief of the Moscow regional FSB. He was close to Korzhakov and was thought to have a direct line to the Kremlin. Well, I called Boris and he said that they'd come to arrest him. 'Who?' I asked. He said, 'Moscow police,' and he named some names. I ran back to the office and said, 'The very people I was talking about have come for him: the Kurgan connection in the police.' Trofimov ordered me to go there immediately and clear things up."

It's a stone's throw from the Lubyanka HQ to The LogoVAZ Club. There Sasha discovered eight armed policemen who told him that they were ordered to deliver Berezovsky to the station to be questioned in the murder of Listyev. A camera crew from NTV was setting up in front of the entrance; someone had tipped them off that Berezovsky was going to be arrested.

"I knew that he could not be allowed to be taken away by these cops, because by morning there would be a report that he'd had a heart attack or was killed trying to escape, and you wouldn't be able to prove anything," Sasha continued. "I pulled out my service gun and FSB ID and yelled, 'Move along! This is our investigation and we'll question him ourselves.' 'We have our orders,' they snapped back. After some arguing they called their bosses, and I called mine. Trofimov said, 'Don't give him up under any circumstances. I'm sending reinforcements. How many are there?'"

Fifteen minutes later twenty of Trofimov's men arrived with their guns. The incident ended when an official police investigator showed up and took a statement from Berezovsky, with Sasha standing guard by his side.

At the time, I had heard that the standoff at LogoVAZ was part of ongoing hostilities between the Moscow city government and the Kremlin. Tensions were running high, almost to the point of violence. Mayor Yuri Luzhkov, a powerful city boss, fought with First Deputy Prime Minister Anatoly Chubais over the privatization of city property. The city police naturally worked on behalf of City Hall, and the FSB for the Kremlin.

"I heard that the confrontation at LogoVAZ was part of politics—City Hall versus the Kremlin—and that the mayor tried to use the murder of Listyev as an excuse to get rid of Boris. Isn't that so? What did the Kurgan gang have to do with it?" I asked.

"It might be," Sasha replied. "I didn't understand politics at all then. I'm an oper, and I followed the evidence, not the politics. But Listyev was not murdered by the mayor. And the mayor was not the one who tried to blow up Boris in '94. So you can't get away from the mob. And the cops are much closer to the mob than they are to their own higher-ups, believe me. I knew for sure that the cops who had come for Boris in '95 were up to no good. But you are right: many thought at the time that it was the mayor versus the Kremlin."

He paused for a bit, glanced over at me, and added, "You and Boris, you're always thinking politics, but you don't see the people—that's your big mistake. In our work the individual is the most important thing. I trusted Boris right away, and Trofimov. I didn't trust Luzhkov, and I never trusted Korzhakov, even though he and

Trofimov were friends. That time in LogoVAZ, I was protecting Boris and I felt Trofimov backing me up, the two people I trusted. I couldn't have cared in the least about the Kremlin or the mayor."

Listyev's killers were never found. The case became just another of a dozen legendary contract killings of the 1990s, from the shooting of the liberal Duma member Galina Starovoitova, to the bombing of the investigative journalist Dmitry Kholodov, to the poisoning of the prominent banker Ivan Kivelidi.

Nevertheless, ORT went on the air as planned and kept its three-month moratorium on advertising. As for Sasha and Boris, they developed a bond shared only by people who have faced mortal danger together—not friendship or attachment, but a special kind of loyalty that no other can surpass.

Boris's first instinct was to repay Sasha for saving his life by simply giving him money—completely typical for Moscow in those days. But he had already learned enough about Sasha to know he wouldn't take it and might be offended. So he decided to give him something that most former Soviet citizens could only dream about: he would take him on a trip abroad, combining the pleasant with the useful. After the attempt on his life and the murder of Listyev, security was not an idle concern, and Sasha was someone he was happy to have around.

A single phone call to Korzhakov was enough to arrange an assignment for Sasha, and with a "cover document" in his pocket—a diplomatic passport in the name of Alexander Volkov, second secretary in the Russian Embassy in Bern—Sasha flew in Berezovsky's private jet for his first trip away from his homeland, in March 1995.

He called Marina from Switzerland and told her, thrilled, "You won't believe it: they don't lock the doors in the hotel and the cops are as polite as your academics!"

"You've had time to deal with the cops?" Marina asked in surprise.

"I'll tell you when I get back," Sasha said.

He gave her presents of French perfume when he returned and

denim outfits for Tolik in graduated sizes for the next five years—an incredible luxury by Moscow standards. "Who knows what may happen, but at least one problem is taken care of," he laughed.

He also told her the story of the Swiss cops. Dealing with them made an indelible impression on Sasha. Boris had been driving a sports Mercedes, with his wife, Lena, in the front and Sasha in the small backseat. With his Moscow habit of paying no attention to the rules, Boris drove at a wild speed, crossing the solid line on more than one occasion. They wound up in the hands of two exceedingly polite policemen. In Moscow, "resolving" a case like that would entail a $20 bill folded into one's driver's license. But that was out of the question here: the group went to the police station in the Alpine town of Chateau d'Oex. Boris, Lena, and Sasha were locked up in a cell with a steel door and a peephole while the police took their papers away.

It didn't occur to Sasha that their salvation was his cover identity. The polite policemen returned two hours later. "We must apologize," they said. "We have no right to detain you, you have diplomatic immunity. It took some time for your embassy to send confirmation, but now everything is in order." They returned his fake passport, expressing no surprise that the second secretary in the Russian Embassy spoke no foreign languages.

In retrospect, Sasha's presence in Switzerland might have been more than just a cursory precaution for Boris. Many years later a Russian defector to the West who had been privy to the goings-on in the SVR, the Russian foreign intelligence service, told me that the Moscow center was extremely alarmed by Berezovsky's plan to privatize Aeroflot, the Russian national airline, which had been a traditional cover for hundreds of spies all over the world. So, in early 1995, a secret cable went out to the Geneva station to monitor Berezovsky's visit, which, as the SVR suspected, had to do with setting up a financial and sales center in Lausanne to place the airline's cash flow out of the control of the spy agency. The intelligence report about that visit was the origin of the famous "Aeroflot case" that came to haunt Berezovsky many years later.

February 8, 1995: Russian troops finally take Grozny. Twenty-seven thousand civilians have been killed in the battle, and the city has been leveled by massive aerial and artillery bombardments. Russian forces carpet bomb many other towns. Civilians cannot escape. Aid groups are refused access. Chechen fighters retreat into the mountains and start a guerrilla war.

For Sasha, the war in Chechnya was at first essentially a sideshow, a distraction, which diverted the Agency's attention and resources from what he saw as the core problem: corruption and crime among the police and the services. He was sure that the war would end quickly, as the president and the generals had promised. For nearly a year he had spent long nights at home at the kitchen table, drawing colored charts of mob connections with the top brass of the FSB and the Ministry of the Interior. He even wrote a memorandum about it, addressed to Yeltsin, which Marina retyped at least a dozen times.

But after meeting Berezovsky, he never sent it. Boris seemed to offer a better way to advance his mission: a direct connection to the Kremlin. He pestered Boris with stories about the ties certain generals had with either the Solntsevo or Kurgan or Podolsk gangs, the world he knew so well. Finally, Boris arranged meetings for him not just with Korzhakov, but also with Mikhail Barsukov, the director of the FSB, and Deputy Minister of Internal Affairs Vladimir Ovchinsky, so that they could hear directly from Sasha what was going on in their agencies.

But the meetings did not go well. As Korzhakov recalled in an interview with *Komsomolskaya Pravda* on December 14, 2006, he did not like Sasha and what he had to say: "This major came, thin, unshaven, shaggy-haired, with worn, unpolished shoes, wearing a pair of Chinese work trousers, his sweater hanging down to his knees. His eyes darted around." Korzhakov heard him out for an hour and a half, and then he "asked around. It turned out that one of my friends worked in the 'bad' department that Litvinenko had 'ratted out.' I had served with him back in Afghanistan. I trusted him, he was a perfectly normal guy, a fighter. I asked him to come see me and I told him about Litvinenko's visit. He said, 'You know me, don't you? You can't believe Litvinenko, the creep makes up denunciations.'"

Ovchinsky was another reluctant listener to whom Sasha made his case. "He was strange, hard to understand," Ovchinsky told the Latvian newspaper *Chas* in an interview on December 30, 2006. "He would come and report to me about our people who were working on organized crime. He tried to expose corruption in the leadership of the Ministry. At first I thought Litvinenko was kind of a Boy Scout, who cared so much about the work . . . He did accuse a lot of people, he mentioned the names of famous professionals. But you see, nothing of what he said was confirmed."

"I was so naïve," Sasha said about those meetings. "I thought that since they were the big bosses, they would take care of it and stop the mayhem in the services. Not in the least. Every time the threads led high enough, it turned out that the person involved was somebody's buddy or relative or comrade in arms. The only thing I achieved is a certain reputation: as the village idiot. And then I discovered that the higher-ups were even more involved with criminals than was middle management. And not surprisingly, they bought up all these mansions and Mercedes cars even though they had measly salaries. The whole system was rotten to the core. I collected a lot of material on the topic."

On our drive to Istanbul, Sasha gave me a three-hour lecture on the life and mores of Kontora circa 1995. How corruption was systematic. How, with the old Marxist ideology dried up, the mission had vanished. How the vacuum was filled by money.

"The FSB continued gathering information," he explained. "And information is a commodity. Information is power. It can be used to solve problems in the marketplace, to put pressure on the competition. The FSB found its market."

The courts did not work, nor did the laws. "If your partner bilked you, or a creditor did not pay, or a supplier did not deliver—where did you turn to complain? I'm not even talking about the primitive rackets from which you need protection. When force became a commodity, there was a demand for it. Roofs appeared, people who sheltered and protected your business.

"First it was provided by the mob, then the police, and soon enough our own guys realized what was what, and then the rivalry began among gangsters, cops, and the Agency for market share. As the police and the FSB became more competitive, they squeezed the gangs out of the market. But in many cases competition gave way to cooperation, and the services became gangsters themselves."

One thing on which his friends and enemies all agreed is that Sasha had a phenomenal memory. He kept hundreds of episodes, addresses, telephone numbers, and names in his head. Altogether they formed a horrifying picture of a criminal wave gradually engulfing the agencies of law and order in the new Russia.

By the time we reached Istanbul on that Halloween night in 2000 we had bonded, and not just as friends and partners in Sasha's flight to freedom. We had discovered parallel tracks in each other's lives, connected by Boris Berezovsky and by two very different approaches to the same goal: keeping Russia open and free.

For him, 1995 was a watershed year. He grew ever more convinced that there was no easy victory in sight in the war he was waging, but he thought that Boris Berezovsky and the people in the Kremlin would help him. For me, 1995 was the beginning of my entrée into the tumultuous world of Kremlin oligarchs and its inner-circle power struggle.

PART II

THE STRUGGLE FOR THE KREMLIN

CHAPTER 3

THE ROBBER BARON

Moscow, spring 1995

We drove through the exclusive Rublyovka neighborhood, an enclave of summer homes of Kremlin inhabitants since the days of Stalin. I had been here before my emigration from Russia, in the 1970s. Outwardly, everything looked as in the old Soviet days: the same ochre-colored walls with barbed wire on top, the same heavy gates with peepholes for guards, the same No Stopping signs along the highway.

We pulled into a driveway. My driver honked, and a security guard in paramilitary fatigues came out of a booth. He stared impassively, then waved us on. An iron gate screeched open, and we drove into a huge pine grove. Beyond the trees stood a brick home in classic government-dacha style: dull blocks of red brick and concrete. The location was impressive, with a spectacular view of the Moscow River. My companion, Arkady Evstafiev, press secretary to First Deputy Prime Minister Anatoly Chubais, explained that it was once the dacha of Nikolai Rhyzhkov, the last prime minister of the USSR.

Earlier that day, when Arkady had telephoned me to say "I'd like you to meet somebody," he wouldn't tell me who it was.

"You will see. I can't talk over the telephone."

Now we were ushered through the house by a butler who looked like a security guard and out onto the back lawn, to a tea table covered with a white tablecloth, set in a pool of sunlight. My host introduced himself with a quip.

"Say, is this like Soros's home, or do we still have some work to do?" It was Boris Berezovsky.

We were waited on by four young, poker-faced fellows in dinner jackets and white gloves, who seemed completely out of place amid the spring greenery or, for that matter, at the harsh, Party-style building. There were several other people at the table, but Berezovsky dominated. He gave an inspiring speech about the future of Russian television, delivered at machine-gun speed, obviously unable to keep up with his train of thought.

Dressed in jeans and a sweater, Berezovsky looked even more out of place, neither an apparatchik nor, seemingly, a capitalist. He was more of a mad mathematician, breathlessly explaining a theorem of profound elegance, while his listeners were preoccupied with petty, mundane concerns. In the flesh, he seemed much nicer than on television; his bald head gleamed in the sun but somehow didn't age his youthful, expressive face. His fierce dark eyes and constant gesticulations conveyed much more energy in person than on the screen.

Berezovsky's opening quip was more than just a nouveau riche icebreaker. He had summoned me because I worked for George Soros, hoping to lure that legendary billionaire into becoming his backer in major privatization deals that were on the horizon. I had more or less guessed why I had been invited to Berezovsky's tea table. What I did not realize was that I was about to enter a new planet of the solar system—BorisWorld—which I would be navigating for the next decade.

———

I tried to respond politely to Berezovsky's quip. El Mirador, Soros's summer home, is a lovely Mexican-style hacienda in Southampton on Long Island. The best I could manage was, "There is some resemblance, although the building is in a different style."

"Well, as soon as we are done with the elections, we'll deal with real estate," Berezovsky replied. "I'd like to invite Mr. Soros to my dacha when he is next in Moscow. We need to learn from him. The way he shorted the pound, what an outrageous guy, top-notch!"

Berezovsky was referring to September 16, 1992, a.k.a. Black Wednesday, when Soros played against the British government on currency markets around the world, forced the British to devalue the pound, and made a billion dollars in a day. This earned him the sobriquet "the man who broke the Bank of England."

Soros's Black Wednesday fame made him a role model for the new breed of Russian capitalists, but George himself was of two minds about the goings-on in Russia. His principal interlocutor there was Anatoly Chubais, and he reacted to Chubais's privatization explosion with a mixture of amazement and disapproval. On the one hand, he could not help but admire Chubais's grandiose feats: in a little over three years, the youthful first deputy prime minister had essentially reversed the revolution of the Bolsheviks, who seventy years previously had shed rivers of blood expropriating private property. Chubais transferred much of that state property back into private hands, almost without bloodshed—that is, not counting the storming of the Supreme Soviet in 1993, or the several hundred victims of "business disputes" across the country.

Yet to Soros, Chubais wasn't doing things quite the way he would. The arrogant, abrasive first deputy prime minister was not just an archenemy of the Communists. He was a radical free-marketeer who assumed the rule of law would somehow automatically follow in the wake of economic freedom. If the economy was opened up, social relations would work themselves out. Soros, on the other hand, was horrified at the ugly consequences of the no-holds-barred brand of capitalism. Their dispute broke into the open in January 1995, at the World Economic Forum in the Swiss ski resort of Davos, where Chubais announced to the world that privatization in Russia had bred a new class of property owners, people who would make up the backbone of the new free Russia.

Chubais came to Davos in place of Yeltsin, who was stuck in Moscow as a wartime president; the New Year's Eve debacle in

Grozny was too fresh. As the delegates gathered to listen to Chubais give his speech, the ferocious fighting in Chechnya continued.

Nonetheless, Chubais's speech was triumphant. He had just completed the first stage of massive privatization, whereby vouchers given to each and every Russian citizen could be traded for equity in state-owned enterprises. Many vouchers, to be sure, were bought up by speculators and "red directors," former Soviet factory heads, but even so, Chubais succeeded in making several million people stockholders.

Most observers had predicted runaway inflation and chaos, but the pessimists were discredited: inflation was held in check. The statistics of privatization spoke for themselves. Yeltsin remained in power, despite the intrigues of the Communists. "Our reform is irreversible!" Chubais proclaimed.

In response, Soros, a widely admired guru in Davos, called the new Russian capitalists "robber barons."

"I was hoping to see an orderly transition to an open society, a market-oriented democratic system based on the rule of law," he complained. "That attempt has basically failed. But you do have the emergence of a new system: robber capitalism."

To be sure, he added, "it is raw and ugly, but a very vital, self-organizing system. It can succeed because there are now economic interests that know how to defend themselves." But the problem is that "the system is creating a tremendous sense of social injustice and a decline in civilized values, the sense of frustration and disorientation that could lead to a political backlash and a xenophobic, nationalistic mood."

Over the years, Soros and Chubais held several conversations, mostly during George's frequent visits to Moscow related to his various philanthropic initiatives. I often joined them, but it was a dialogue of the deaf with the dumb. Chubais, the free-market worshipper, kept repeating that private property would eventually resolve all social and political problems; that democracy and freedom, social morals, the rule of law, and a liberal system of government would flow from capitalism just as surely as efficient prices flowed from Adam Smith's invisible hand.

Soros, on the other hand, somewhere between a Keynesian and a covert socialist, believed that in moments of crisis, state interference was unavoidable. He advised Chubais to reintroduce customs tariffs to protect the most vulnerable sectors of Russia's economy and to support Soros's own campaign in Washington to create a social safety net for Russia, paid for by Western economic aid, a "social Marshall plan" that would prime the pump of demand by putting billions of dollars into the hands of ordinary Russians. Chubais wanted Soros to lead the way by investing in Russia himself, but Soros was too busy setting up multimillion-dollar charities and did not want to mix business and philanthropy. Besides, with the Communists gaining strength, he considered Russia too risky for investors.

Now, at Berezovsky's tea table, it was Boris's turn to try to lure George into a business partnership. Boris ardently believed that sooner or later, his 200 million ORT television viewers would turn into an enormous advertising market and his investment in the network would be richly rewarded. Meanwhile, however, he faced a deficit of $170 million, and he couldn't afford it. He explained that he wanted to ask Soros for a loan of $100 million or so, with collateral in ORT shares plus an option to buy more. It was a package potentially worth a billion, he claimed. Moreover, by supporting the new progressive TV, Soros could really help democracy in Russia. After all, he noted, Soros had given $100 million to help Russian scientists without getting anything in exchange.

"By the way, why does he call us robber barons? Does he think that we're all gangsters here, like Al Capone?" Boris inquired.

"Not exactly," I said. I told him the story of the American tycoons and financiers of the Gilded Age. I told him about their mansions in Newport, where children are now taken on tours, just as Soviet children, as both of us well remembered, were taken to Lenin's Tomb. "Those people are remembered not for how they made their money—they were no angels—but for building American industry and for their philanthropy. That was how Carnegie Hall, the Rockefeller Foundation, and Vanderbilt University came about. This is why Soros gives money to Russian scientists. He wants to be remembered not as 'the man who broke the Bank of England' but as a sponsor of democracy in the ex-USSR."

For an instant, Boris seemed reflective. But his comeback was as quick as ever. "How interesting. Well, we will do that, too, as soon as we can. Have you heard about my Triumph Fund? It gives prizes in the arts. What if I were to contribute to your Science Foundation, put in a million and a half or so, would Soros agree?"

From the moment I met Berezovsky, I couldn't rid myself of the thought that he did not fit in the ecosystem of the Russian power establishment. He was the Great Gatsby of Rublyovka, his mercurial temperament and grand visions incompatible with the lethargic but murderous ethos that permeates the Kremlin walls.

The inauguration of LogoVAZ Fellowships for Young Scientists at the Soros Foundation took place in the summer of 1995 in Moscow at the Great Hall of the Ministry of Science. As television cameras whirred, George and Boris shook hands. George gave a speech about passing on the philanthropic baton to a new Russian capitalist class. "Capitalism in Russia is only beginning; after all, you have to make money first in order to give it out. I'm very happy that things are going so well for you and that you have the same understanding I do of the importance of science and education." Boris beamed.

As we drove away from the ceremony, however, George's tone was different. I mentioned the Great Gatsby parallel. "Indeed," George said. "I sympathize with him, but I'm afraid that he will end up badly. He is climbing up and doesn't know where to stop. And the higher you climb, the farther you fall."

By the end of the summer, Soros's forecast for Russia had considerably worsened. Yeltsin, he said, was caught between a rock and a hard place, coping with a social crisis amid pressure from the International Monetary Fund and the World Bank, which supplied the bulk of his budget, to keep spending at bay. In Chechnya, he seemed to have lost control over the army, and the war's violence was spiraling upward.

Spring 1995: Chechen ambushes accelerate, and separatists mine roads throughout the war zone. On June 14, eighty rebels led by warlord Shamil Basayev seize a hospital in the Russian city of Budyonnovsk, seventy miles from the Chechen border, taking more than fifteen hundred hostages. A tense standoff, interrupted by botched Russian attempts to retake the hospital, finally leads to a deal: most of the hostages are released in exchange for Yeltsin's agreement to a cease-fire to the war, allowing negotiations. The militants return to Chechnya as heroes. Russian Prime Minister Viktor Chernomyrdin, who conducts televised negotiations with Basayev, emerges as a leading dove in the Kremlin.

"Russia is falling into a black hole which will drag the entire region with it," Soros gloomily predicted late that summer. He asked me to gradually wind down the science program so that we wouldn't be "burning cash for nothing."

He was still reluctant to consider a loan for ORT. "Boris needs a strategic partner, and I don't understand anything about television," he said. "I can introduce him to someone."

But that potential partner, an investor in one of the big American networks, did not want to give Boris a loan either. Instead, he simply offered to buy a chunk of ORT. Boris said that wasn't possible, as the Communists in the Duma would kick up an incredible fuss once they found out that Channel One was being sold to Americans. Well, if that's how it was, the strategic partner said, then even a loan would bring a huge political risk. The deal didn't go through.

The only good news was that the success of the revamped Channel One exceeded all expectations. A new team headed by the liberal journalist Konstantin Ernst, a young intellectual with shoulder-length hair, revamped programming, changed the format and style of the news, and produced entertainment broadcasts targeted at young viewers. The network strove to create a vision of dynamic, prosperous, Westernized Russia, a place where you wanted to live, if only the Communists didn't drag it back into the Soviet past. The ratings rose steadily, gradually overtaking NTV, but the main problem remained unresolved: the network continued to run huge losses. Boris constantly searched for money to keep it going. He thought he just needed to buy a year's time, until the presidential election.

He was certain that after Yeltsin's victory, foreign investors would line up to see him. Once, as we sat on the terrace of The Club drinking an incredibly good bottle of Chateau Latour, his favorite wine, I asked him what he would do if Yeltsin didn't win. He looked at me as if I were an idiot. "What do you mean, not win? That can't happen! Did you ever get into a fight when you were a kid?"

"No," I admitted.

"Well, you cannot get into a fight thinking that you may be beaten. And not just beaten, but hung from a lamppost! Well, we can't even think of losing. These aren't your municipal elections in Cincinnati. This is a revolution, old boy!"

Chubais, despite his Davos speech, was still scrambling. His voucher program had privatized more than half of the economy, but in the form of a massive number of small and medium-size businesses. He had not yet touched the biggest companies: oil and gas, minerals, telecommunications, military industries. These enterprises were still operated by their former Soviet managers, many of whom were siphoning off funds through third-party sales outlets, laundering the proceeds or stashing them abroad in offshore tax havens.

The managers of these large state-owned enterprises were known collectively as "the director corps," and they constituted a powerful lobby whose Kremlin advocate was Oleg Soskovets, a veteran of the Soviet military industry, who held the other first deputy prime minister portfolio and was Chubais's chief rival in the Cabinet. Along with the Communists in the Duma, the director corps presented the principal obstacle to further privatization, as its members were eager to reintegrate into a planned economy should the Communists return to power.

Chubais, who strove to make the Russian economy 100 percent private, felt that his time was running out, so at some point in mid-1995 he came up with an extraordinary strategy: the state should take its biggest industries and privatize them in one big push. Let capitalists take over these companies. Rather than deceitful managers skimming income, have the owners start paying corporate taxes. At best, the new owners could help Yeltsin fight off the Communist onslaught. At worst, let the Communists, should they win, try to renationalize private property.

But this time Chubais could no longer afford to give out privatization vouchers free to every Russian. He needed cash. At the time, state budget receipts were only $37 billion, whereas expenditures were $52 billion, generating nearly a 30 percent deficit. Oil exports at the price of $15 per barrel were not generating enough cash. Taxes were not collected, and salaries of state employees had to be paid. The war in Chechnya was costing more and more each month. Foreign investment trickled to a minimum. So he turned to the only place where one could find cash in the country: the emergent banking sector, where no Soviet holdovers existed. It was a 100 percent novel, privately owned industry that originated from scratch.

As Chubais himself later explained, "In 1996, I had a choice between the communists coming to power, or robber capitalism. I chose robber capitalism."

Chubais handpicked a dozen bankers whom he knew would never cave in to the Communists and offered them some of the crown jewels of Russia: gas, minerals, and elements of the infrastructure industries, in exchange for all the cash they could raise. The government got loans from the banks secured by shares in the enterprises. If the loan was not returned on time, then the bank could auction the shares off—a pure formality, since the bank itself controlled the process.

The loans-for-shares auctions involved twelve enterprises in all: six oil companies, three factories, and three shipping companies. They garnered $1.1 billion for the government. The lucky robber barons became some of the richest men on earth—assuming they could hold on to their assets after the elections.

As for Boris, he wasn't initially planning to take part in the auctions, as he didn't own a bank and didn't have that kind of money. He also had the insatiable TV network hanging around his neck, which devoured all the profits from his automobile business. But among all the new oligarchs, he was the closest to the Kremlin, and so he figured out a way to turn his weakness into a strength: he explained to Chubais and Korzhakov, the two principals in the Kremlin, that in order to support ORT, he needed some sort of cash generator. After all, the state owned a 51 percent stake and should bear some responsibility for the unprofitable network. He got the go-ahead. An additional "auction" was hastily announced for a controlling stake in Sibneft, the Siberian oil company that was the seventh largest oil producer in the Russian Federation. Chubais's economists valued it at a minimum of $100 million.

But Boris didn't have $100 million. He could scrape up only about half that amount.

October 6, 1995: A bomb critically injures Anatoly Romanov, the Russian commander in Chechnya and one of the rare doves in the military, who was in the midst of peace negotiations with the rebels. The cease-fire that has been holding since June is shattered. Rumors abound that the attack on Romanov is the work of "the Party of War," a cabal of top military and security mandarins unhappy about Yeltsin's attempts to reach a negotiated settlement. The defense and interior ministers openly call for an all-out war.

One day in the early fall, Boris called to invite me to The Club to discuss "an urgent matter."

For most people in Moscow, The Club was a famous and mysterious place. A visit there was proof of one's status. The quality of wine and the artistry of the chef were legendary. In the wake of the assassination attempt on Boris in 1994, the security was impressive, including metal detectors, closed-circuit television monitors, an ID registry, and the presence of many attentive young men with the demeanor and habits of the old KGB Kremlin guards.

Over the bar, which also served as a waiting room, hung the first HDTV in Moscow. There was a white grand piano, played occasionally by one of Boris's old friends, an elderly Jew in a white suit. In the corner stood a stuffed crocodile, for reasons unknown. Boris was always behind schedule, so his visitors usually had to wait. The atmosphere was supposed to help time pass pleasantly for his unending stream of visitors.

On any given day at The Club you could rub elbows with ministers and TV personalities, deputies of the Duma and top journalists, provincial governors and Western fund managers, as well as people no one knew, such as an unremarkable young man in a jeans suit who often sat in a corner: Sasha Litvinenko. Sasha and I saw each other at The Club several times before we were ever introduced.

This time I was rushed straight through the bar into Boris's office via a small foyer, in the middle of which was a little burbling Baroque fountain.

"What do you think, would George be interested in an investment project of about $50 million?" Boris began before I even got in the door.

After the fiasco over the loan for ORT, it seemed pointless to go to Soros with another proposal like this, but before I had a chance to say a word Boris began throwing information at me. "This time, I don't have an unprofitable television station but a real, profit-making oil company, vertically integrated, with an oil field, a refinery, and an export terminal—a crown jewel of the Soviet energy complex. We are gearing up for the auction and are just a bit short of cash. So I'd like to propose to George to go into this with me 50–50."

"Wait a minute," I objected. "They don't allow foreigners into these auctions."

"Not a problem," exclaimed Boris. "A Russian legal entity is set up, with George having 50 percent minus one share. By world standards, the oil reserves here would be worth maybe $5 billion. Less the political risk, of course. Tell George he must agree. Here's the documentation package. This is really urgent. I could fly to New York at any minute."

I carried the offer to New York and was surprised to discover that Soros was willing to consider it. He pondered it for two weeks. I watched him, making bets with myself: would he cross the line and join in the gold rush of robber capitalism?

George Soros does not hide the fact that he is made up of two personalities: a shrewd fund manager acting in the interests of his shareholders, and a social reformer who strives to change the world for the better. To avoid a conflict of interest, he prefers not to do business in those countries where he does philanthropy. But this was an opportunity of a lifetime.

In the end, he declined. "This package is worth nothing," he said. "I'll bet you a hundred to one that the Communists will win and cancel all these auctions. And my advice to Boris is this: he should not do it either. He is putting into this all he has got, and he will lose it all."

Soros was not alone in this evaluation. Boris went around to all his Western and Eastern partners, from the bosses of Mercedes in Germany to the owners of Daewoo in Korea, but nobody wanted to buy into Sibneft. Everyone thought that Chubais's gambit with dubious auctions would not last a month after Yeltsin's departure, which seemed all but certain.

In the end, Boris did find a partner, an unknown oil trader named Roman (Roma) Abramovich. Roma was a shy, rosy-cheeked fellow of twenty-nine, slightly pudgy, who wore jeans and a sweater and who drove to The Club on a motorcycle. Where he got the $50 million no one knew.

"Let me introduce you," said Boris one day at The Club when I returned with Soros's rejection. "This is Roma, my new partner. He is very interested in philanthropy, and I think we need to put him on the board of the new foundation."

Boris was talking about my latest project, the Russian Society for Science and Education, which I was trying to organize with donations from various budding oligarchs.

I started my spiel about the Gilded Age and the pillars of American philanthropy. Roma listened politely, lowering his gaze and smiling shyly in response to Boris's cooing that he was one of those young people Russia needed "to make it into a normal country."

"Well, what do you think? A wonderful guy, we need more like him!" Boris enthused after Roma left without ever having said a word.

Boris would come to regret bitterly the day that he brought Roma into his circle: five years later, taken control of Sibneft and ORT, the shy young man would become the next gray eminence of the Kremlin and the richest man in Russia.

CHAPTER 4

THE DAVOS PACT

January 9–18, 1996: Chechen rebels led by the warlord Salman Raduyev attack the town of Kizlyar, Dagestan, inside the Russian border. They take with them 160 hostages but are encircled by Russian troops in the border village of Pervomaiskoye. Sasha Litvinenko, among other FSB men, is there, in the trenches with the regular army. After a weeklong siege, and several futile attempts to take the village, Russian commanders insist that there are "no hostages left" and launch an intensive bombardment, killing many hostages and some rebels. The next morning, Raduyev and the bulk of the rebels escape through Russian lines, taking twenty hostages back to Chechnya. Litvinenko is stunned by the army's brutality.

Davos, Switzerland, February 3, 1996

Vladimir Gusinsky, nicknamed "Goose," answered the phone at his hotel room in Davos. When he heard the voice of his caller, he was speechless. It was his archenemy, Boris Berezovsky.

They were both attending the World Economic Forum of 1996.

"Volodya, don't you think that we should let bygones be bygones, and sit down and talk?" Boris said.

A former theater director and a leader of Moscow's Jewish community, Gusinsky, forty-three, was at one point considered the wealthiest man in Russia—that is, before the loans-for-shares scheme created a new, richer breed of oligarchs. He owed his fortune to his friendship with Mayor Yuri Luzhkov. Goose's Most-Bank was the principal depository of municipal funds. His real estate company snapped up the best properties made available in city-controlled privatizations. He also owned a newspaper, a weekly news magazine, a radio station, and NTV. The network loved to give the Kremlin headaches, attacking its policies day and night and mocking its officials on *Kukly* (The Puppets), the popular political satire program. In his political outlook, Goose, a bespectacled intellectual, was close to Grigory Yavlinsky, the left-of-center democratic politician and a friend of George Soros. Gusinsky did not like Yeltsin and he feared the cabal of military and state security types in the president's circle.

The twists and turns of Goose's rivalry with Berezovsky had been the talk of Moscow for months. At one point, Goose even had to flee the city for London for five months, after Boris's Kremlin pal, General Korzhakov, sent some goons to harass him in what became known as the Most-Bank raid.

On that memorable day in December 1994, Goose's motorcade left his country dacha as usual. In the lead was a fast car with watchers scanning both sides of the road. Then came Goose's armored Mercedes, followed by an SUV swaying from side to side to make sure that no one attempted to pass, and finally a windowless van carrying a team of former paratroopers led by a fierce, egg-headed gorilla nicknamed Cyclops.

Suddenly, word came through the guards' earphones: "We have company." Someone was tailing the convoy. Gusinsky's driver floored the gas pedal and they screeched up to the Most-Bank headquarters, located in one of the city's tallest buildings, which also housed City Hall. It was formerly the headquarters of Comecon, the economic command center of the Soviet bloc. Shielded by bodyguards, Goose quickly disappeared inside and rushed straight into the safety of the mayor's office.

Moments later his pursuers arrived, about thirty strong, in flak jackets and balaclavas, armed with automatic weapons and grenade launchers. For the next two hours, in horrified disbelief, Goose watched from the mayor's window. The attackers, who evidently belonged to a branch of the secret service, disarmed his men and put them facedown in the snow, where they remained for nearly two hours, in full view of a crowd of spectators and TV cameras. The city police, called to the scene, exchanged a few words with the attackers and then quietly drove away. So did an FSB squad, alerted by Most-Bank staff, who thought a robbery was in progress.

Eventually the assailants left, as mysteriously as they appeared, without identifying themselves or explaining the reasons for the raid. The next morning Goose took his family to London and the safety of the Park Lane Hotel, where he remained for several months. The managers of his vast business empire shuttled back and forth from Moscow to London.

The mystery of the Most-Bank raid cleared up a few days later when Korzhakov confessed. His people had roughed up Goose's men, ostensibly as part of a search for unlicensed weapons. Korzhakov claimed he was just being cautious. Goose's convoy was taking the same route as the president on his way to the Kremlin, so he couldn't be too careful. But the general also suggested that the raid was partly a matter of personal pleasure. "Hunting geese is among my favorite hobbies," Korzhakov gleefully told the Russian weekly *Argumenty i Facti* on January 18, 1995. Many felt it was his revenge for NTV's criticism of the war in Chechnya, launched in December, and for mocking him as a hopelessly dumb puppet on the *Kukly* show.

At the time, many believed that the Most-Bank raid was encouraged by Berezovsky. After all, he was friendly with Korzhakov. Four months later, when Berezovsky was nearly taken away by Moscow police in the aftermath of Listyev's murder on March 1, 1995—and saved by Sasha Litvinenko—the same logic suggested that it was the mayor's revenge for the Most-Bank raid.

Now, in February 1996, Berezovsky and Goose were direct competitors in network television, and yet Berezovsky had the nerve to call and invite Goose for a drink. But Goose thought that he knew what it was all about. The way things were going, he would dine with the devil himself if he could get some guidance on how to prevent the catastrophe looming in Russia's presidential elections.

———

Just a few months earlier, the privatization dream machine had ground to a halt. For months, lucky bankers had been waking up to discover that they were now industrialists. But in December, without explanation, the government canceled three loans-for-shares auctions in the aviation industry, including a deal for KB Sukhoy, the producer of the famous fighter jets. Rumors flew that the stoppage was the work of Defense Minister Pavel Grachev, one of the Kremlin's leading hawks.

Chubais's standing grew more and more shaky. As the June elections loomed in everyone's mind, he was unquestionably becoming Yeltsin's main liability. Communist propaganda made him Public Enemy No. 1. The chant "Retire Yeltsin, Jail Chubais!" reverberated at rallies. His enemies ruthlessly exploited Chubais's non-Russian surname and his peculiar looks, especially his red hair. In Russian folk tradition, a redhead is someone to watch out for, a devious and suspicious character. In support of this view, an ancient edict of Czar Peter the Great prohibiting redheads from giving legal testimony was handily discovered in the archives and trumpeted on the airwaves.

By early January, a split had developed in Yeltsin's inner circle. An anti-Chubais faction, headed by Korzhakov, began whispering into the president's ear that it was about time he sacrificed "the privatizer" to raise his popularity at least a little bit.

Korzhakov's group included Sasha's top boss, FSB director Mikhail Barsukov, and First Deputy Prime Minister Oleg Soskovets, a man whom Korzhakov hoped one day to install in the president's office. The liberals who supported Chubais included Foreign Minister Andrei Kozyrev, Chief of Staff Sergei Filatov, and the journalist Valentin Yumashev, whose friendship with Yeltsin's daughter would eventually deepen into marriage and who would become a major Kremlin power broker in his own right. Prime Minister Viktor Chernomyrdin, the former Soviet gas and oil chief, maintained strict neutrality, as did Boris Berezovsky. An important trump card for

Chubais was his favor with the West, from the Clinton administration, to the World Bank and International Monetary Fund, to the flock of Harvard University advisers who were helping him build such capitalist institutions as a stock market and a tax service. But that card was, if anything, a liability in the public's mind.

On January 17, 1996, Yeltsin opened his election campaign with a bombshell. He fired Chubais and several liberal members of his Cabinet, claiming, "Chubais is to blame for everything." The phrase thundered throughout Russia. It was a total defeat for the reformers. To manage the economic portfolio in place of Chubais, Yeltsin appointed Vladimir Kadannikov, the director of the Volga Automobile Factory, the plant that Boris had been trying to privatize at the time of his attempted assassination. Pro-Western Foreign Minister Andrei Kozyrev was replaced with an arch-hawk, the foreign intelligence chief Evgeny Primakov. The liberal Chief of Staff Filatov resigned, and another hardliner, Nikolai Yegorov, was put in his place.

In one fell swoop, Yeltsin appointed Chubais's nemesis, First Deputy Prime Minister Oleg Soskovets, to chair his reelection committee, with the two generals as his deputies: the FSO's Korzhakov and the FSB's Barsukov. At the time, according to opinion polls, the Communist candidate, Gennady Zyuganov, was in the lead, with 24 percent of likely voters; Grigory Yavlinsky, the socialist democrat friend of Soros, stood at 11 percent; the fascist Vladimir Zhirinovsky had 7 percent; the maverick paratrooper Gen. Alexander Lebed had 6 percent; and Yeltsin had a meager 5 percent, just above the margin of error. Half of those surveyed remained undecided.

When Berezovsky arrived in Davos on February 1 he discovered that Gennady Zyuganov, the potential future Communist president of Russia, was one of its main attractions. Western CEOs "flew to him like flies to honey," in his words. Meanwhile, Chubais, unemployed, roamed the Swiss ski resort "like a lonely ghost." He was old news.

Zyuganov, a husky, balding apparatchik of fifty-one, did his best to portray himself as a Western-style social democrat.

"We want a mixed economy," he said in William Safire's column in *The New York Times*. "Communism means collegiality, sustainable development, spiritual values, major investment in the human being."

"I was shocked to see all these Westerners, including Soros, snowed by Zyuganov," Boris recalled. "They didn't get that Zyuganov was nothing but a front for the old Central Committee! They would start jailing people immediately. How could the West not understand this?"

But the West, by all accounts, had already written Yeltsin off. According to a CIA analysis leaked to the press, the Russian president was an alcoholic who had suffered four heart attacks and would lose the ballot if he managed to live that long. The choice in Russia was between the Communists and a coalition of the military and secret services.

"Your game is over," Soros told Boris when they met in Davos for breakfast. "My advice to you is to take your family, sell what you still can, and get out of the country before it is too late."

But Boris was stubborn and adventurous. The conversation with George had the opposite of its intended effect: it only added to his urgent desire to win at all costs. He picked up the phone and called Goose.

Goose was an essential ally for Yeltsin on two accounts. First, his pal, Mayor Luzhkov, a stocky, bald man in a proletarian cap with the demeanor of Mussolini, was in control of Moscow, where 10 percent of the electorate lived. Without Luzhkov, no victory at the city's polls was possible. Second, Gusinsky's NTV was particularly popular among Russia's educated class, which made up about 15 percent of the vote.

When Boris sat down with Goose for a drink, he went straight to the point: "Volodya, do you know what the Communists will do when they get to power? They will put you in jail for being a rich Jew."

Goose agreed. Boris then launched into his pitch. The situation was salvageable only if they joined forces. Goose had to discard Yavlinsky and get Mayor Luzhkov to endorse Yeltsin's candidacy.

Boris even wanted to bring Chubais back into the game. Boris never did anything halfway.

Gusinsky had good reasons to refuse. He had a number of long-standing grudges against the Kremlin crowd, from Korzhakov's thugs holding his men facedown in the snow to Chubais cutting his bank out of the loans-for-shares bonanza. As for the mayor, it would be quite a challenge to make him work with Chubais: they were in perpetual conflict over privatizing Moscow-based enterprises, arguing whether they were municipal or federal.

"If the Communists come to power . . . ," Boris started again, but Goose interrupted him by reciting Boris's own arguments: the Communists aren't going to care whether the privatizations were for Moscow or for the Kremlin, they would rescind them all; Yavlinsky was a nonstarter—being a Jew, he would never get more than 12 percent of the vote. By default Yeltsin appeared to be the lesser of all evils. Goose was already ready to say yes.

But, Goose added, Yeltsin's secret services and the military were no less a threat than the Communists. And the war in Chechnya should be stopped at any cost. Boris could not have agreed more. They shook hands on a deal. Common enemies have united stranger bedfellows, but nobody in Moscow predicted this pairing.

Boris began calling fellow Davos oligarchs who had fallen into various states of dejection, inviting them for a strategy meeting. Chubais was invited, too. Upon seeing the archenemies Berezovsky and Gusinsky chatting like old friends, a spark was lit, and the "Davos group" was born. Boris was authorized to seek a meeting with the president for the group.

To get to the president over the head of Korzhakov, Boris used his connection with Tanya-Valya, as the inseparable duo of Tatyana, the president's daughter, and Valentin Yumashev, the journalist, was known. He had no doubt that the all-powerful FSO director would learn of his role, and their relationship would be finished. Korzhakov blacklisted anybody who bypassed him to see the president, even on a completely innocent errand. And this was no innocent errand: Boris was plotting to reverse Korzhakov's coup.

Sometime in late February Yeltsin met with the Davos group in the

Kremlin. It was Boris's first serious meeting with the president. He wasn't sure how to conduct himself with this enigmatic man, who combined seemingly incompatible traits: decisiveness in times of crisis with inertia bordering on stupor in the periods in between, an autocrat who protected free speech and civil liberties, a former Communist Party boss who hated the Communists, a Soviet through and through who had single-handedly disbanded the USSR.

Yeltsin looked ill. Right before New Year's Eve, he had suffered yet another heart attack, which his staff managed to hide from the press. His bloated face and big ex-athlete's body, wasted by alcohol and heart disease, exuded fatigue. Berezovsky knew that Yeltsin's wife was trying to talk him out of running for a second term. He also knew that his closest confidant, Korzhakov, was now pushing the president to replace the moderate prime minister Chernomyrdin with the hawk Oleg Soskovets, which would make him the official successor should the president be incapacitated (perhaps by a final heart attack).

"Boris Nikolaevich, we'd like to raise the issue of the coming elections," Berezovsky began. "We have the feeling you're headed toward catastrophe."

"But I'm told that the situation is improving, that the polls are skewed, and for the most part, people will vote for me," the president said, frowning.

From Yeltsin's neutral tone, Boris couldn't make out whether he was completely out of touch with reality or just teasing them.

"Boris Nikolaevich, you're being deceived!" Berezovsky retorted. The members of the group chimed in: "What's going on around you is a disaster. People see it, so many in the business community are trying to cut a deal with the Communists and the rest are packing their bags to flee abroad. If we don't reverse this situation now, in a month it will be too late. And our motivation is pure: if you lose, the Communists will hang us from the lampposts."

"Well, what are you proposing?" Yeltsin inquired, again in a neutral tone, displaying neither consent nor objection.

"Give us an opportunity to help your campaign," Boris pleaded. "We have the media, money, people, contacts in the regions, and the main thing: determination. We just need a word from you."

"I already have a campaign staff," said Yeltsin. "Are you suggesting that I fire Soskovets and put you in charge?"

"No, of course not. Create another entity—say, an analytical group. Let it work alongside your staff. And we propose Anatoly Borisovich Chubais as its leader."

"Chubais? Chubais . . . Chubais is to blame for everything," the president said, quoting himself. He paused, still revealing little behind his impassive mask. But then he flashed a hint of a smile. "Well, okay, since he's to blame, let him clean up the mess. All right, give it a try," he said.

After the meeting Boris stayed behind for fifteen minutes to discuss details. He worried that the president was not completely sold on the plan. He mentioned that he had heard of Korzhakov's idea to suspend the elections.

"We will win, democratically, Boris Nikolaevich. Any other way would lead to massive bloodshed," Berezovsky argued. But as he left he was still not sure whether he had carried the day. Yeltsin held his cards close to his chest.

The very next day, people began working feverishly at "Shadow HQ," as the endeavor became known in its narrow circle. It was kept secret from the press and the public. Within days, Boris and Goose managed to pull together a team of the best brains in Moscow, from pollsters to speechwriters. They worked out strategies to reach out to the young, pensioners, and the military; they scheduled rallies and concerts; they enlisted performers and pop stars; they courted regional power brokers; in short, they used every trick they could find in the Western book of campaigns, previously unknown in Russia. Their sluggish opponents never responded but just hoped to win by making speeches in the archaic style of the Soviet Politbureau.

Work at Shadow HQ continued 24/7 in total secrecy. Chubais managed finances and logistics, Boris determined general strategy, and Goose brought in his star creative genius, NTV president Igor Malashenko, to coordinate the media campaign. Yeltsin's ratings in the polls began to climb almost immediately.

Years later, as an exile in America, Malashenko recalled the drama and the irony of those days.

"I first was taken to see Yeltsin on March 6, under a veil of total secrecy. I told him straightaway that I will make him win. He did not seem to believe me. My impression was that he agreed to work with us only to be able to say to himself that he had exhausted all options. I said that I needed his help with aggressive news management on a daily basis.

"'What do you mean?' he asked.

"I told him how Ronald Reagan would go to an automobile plant to make a speech about the economy, or to a flag factory to generate patriotic images. He was amused by the flag factory idea. My people rushed to look for a flag factory in Moscow. But when we found one, I dumped the idea: it was a miserable hole, filled with embittered workers, hungry and dressed in rags, who hadn't gotten their wages in months, one of those sinking places. There was no demand for Russian flags in those days."

––––––––––

Korzhakov flew into a white rage when he learned about the Shadow HQ. The triumvirate of Chubais-Boris-Goose, backed by cash from the loans-for-shares oligarchs, was as much a challenge to him as were the Communists. He wanted Yeltsin to be the president, but on his terms, whereby the dominance of the secret services would be guaranteed. When he learned Berezovsky had made an impression on Yeltsin with his frank depiction of the president's bleak prospects in the polls, he changed tactics: his entire team began to whisper to the president that the situation was so bad that no smart campaigning could save him from a humiliating defeat. He even brought over a team of American consultants and tasked them with producing an independent assessment that the elections were not winnable.

The only solution, he argued—and no doubt believed—was to postpone the elections and impose a state of emergency.

By mid-March, two irreconcilable political centers had formed around the president: one strove to solve the Communist problem by throwing money at it, the other, by crushing it with tanks.

March 6, 1996: Hundreds of Chechen fighters infiltrate Grozny, override Russian units, and hold the city for three days before escaping back to the mountains with large amounts of captured weapons and ammunition. The surprise assault is the first rebel effort to retake Grozny since it fell to Russian forces in February 1995.

George Soros arrived in Moscow on March 15, 1996, to meet with Prime Minister Chernomyrdin and get his blessing for a new project: connecting Russia to the Internet. At that time, few people in Russia had even heard of the Net, but to George it was clear: if there was something that could drag this country out of its eternal provincial swamp, it was integration into the worldwide information network. The plan called for thirty hubs at main university campuses throughout the country, with links to the surrounding urban communities. It would connect broad progressive circles across the country: journalists, nongovernmental organizations, liberal local politicians, and the educated class at large.

When I first came to George with the idea, I didn't particularly expect that he would fund it. After all, he was still predicting that Russia was about to undergo a "catastrophe of cosmic dimensions." But to my surprise he agreed, saying, "Even so, there is life after death." He allocated $100 million over five years, with the caveat that the Russian government match the funds with contributions in the form of free telecommunication channels to link the hubs with each other and the rest of the World Wide Web. For that, we needed to see the prime minister.

The problem, however, was that Chernomyrdin didn't want to see George. Someone had told him that Soros had fraternized in Davos with Zyuganov and was helping Zyuganov reconstruct himself as a moderate social democrat. I had to use all my personal chits with Berezovsky, and he, in turn, with the prime minister, to secure an appointment.

On the day of the meeting, the Communists sponsored a resolution in the Duma denouncing the Belovezh Agreement. This was the famous pact that Yeltsin had signed in 1991 with the presidents of Ukraine and Belarus, officially terminating the USSR. The news of the Duma's maneuver exploded across the entire former empire, from the Baltics to Central Asia, provoking panic in the former republics of the Soviet Union. Yeltsin denounced it as election-year posturing. Even the former head of the USSR, Mikhail Gorbachev, who had lost his job as a result of the Belovezh Agreement, told Reuters news service, "I am the one who is expected to applaud this because my presidential post would now become real again. But to talk about the revival of the Soviet Union now . . . means to ignore the new realities."

Chernomyrdin received us at the White House, the seat of the government on the banks of the Moscow River. Aside from Yeltsin and Primakov, he was the last major Soviet-era holdover in the Russian government. Those roots were evident in his large, solid figure, his big head with the heavy, square jaw, his deep-set eyes, and the bass voice of a man used to giving orders. But that was evidently their limit, because he immediately fell upon us with a very un-Soviet, angry invective against Zyuganov, the leader of the Communists, calling him a "wolf in sheep's clothing."

"Some Western figures, as we hear from Davos," said Chernomyrdin, looking pointedly at Soros, "see in him a moderate leftist. This is Western naïveté, Mr. Soros, the kind Comrade Lenin understood best of all, when he said that the capitalists would sell him the rope with which he would hang them. But I know these people well, Mr. Soros, I was yoked with them for thirty years, I can see right through them. Did you hear what they got up to today? They want to restore the Soviet Union! And they will restore it, if they have their way. So don't deceive yourself, Mr. Soros, nothing good will come of them, and we will not let them back into power, whatever the cost."

After listening to a ten-minute lecture about the horrors of Communism, Soros finally got a chance to assure the prime minister that he was far from supporting Zyuganov, especially after the resolution in the Duma. He shared the universal concern of the West about the outcome of the presidential elections.

"Yes," sighed Chernomyrdin. "That's our main concern, I can assure you, Mr. Soros."

By the end of the conversation the prime minister's feelings toward the West appeared to improve. In any case, the university Internet centers obtained free government connectivity.

George was happy with his new acquaintance.

"Do you know that this man controls Gazprom?" he asked as we drove away from the White House. "Maybe he is even richer than me!" Briefly, I saw the face not of a philanthropist, but of an investor. Possibly a very hungry investor.

"Guess how many people read the transcript of your conversation?" Sasha Litvinenko asked when, years later, I described to him our meeting with Chernomyrdin.

He explained that in early 1996, one of his agents reported that someone was selling transcripts of conversations from Chernomyrdin's office, which was bugged, along with conversations from the office of his chief of staff. The buyers included some Chechens in Moscow, who sent them to the separatists in the mountains. It was doubly a scandal: first, that someone was bugging the prime minister, and second, that the transcripts were reaching the enemy.

"We began to work on this lead and established that Korzhakov's people were running the bug. That meant that Korzhakov's office had been penetrated. As soon as I submitted the report, Korzhakov himself came, seized all the materials, and said he would investigate it himself."

By then, Sasha found it harder and harder to sort through the arcane political connections of the top brass. Sasha's mentor, Gen. Anatoly Trofimov, the head of the Moscow FSB, was close to Korzhakov. But if Korzhakov was bugging Chernomyrdin, Sasha was unsure of what should and shouldn't be reported, and to whom.

At the same time, some people in the Agency were beginning to wonder about Sasha. It was not a secret that Sasha was connected to Berezovsky. But was he Berezovsky's man? Or the opposite, an Agency mole in Berezovsky's circle?

Shortly after the wiretapping investigation, one of the director's aides called Sasha into his office. He came straight to the point. "Listen, Gusinsky is once again friendly with Berezovsky and has gone over to Chernomyrdin's side. He's left the mayor. The director is very interested in this connection: Goose, Berezovsky, and Chernomyrdin. So start developing this line and report personally to the director, through me."

Sasha naïvely asked, "What's wrong with Berezovsky and Gusinsky making peace? I think this is only for the good. Besides, perhaps some order will be restored in Moscow if the mayor quiets down a bit."

The aide, who himself was not sure what was going on, offered his own interpretation: "You want these two Jews to be together? Nothing good will come of it. For us, it's a good thing when the Jews quarrel among themselves. So, have you understood the assignment? Then you are free to go."

Sasha had both official and unofficial reasons to be pleased when Boris called him in mid-February and proposed that they meet. He was doing what his bosses wanted him to do, and in the process he hoped he would learn why he had been given the assignment.

When they met, Sasha chatted about Chechnya and what he had seen in the trenches at the siege of Pervomaiskoye. He was still in shock from it. Boris had no time to listen, as usual, and he had his own agenda.

"We'll work on Chechnya after the elections, and I promise you, we will end this mess," said Berezovsky. "But for now, here's what you need to know. Until quite recently, I was on very good terms with your bosses, Korzhakov and Barsukov. But now we've split.

And I want to warn you that you may have problems if you remain connected to me."

Boris explained his quarrel with Korzhakov: Korzhakov wanted to cancel the elections, but Boris thought that if that were to occur, the Communists would bring people out into the streets. Federal troops, certainly the FSB, might be ordered to shoot at the crowd.

"I don't want to pressure you, Sasha," Boris said. "I just want you to understand that very soon you'll have to pick which side you're on."

Up until that moment Sasha had had no reservations about his special relationship with Boris. He was not particularly savvy politically. He relied only on the general conviction that he was working for the government, led by the president. He divided the world into "us" and "them," and so Boris, as a member of the establishment and an adviser to Yeltsin, was part of "us" and someone whom the services were supposed to serve. Besides, his bosses—Korzhakov, Barsukov, and Trofimov—had encouraged their relationship all along. It was only now that Boris was being described as an "operative object."

What he heard from Boris shook him to the core. For the first time in his life he faced a value judgment that could bring him into conflict with his official duties. Of course, Korzhakov and Barsukov were his commanders and Boris was an outsider. Yet he trusted Boris's judgment.

Boris did not want an answer right away. He added that he would understand if Sasha distanced himself. However, he wanted one last favor: to set up a meeting for him with General Trofimov, the Moscow FSB chief, the man who had protected him from the city cops after the Listyev murder.

Trofimov, a short, thin man with the demeanor of an accountant, was a legend in the services. He had a reputation as incorruptible. Even the former Soviet dissidents whose cases he managed in the 1980s had accorded him a measure of respect. Some said that he was close to Korzhakov, but Boris doubted it; he believed that Trofimov's only true loyalty was to Yeltsin. Trofimov was the one who had arrested the leaders of the parliamentary putsch after the storming of the White House in 1993. Boris was confident that Trofimov harbored no political ambitions, and he wanted to sound him out in advance of the gathering storm: the position of the Moscow FSB chief would to a large extent determine the outcome if Russian politics deteriorated into street-level confrontations.

The next morning, Boris came to see Trofimov at the Moscow FSB office. Sasha waited outside.

"I do not know what they talked about, but when I escorted him out after the meeting, out in the street I spotted surveillance," he recalled. "Two guys standing across the street with an attaché case."

Sasha knew the device well; it was a standard clandestine camera. The agents were positioned just as he had been taught, standing at an angle to each other. One was holding the attaché case perpendicular to the door of the FSB building, with the camera in its side pointed at Sasha and Boris. The other provided cover by pretending to talk.

"I pointed them out to Berezovsky. He jumped into his Mercedes and sped away, and I rushed toward them, but they were gone. So I went back to my boss and told him about the surveillance."

Trofimov smiled and said that it was not the FSB. He suggested that Sasha inquire at the FSO, Korzhakov's agency.

"I called General Rogozin, Korzhakov's second in command, and I couldn't believe it as I heard myself ask, 'Georgy Georgievich, Anatoly Vasilievich here wonders whether it was you who was carrying out surveillance of our building.' And Rogozin only laughed and said, 'We should keep a watchful eye on the oligarchs, Sasha.'"

He expected Trofimov to give him at least a hint about what to do next. But the general was reticent. For the first time in his life, Sasha decided not to choose sides, "because I could not make any decision."

"It was a very difficult time for him," Marina recalled later. "He lost weight, and could not sleep at night."

———

In the meantme, a similar dilemma tormented the president. He had to choose between the same two camps: Berezovsky and the Shadow HQ, or Korzhakov and the secret services. Yeltsin lost sleep too, but unlike Sasha he could not afford the luxury of procrastination. In his memoirs, *Midnight Diaries,* he describes the lonely agony of indecision and soul-searching in 1996: Could he be certain that the election was all but lost? Did the end of stopping Communism justify any means, including suspending the Russian Constitution? Would it be acceptable to use force and shed blood to prevent the bloodbath that the Communists would undoubtedly unleash if they took power?

On March 17, 1996, he made his decision.

At 6 a.m. on that day, Berezovsky was awakened by a phone call from Valentin Yumashev.

"It's all finished," he said in panic. "Boris Nikolaevich has just given a green light to cancel the elections."

After a late night with Korzhakov and his buddies, the president had authorized three decrees. He would dissolve the Duma, ban the Communist Party, and postpone presidential elections for two years.

Boris had two ways to get Yeltsin to change his mind: through Chubais, and through Prime Minister Chernomyrdin. By the time Yeltsin convened a secret meeting of his senior ministers to announce his decrees, Boris had pulled both of these strings for all they were worth.

Yeltsin began the meeting by saying that he had drastic steps to propose in response to the recent Duma resolution reinstating the USSR. Yet he admitted that this was just a pretext. He was fully aware that he would be violating the Constitution, but it was a necessary step to rid Russia of the scourge of Communism once and for all. He would take full responsibility.

Dead silence fell in the room. Then, after a long pause, Prime Minister Chernomyrdin spoke out against the decision, arguing that there was no need for such drastic measures when the president's numbers were actually improving. Then, quite unexpectedly, Interior Minister Anatoly Kulikov also spoke up. He suggested, ominously, that he could not guarantee the loyalty of his forces should the Communists call people into the streets—and he tendered his resignation. It was a powerful statement.

But it did not single-handedly change Yeltsin's mind. Everyone else—the FSB, the military, the intelligence and foreign services, and the two first deputy prime ministers, Soskovets and Kadannikov—were supportive of the decrees. We are firmly in control, they said, and after all, you are not going to abolish the Constitution, you are just going to suspend it for two years for a greater good, Mr. President.

Korzhakov was triumphant. In his hands he held a leather folder stamped with the presidential seal that contained the three decrees. Crack units of the FSB stationed around Moscow were placed on alert, ready to move into the city to secure media and communications centers. By speaking against the plan, Chernomyrdin just might have sealed his resignation and made it more likely that Korzhakov would get his wish that Oleg Soskovets would be installed as prime minister. Chubais, Goose, and Boris would not last long in such a regime.

But Kulikov's and Chernomyrdin's responses had puzzled Yeltsin, and the president hesitated. In a maneuver that must have thrown the hawks for a loop, he retired to his study for a final moment of reflection. The thick silence of the Kremlin descended on his shoulders. Yeltsin was alone in the famous room where Ivan the Terrible, Peter the Great, Stalin, and Khrushchev had each once plotted. As Yeltsin recalls it in his memoirs, he wrestled with a terrible choice: Would he be the ruler to go down in history as the man who had a chance to free Russia for the first time in a thousand years, and blew it?

And then he heard a noise. It was his daughter Tatyana who stormed into the room.

"Papa, you must hear another opinion."

While Yeltsin had been discussing the would-be coup with his generals, she and Valentin Yumashev, the Tanya-Valya team, had brought into the Kremlin the only man who had the brains, the clout, and the chutzpah to try to change Yeltsin's mind: Anatoly Chubais.

When Chubais entered the room, his face was crimson, his usual color in moments of extreme excitement. He did not waste time on niceties. He denounced Yeltsin's idea as "madness." He spoke about the civil war that such a move would unleash, and about the KGB hacks, Korzhakov & Company, whose true agenda was to control the presidency. He boasted of his confidence that Shadow HQ would bring Yeltsin to victory in the election if it were to go forward.

In the end, after enduring a shouting match with Yeltsin, something he had never done before, Chubais changed the president's mind.

Yeltsin returned to the meeting, canceled the decrees, and told the Korzhakov team to steer clear of the campaign. Chubais received a green light to do what he saw fit.

Activity at Shadow HQ resumed at full speed. Working in concert, ORT and NTV strove to offset Zyuganov's propaganda on the many regional TV stations that were controlled by the Communists. In living rooms, on banners, and on billboards, Yeltsin's campaign slogans "Vote with Your Heart!" and "Choose or Lose!" were ubiquitous. Goose delivered Luzhkov's support and blanketed Moscow with photographs of the president and the mayor together. Berezovsky met with General Lebed and agreed to secretly fund his campaign, to split the Communist vote.

April 21, 1996: Chechen President Dzhokhar Dudayev is assassinated by two guided missiles homing in on the signal from his satellite telephone. He had been speaking with a liberal Duma deputy in Moscow, discussing a peace initiative. Dudayev is succeeded by Zelimkhan Yandarbiyev.

May 27, 1996: President Yeltsin and Prime Minister Chernomyrdin meet with Yandarbiyev at the Kremlin to sign a cease-fire in the seventeen-month war, in which an estimated forty thousand people have died.

On June 16, after an ardous campaign that took him all over the country, Yeltsin managed to eke out a plurality of 35 percent of the vote, just ahead of the 32 percent for his Communist rival Zyuganov. By the rules of the new Russian electoral system, it set the two of them to face each other in a runoff on July 4. Berezovsky's strategy of diminishing the social democrat Yavlinsky and secretly helping Lebed paid off: Lebed, the former paratrooper, finished a strong third with 15 percent, heavily denting the Communist base, while Yavlinsky finished fourth with only 7 percent. Vladimir Zhirinovsky earned only 6 percent of the vote.

There was no doubt in the president's mind that he owed his first-round win to the work of Chubais, Goose, and Berezovsky. On the morning of June 17 he gathered the team in the Kremlin to start planning for the second round. The mood was jubilant. The coalition of reformers and oligarchs seemed to be firmly in charge in the Kremlin.

Not only that, but Yeltsin even managed a masterstroke on the very next day. He got Lebed's endorsement in exchange for naming him secretary of the National Security Council, with a mandate to find a quick solution to the Chechen conflict. It all but sealed Yeltsin's victory in the second round.

One day later, Korzhakov made his move.

Sasha Litvinenko sensed that something was cooking on the afternoon of June 18. A fellow oper complained about an extra load of work that had suddenly fallen on him just as he was about to go home: Director Barsukov urgently wanted all available information on Chubais, Berezovsky, and Gusinsky.

"A thought went through my mind immediately: they are preparing to arrest them," Sasha recalled.

"Did you think of warning Boris?" I asked.

"No," he said. "That would be treason, and I was not at all up to it. I was not happy, of course. I thought of Boris as a friend, and I knew the whole thing was political, but you know, that's the whole point of wearing a uniform: you don't question your superiors."

"Would you have arrested him if you were ordered?"

"At the time I would. I was a loyal officer. That was what I was trained to do: obey orders. But it would not have given me any pleasure."

"Would you have shot at the crowds if you were ordered?"

"I don't know. Lucky me, I was never asked to."

On that afternoon in 1996 Sasha wondered why he had been left out of any preparations that were going on. After all, he was the Agency's "Berezovsky connection." Was his loyalty in question? Or were they saving him for some special task? Just as he was leaving for home, his phone rang. It was General Rogozin, Korzhakov's deputy.

"Sasha, can you stop by my office tomorrow at four?" he asked.

This is it, Sasha thought. They want to use me against Boris. Just as Boris had warned. God help us both.

But he never met with Rogozin. Just as Sasha was entering the deputy's waiting room the next afternoon, Rogozin ran out in great haste.

"Georgy Georgievich, shall I wait for you?" Sasha inquired.

"Don't wait, I have a situation to deal with. Let's talk tomorrow," cried the general as he ran down the hall.

The conversation never happened.

In the early hours of the evening on June 19, 1996, Igor Malashenko, Goose's right hand and the creative genius of NTV, stopped by The Club. There he found Berezovsky and Chubais sitting on the veranda. Boris was in a festive mood, sipping his favorite Chateau Latour, whereas Chubais was increasingly worried.

For the past four hours he had not been able to locate his closest lieutenant, Arkady Evstafiev. It was not like Arkady to disappear without warning. Chubais made frantic phone calls all over town, telling everyone he knew to look out for Arkady.

Suddenly, word came that Arkady and Sergei Lisovsky, the owner of the talent agency Media International, had been arrested by Korzhakov's people as they were leaving a government building, carrying a box filled with half a million dollars in cash.

According to Malashenko, "Stunned silence fell over the terrace." No one was surprised by the cash: Lisovsky's agency was coordinating campaign performances for Yeltsin, and his rock stars and pop singers only sang for cash. But that Korzhakov chose to move against Chubais's people was ominous. Clearly, another shoe was waiting to drop.

"Let's move off the terrace and get inside," someone suggested, fearing for the group's safety.

Several more people arrived: Gusinsky, surrounded by his security detail led by the fearsome Cyclops, armed with a huge pump gun; curly-headed Boris Nemtsov, a rising star of the liberal movement; and Alfred Kokh, the state properties minister.

Malashenko later reconstructed the events of that night: "The two coolest heads, as usual, were Boris and Goose. They sat down with Chubais to review our assets": the two TV networks, a direct line to the president in the persons of Tanya-Valya, and, as allies, probably the prime minister and possibly General Lebed.

Tanya-Valya were destined to save Russian democracy for the third time that year. They arrived at The Club just after midnight. In everyone's retrospective judgment, it was perhaps the single most important development of the affair. By the early morning hours, snipers had deployed on the roofs and the building was surrounded. Yet they would never dare an assault with the president's daughter inside.

With the security of The Club ensured by Tatyana's presence, everyone's mind turned to the fate of the two detainees, Evstafiev and Lisovsky. It was at that point that Chubais picked up the phone and yelled at Barsukov, the FSB director: "If a single hair falls from their heads, you are finished!" Of course he did not have much to back up his threat, but the sight of Chubais shouting at Barsukov raised everyone's morale.

As soon as she arrived, Tatyana called her father. She insisted that he be woken. "Papa, you have to watch the news," she said, "something important is happening." By then, the NTV announcer Evgeny Kiselev was on his way to the newsroom. Berezovsky called General Lebed and sent someone to bring him to the studio as well.

"This was perhaps the most important newscast in NTV's history," Malashenko recalled. "Ironically, the broadcast was aimed at an audience of only one: the president. If not for Tatyana's wake-up call, everything would have been lost."

———

Usually when in Moscow, I went to bed late and kept my TV on. At about 1 a.m. that night, I heard NTV make an announcement of an emergency special report, coming soon. An hour later, somber Evgeny Kiselev appeared on the screen to say that a coup d'état was in progress: two Yeltsin campaign workers had been arrested by the secret services. The coup's aim was to destabilize the government and declare a state of emergency. Then General Lebed came on the screen and declared in his deep voice that any attempted coup "would be crushed mercilessly." Fifteen minutes later the report was repeated by ORT.

I could not understand what I was hearing. I picked up my phone and called Boris at The Club. He was at a peak of excitement.

"Just watch," he said. "The idiots have lost. They did not understand the power of the media."

The president watched the program, placed one phone call, and went back to bed. Arkady and his companion were set free at 4 a.m.

Later that morning, Chubais received a summons from the president's office.

"I will demand that he fires Korzhakov and Soskovets," he said to Boris as he was leaving for the Kremlin.

"Barsukov should go too," said Boris. "If one of them stays, sooner or later it will start all over again. I will make sure that TV crews wait outside." By then Boris knew that the best way to guarantee that the volatile president would not change his mind was to immediately put his decision on the air.

At 9 a.m., in a nationally televised address, Yeltsin fired Korzhakov, Barsukov, and Soskovets.

When Sasha Litvinenko came to work the next morning, the Agency brass "looked shell-shocked."

But a Barsukov assistant called him into his office and said, "Tell Boris that if Korzhakov or Barsukov are arrested, he is dead." He dutifully delivered the message.

———————

July 8, 1996: Four days after Yeltsin's decisive victory in the runoff election, hostilities resume in Chechnya. Each side blames the other for violating the truce.

PART III

THE DRUMBEATS OF WAR

CHAPTER 5

THE REBELS

August 6, 1996: Thousands of rebels led by Chechen commander Aslan Maskhadov pour into Grozny, encircling several thousand federal forces. After two weeks of intense fighting, the Russian army abandons the capital. Over the objection of his generals, who want to raze Grozny with a massive bombardment, President Yeltsin authorizes National Security Adviser Alexander Lebed to seek a settlement. On August 31, Lebed and Maskhadov sign the Khasavyurt Accord, granting the rebels de facto control of the republic, promising prompt withdrawal of troops and free elections. The issue of formal independence for Chechnya is deferred until 2001.

Grozny, September 1996

Akhmed Zakayev, the security adviser to the interim Chechen president, settled into his new offices in one of the few buildings still intact in Grozny. He had been through hell over the past two years.

Before the Soviet Union collapsed, Zakayev had been a leading actor in the Grozny Drama Theater, performing Shakespeare and Russian classics, dreaming of a Chechen cultural renaissance that would follow the end of Communism. After the USSR fell and Chechnya declared its independence, he became the head of the Chechen National Actors Guild, a "would-be Chechen Ronald Reagan," he joked. But then came the war. He traded his stage costumes for the fatigues of a hardened guerrilla, a green band with Islamic inscriptions across his forehead and a Kalashnikov by his side. In August he had led the assault on Grozny from the south, against a Russian force that outnumbered his men several-fold. Now he was happy to return to civilian life and assume his new post in the government of interim President Zelimkhan Yandarbiyev.

That very month, as the rebel government struggled to assume control of the restive guerrilla movement, Sasha Litvinenko went on a raid in Moscow. In a strange twist of fate, that raid would threaten to undermine the fragile Chechen peace accord.

———————

The fragility of the peace had a lot to do with the absence of one man: the late Dzhokhar Dudayev, the only leader, in Zakayev's view, who could unite the warring factions and personalities of the Chechen resistance.

Zakayev first met him in early 1990, when Dudayev was an air force general stationed in Tartu, Estonia. He was the only ethnic Chechen to reach such a high rank in the Soviet military. Initially Zakayev was suspicious of the smooth forty-six-year-old officer with an immaculately groomed, pointed moustache and ridiculous Soviet army cap. To become a general, one had to be 100 percent loyal to the Communist Party. A nonethnic Russian also had to be totally assimilated and married to an ethnic Russian. Dudayev was all of these things. He could barely speak Chechen. But when Zakayev heard him address a conference about the rebirth of the Chechen nation, he was overwhelmed. Here was a man, he saw, who could lead their people to freedom. As an actor, Zakayev appreciated Dudayev's charisma. Perhaps it was the influence of Estonia, one of the most rebellious Soviet republics. Estonians revered Dudayev for ignoring orders from Moscow to shut down Estonian TV during massive anti-Soviet disturbances.

After the collapse of the Soviet Union, Dudayev returned to Chechnya, became active in politics, and was quickly elected president. He proclaimed independence in November 1991. Zakayev watched from a distance until one day in November 1994, when Dudayev called to offer him a cabinet position as minister of culture.

One month later, the first Chechen War began.

As with many wars, it started as a result of a miscalculation on both sides. When the Soviet Union collapsed, the Chechens were under the impression that they would be free, like other Soviet republics. These expectations were reinforced by the Kremlin's decision to apportion state property. The Red Army, as it left Chechnya, transferred all its possessions to the Dudayev government—tanks, guns, aircraft, weapons, and ammunition. It was a decision the army would later regret.

But Chechnya was not a full republic of the USSR, like Estonia and Georgia. It was just one of eighty-six provinces of the Russian Federation, and an autonomous ethnic region. In Moscow's view, it was not entitled to full sovereignty. The Chechens protested and declared independence unilaterally, as did Tatarstan, another predominantly Muslim region, landlocked in the center of Russia. In February 1994, President Yeltsin went to Tatarstan and signed a treaty on the mutual delegation of powers with its strong-man president, Mintimer Shaimiyev. For all intents and purposes, Shaimiyev was granted control of local affairs in his nation of 3.7 million, leaving to Moscow the regulation of defense, currency, federal law, and collection of federal taxes, among other things.

The Chechens expected similar treatment, and probably would have been willing to give up their formal independence if they could otherwise manage their own affairs. But Moscow offered no negotiations. As a mountainous nation of only 1.1 million, Chechnya seemed insignificant in comparison to Tatarstan. Talks were delayed and postponed. By mid-1994, the mood in Moscow was rapidly changing, and Yeltsin could not afford to grant another region even token sovereignty. Instead, he decided to undermine Dudayev and install an administration loyal to Moscow.

In the summer of 1994 he authorized a covert operation supporting anti-Dudayev forces, comprised mostly of Moscow-based

Chechen expatriates. Dudayev crushed the insurgency and captured a number of Russian soldiers posing as dissident Chechens. He paraded them on TV and publicly denounced Yeltsin as a liar. Yeltsin was enraged. In December 1994 he unleashed the full force of the Russian army, on the strength of assurances by Defense Minister Pavel Grachev, who bragged that "a paratroop regiment would take Grozny in two hours." Sasha Litvinenko and a group of his FSB friends saw a broadcast of Russian columns advancing on Grozny and were awash in patriotic fervor. They applauded and toasted to a quick victory.

"What are you happy about, silly?" Marina asked him at the time. "People will get killed. And it is a war in our own country, isn't it?"

But back then he would not even call it a war. He repeated the defense minister's boasts about a two-hour job for a paratroop platoon. And he dismissed the Chechens, those primitive shepherds, who could not possibly fight the Russian army.

Some weeks into the war, when NTV showed horrific pictures of the destruction of Grozny, Sasha's comments became less flippant but no more sympathetic to the Chechens. The bandits were putting up resistance, fighting for every house, he said. Bombardment was the cheapest way to smoke them out; it cost fewer Russian lives than hand-to-hand combat. The Chechens were the enemy. He was an officer. War is ugly, but it was necessary to preserve the integrity of Russia.

His moment of truth came in January 1996, during the siege of Pervomaiskoye. He called Marina unexpectedly from work to say that he was leaving for Dagestan and asked her to turn on the TV. For two weeks Marina was glued to the screen, hoping to see his face among the Russian troops that surrounded the unfortunate village where a band of insurgents held some 120 hostages. It was clear to Marina that something very wrong was happening, and the fact that Sasha did not call home—very unusual for him—added to her anxiety.

As the hostage drama unfolded, she saw the absolute helplessness of federal commanders, who could not explain how fewer than three hundred pinned-down rebels held out against thousands of federal troops, who could not take the village after artillery and aircraft had pulverized it for four days. Nor could they explain why the bombardment was allowed in the first place, while most of the hostages were still alive. Nor how the insurgent commander, Salman Raduyev, and his "Lone Wolf" band of fighters were able to break out of the village through three lines of encirclement.

Two days after everything was over, the doorbell rang. It was Sasha.

"At first, I did not recognize him," Marina recalled. "He was a different man, exhausted, with an empty stare. He could barely walk, he had frostbite on his feet."

It took him some days to recover, and then he did something that he had never done before. He told her what had happened.

Marina was horrified by Sasha's story. His group, a bunch of big city opers from the FSB, was thrown into the middle of a military operation without any equipment, protective gear, or even an adequate supply of food and water. They were ordered to storm the village on foot across an open field, but had to retreat when they were exposed to friendly rocket fire. They slept in an unheated bus in the freezing cold. They had some canned food, but no spoons or forks or even knives to open the cans. They were abandoned for two days in the bus without any orders or communications from anyone. Finally Sasha managed to navigate through the frozen fog to a heated command tent, where he found a group of generals, dead drunk.

On the third day of the siege a commando unit suddenly appeared out of the fog, and Sasha recognized its commander, an old friend from officers school. The new arrivals were equally disoriented, but at least they were properly equipped, dressed, and trained. The commander adopted the hapless FSB troop, which Sasha believed saved them from freezing to death.

"In Pervomaiskoye, we did not see any command or control or coordination," Sasha told me later. "We were on our own, fighting the elements as much as we fought the Chechens, perhaps even more. Which made me wonder, who the hell were our commanders?"

On the last day of the operation they captured a Chechen boy, perhaps seventeen years old. They had finally taken the village after most of the terrorists had filtered out. It was a terrible sight: craters from bombardment, burned-out houses, and everywhere the bodies of rebels, villagers, hostages, and Russian soldiers.

The boy had apparently strayed away from his comrades and walked right into their hands.

"He was very scared, expecting that we would beat him," Sasha recalled, "but I took him aside to talk. He was an intelligent-looking boy from Grozny, spoke clear, educated Russian. I was interested to know how he ended up among the terrorists. Wouldn't he rather be in school? And he told me a remarkable thing: 'I hate the war, but it has to be done. When it started, our whole class went.' I remembered my grandfather's stories of his whole class volunteering to go to the front during the Great Patriotic War with the Germans. And I thought that these were not terrorists, even though they attacked civilians. Entire classes of schoolboys don't join terrorist organizations. This was a people's war."

He also found a field journal on a dead Chechen commander. What a contrast from the typically messy methods of Russian commanders! At the end of each day, the Chechen took stock of his personnel, ammunition, and supplies in an organized and cool-headed manner.

"It was in Pervomaiskoye that I realized that it would not be an easy war to win, but I still thought it was necessary for Russia. It did not yet cross my mind that perhaps we should have left the Chechens alone," he said.

In the Chechen notebook, Sasha found some Arab names among the fighters, his first indication of the presence of foreigners. This was a significant discovery. He handed over the notebook to his commanding officer. The next day, the FSB director displayed the list to reporters as evidence of "foreign mercenaries" involved in the raid. Even Yeltsin himself, in a broadcast from the Kremlin, mentioned the captured diary.

Sasha was in the audience for FSB Director Mikhail Barsukov's press conference from Dagestan on January 20, 1996, which was broadcast nationally on ORT. He heard his boss say, "We used Grad [rocket] launchers mainly to exert psychological pressure . . . so that the local population, including the Chechens, could see. . . . There were three Grad launchers but only one was used. It was shelling an area 1.5 kilometers from the village, and on the other side of the Terek [River] on Chechen territory, where rebels who had come to help the bandits might concentrate."

Sasha could only curse quietly. When he had run across the muddy field toward the town, those Grad missiles were exploding all around him, killing two of his friends. How could Barsukov lie like that to the whole world? Even Yeltsin repeated those lies in a later broadcast from the Kremlin. He described Pervomaiskoye as "a Dudayev stronghold with earthworks, pillboxes, underground passageways between the houses, lots of special constructions, and heavy combat equipment. When I said, here in the Kremlin, that the operation was planned to last just one day, we did not know that under the ground there was a vast Dudayev stronghold. It had been set up long ago and maintained."

It was all lies. The experience shattered Sasha's trust in the system, but he was still adamant that the war must be won. He did not hate the Chechens, but he was a patriot. He could not accept losing a war to them.

It took two years and forty thousand dead, but in the end Russia did indeed lose. Chechnya suffered enormously, and never more than on April 21, 1996. Zakayev was supposed to be with President Dudayev that day but had to go home to his father's funeral. That funeral probably saved his life.

Dudayev, his poet wife, Alla, and four aides went out into the mountains in two vehicles, a van and an SUV. At about 6 the sun had set in the valley, but there was still plenty of light on the hillside where they stopped. Alla was supposed to speak live on Radio Liberty, to make an appeal for peace to the women of Russia and to read one of her poems. But first Dudayev wanted to make a call to the Duma member Konstantin Borovoi in Moscow, who was a leading peace advocate. The president had a satellite phone, given to him by highly placed friends in Turkey. Zakayev had been wary of it, warning that missiles could home in on its signal. Dudayev reassured him: this was

American technology, not available to the Russians. And Dudayev knew what he was talking about. After all, he had been an air force general.

As for the Americans, Dudayev said, trusted sources in the Turkish government assured him that the United States was not helping Russia militarily. The American Radio Liberty in Prague was one of the main information outlets for the rebels. Also, Dudayev said, Yeltsin was moving toward a settlement with him. After the war, surely, the Americans would want to deal with him because he was the only one who could guarantee stability in the oil-rich region and contain "the crazies"—the radical Islamists. Why would America want to harm him?

While the president and his aides placed the satellite telephone on the hood of the SUV, set the antenna, and dialed Moscow, Alla and her bodyguard, Musa, stepped aside to the edge of a ravine.

When Alla heard airplanes Musa reassured her: they were too high to pose any danger. But suddenly, two missiles flew down, one after the other, with a sharp whistling sound. The shock wave knocked her off the edge of the ravine; she stopped herself from falling only by clinging to some branches. When she pulled herself back up, the SUV was destroyed. The missiles had scored a direct hit. Musa was holding the dying president in his arms.

The Moscow press trumpeted the assassination as a triumph of a new technology developed at a secret FSB weapons lab, but Zakayev did not believe a word of it. Such precision was simply out of the question for the Russians. The president himself had said that the technology was American. Zakayev was convinced that the fateful telephone contained a special homing chip that had been planted in Turkey, and that the Americans, using their own satellites, guided the Russian missiles to their target.

———————

During the first Chechen War, Sasha Litvinenko was one of Zakayev's enemies. Only much later in London would they become friends. But Zakayev knew about Sasha before he even knew his name.

"We were aware of an intelligence officer who often came from Moscow almost from the first day of the war. He operated from the FSB headquarters in Nalchik," Zakayev later told me. Nalchik was Sasha's hometown and the capital of Kabardino-Balkaria, another Muslim province of Russia in the North Caucasus.

"We ran an agent of our own at Nalchik FSB," Zakayev added. "He reported that the officer's name was Alexander Volkov, and that he was a local. It was no trouble for us to establish that his real name was Litvinenko, since many people knew his father's family."

Most of Sasha's work during the war was in Nalchik. The only exception came when he took part in the siege of Pervomaiskoye, Dagestan.

"He was pretty damn good," reported Zakayev. "He planted agents in our midst. This was extremely difficult, you know, to find a Chechen who would work for the Russians. And he managed to recruit not one but three. We caught them in the end, thanks to our man in Nalchik. But still, it shows Sasha's talent as an oper."

There was another successful operation of Sasha's about which Zakayev learned only years later. At the beginning of the war, Khamad Kurbanov, the representative of Dudayev's government in Moscow, was detained by the FSB. At Sasha's suggestion, he was released and permitted to settle in Nalchik, where Sasha continued to practice his oper craft on him. Kurbanov's communications led the FSB to Chechen diaspora figures cooperating with the separatists in Russia and Europe.

"If you knew about Sasha, why didn't you take him out?" I asked Zakayev one night over dinner in his London house.

"Mostly because we did not want to compromise our own man. But now I will say that it was Allah's will, because otherwise I would not have had the luck of knowing him in London."

Alla Dudayeva, the president's widow, also knew Sasha during the war. After her husband's death, the rebel leadership decided that Alla should go to Turkey. She and her bodyguard, Musa, were carrying false passports when they were spotted in the Nalchik airport as they were about to board a plane on May 27. Lieutenant Colonel "Volkov" rushed in from Moscow to interrogate her.

"Although Alla was not mistreated, she was very scared," Zakayev recounted. "The people who held her were really fearsome. So when an unexpectedly kind officer came from Moscow, he immediately gained her confidence. She said that Sasha 'displayed an unusual intelligence and sensitivity for the KGB.'"

Sasha had told me what happened. They kept Alla at a former dacha of Stalin's in the mountain spa resort of Kislovodsk. She was guarded by FSB field officers who were accustomed to roughing up captured fighters, not dealing with a grieving woman. They were ordered to treat her diplomatically.

Sasha's task was to find out two things: first, whether her husband was indeed killed, or whether he could have survived the attack and was recovering in one of the mountain villages. Second, if he was dead, where was he buried? The Russians wanted to prevent his grave from becoming a martyr's shrine.

Sasha arrived just as Alla and her captors sat down in awkward silence for lunch in Stalin's luxurious dining room. Alla, forty-nine, a fragile blond woman dressed in black, with distinctly Slavic features, was "very tense and anxious," Sasha recalled. To soften her up, he had to use all of his charms. He began by telling her that he respected her feelings. He expressed condolences. Although she suspected that it was just part of a good-cop/bad-cop routine, she was still moved. After lunch they continued the conversation, recorded by a hidden camera, and she told him the story of her life, from childhood as an officer's daughter at a military base in the Soviet North, to a general's wife, to the first lady of her adopted mountainous nation, to the comrade in arms of a guerrilla leader.

By the end of the hour Sasha was confident that Dudayev was indeed dead. He was just coming to his second task—locating the grave—when he learned that President Yeltsin had pardoned Alla Dudayeva and she was free to go.

When the war ended with the Khasavyurt Accord, Sasha agreed with most of his fellow FSB officers and the military brass: it was a humiliation. All of this suffering, destruction, and the death of his friends were for nothing. Since the agreement had been negotiated by General Lebed, Sasha and his fellow officers now considered Lebed a traitor, someone who, for the sake of politics, betrayed the soldiers in uniform, those who had fought and died. By contrast, the general public accepted the Khasavyurt agreements with relief, which boosted Lebed's chances as a potential successor to Yeltsin in the presidential elections that lay four years ahead.

In September 1996, as Akhmed Zakayev assumed his new office, the prospects of maintaining stability were shaky, at best. Nearly half a million people, 40 percent of Chechnya's prewar population, had been uprooted and were now living in overcrowded villages or languishing in refugee camps. Grozny, which only two years ago had been a flourishing city of four hundred thousand, lay in ruins. The economy was all but destroyed. Thousands of youngsters, brandishing Kalashnikovs, roamed the streets.

The warlords Shamil Basayev and Salman Raduyev, who had led spectacular raids against the Russians, showed no intention of disbanding their militias and accepting central authority. On top of that there were two Russian brigades stationed in Chechnya, and neither one showed any sign of leaving, in spite of what had been agreed with General Lebed at Khasavyurt. There was a Party of War in Moscow plotting against Lebed. From where Zakayev sat, the precarious peace depended greatly on Lebed's stature and job security.

One night in September, Sasha Litvinenko led a squad of opers in a raid of a large private security company in Moscow that was suspected of kidnappings and extortion. The company was run by former officers of the GRU, the intelligence arm of the Ministry of Defense, an old rival of the FSB. When Sasha's men opened a huge safe, he was surprised to find a general's uniform and a bunch of files marked "Top Secret."

"You have no right to see these documents," said the company director, turning pale.

"That is just what I am going to do," retorted Sasha. "As for you, you have no business having them in your safe. For all I know you could have stolen them. How did they get here?"

"They belong to General Lebed, the NSC secretary. He believes his office is not safe."

Sasha locked the door and began studying the files.

The documents were indeed Lebed's. Among them were his ID and a bunch of personal photographs. There was a file detailing corruption in the Ministry of the Interior, implicating several top officials in a variety of misdeeds. Several of the names were familiar to Sasha.

Another file contained a GRU report on Chechnya, including details of the assassination of Dudayev. Sasha learned that, contrary to what everyone thought, the GRU played only an auxiliary role in the killing, providing the planes that fired the missiles. The report suggested that the mastermind of the operation was his FSB colleague, Gen. Evgeny Khokholkov. The report also alleged that Khokholkov was involved in a separate covert operation in which the American guidance system for the missiles was obtained and from which huge sums of money went missing.

The third document was a draft decree by Lebed creating a "Russian Legion," an elite special force of fifty thousand men, subordinate to the National Security Council; it would carry out special operations against those posing a "threat to state security."

In short, Sasha was looking at General Lebed's deepest secrets: two files that gave him leverage over the FSB and the Ministry of the Interior, with the ability to threaten its hawkish directors with exposure to two major scandals; another that created an army under Lebed's control. Together, they helped explain how Lebed planned to fight his political battles with the Party of War.

By the time Sasha acquainted himself with the contents, an official investigator had arrived.

"I cannot process this," he said, when he saw the files.

"What do you mean? It is your official duty," Sasha insisted.

"These documents have nothing to do with the case I am investigating."

"The law says that all materials prohibited for open circulation should be confiscated. Top secret documents are obviously prohibited for circulation."

But the investigator flatly refused. Sasha called Gen. Vyacheslav Volokh, his boss in ATC. Volokh heard him out, promised to call back in a minute, and never did. The investigator suggested that once he finished with his official duties and left, Sasha could initiate a new case of his own.

But Sasha knew better. He called Anatoly Kulikov, the minister of the interior. He knew Kulikov personally through his friendship with a young officer who was like an adopted son to the minister, a son of his late friend. He had never used this connection before, but he needed it now, and he knew Kulikov was a fierce rival of Lebed.

Ten minutes later Kulikov called back.

"Anatoly Sergeevich, we found some Lebed material, top secret," Sasha said.

"So why are you calling me? You have your own superiors."

"My superiors cannot decide what to do."

"Understood." Kulikov's tone shifted. "Is there something there?"

"Some secret memos and compromising files on the whole leadership of the Interior Ministry," reported Sasha.

"Myself included?" inquired Kulikov.

"No, just your deputies."

"Okay," he said with relief. "I will send someone to process them officially."

Gen. Alexander Lebed knew that Interior Minister Anatoly Kulikov was plotting against him. They were on a collision course, and it seemed inevitable that one of them would eventually leave the government. He even joked that "two avians cannot live in the same hole," a wisecrack on their names: Lebed means "swan" in Russian, and Kulikov means "snipe." What particularly worried him was that Kulikov appeared to be forging an alliance with Anatoly Chubais, the Kremlin chief of staff who was now effectively running the presidency.

Yeltsin seemed increasingly weak with every passing day. His heart surgery was scheduled for early November, and no one knew whether the old man would survive it. Constitutionally, Prime Minister Chernomyrdin was next in line, but most people regarded Lebed, who had finished third in the first round of elections, as the heir apparent. Except among the Party of War, Lebed had earned great popular credit by stopping the war in Chechnya. Should the old man die and an election be scheduled, he would easily beat Chernomyrdin. The last person that Chubais needed at the helm was the maverick chain-smoking general, who used to come to official Kremlin functions sporting white socks in black shoes and a bright checkered suit.

On October 13, Lebed made a fatal mistake. Seeking to boost his standing against Chubais, he joined forces with General Korzhakov, the discharged former head of Yeltsin's security who still had a lot of influence in the security services. They appeared together at a rally in Tula, an industrial city one hundred miles south of Moscow. It was the heart of Lebed's former constituency and the district from which Korzhakov planned to run for the Duma.

"I have found a worthy replacement," declared Lebed in his deep bass, the same voice that only three months earlier had pledged to crush a would-be coup led by Korzhakov. Korzhakov spoke next. He accused Chubais of running an "unconstitutional regency" in the Kremlin.

By appearing with the secret police general who was anathema to the liberals, Lebed sealed his own fate. The reformers promptly joined forces with the Party of War to stop Lebed. Boris Berezovsky flew to New York to show George Soros the Russian Legion memo that Sasha had found in the September raid.

"You should not be misled by Lebed's peacemaking role in Chechnya," explained Boris to George. "People in the West compare him to de Gaulle, but he is at best a Pinochet, at worst a Franco. Would you care to share this with whomever it may concern in Washington?" Later that day I faxed the memo to my contact at the Russian desk of the State Department.

The showdown in Moscow was fast approaching. On October 15, after a hostile grilling by Duma deputies, Lebed delivered an incriminating file on Kulikov to Yeltsin's office.

The next day the Snipe struck back at the Swan. Kulikov, a stocky man wearing his bemedaled general's uniform, went on live TV to accuse Lebed of plotting to seize power by force and of undermining the Constitution with his Russian Legion, which (he explained by reading from the memo) would be tasked with the "identification, psychological treatment, isolation, recruitment or discrediting or liquidation of political and military leaders of extremist, terrorist and separatist movements as well as other organizations, whose activities threaten national security."

The next morning Prime Minister Chernomyrdin called a top-level security meeting which turned into a shouting match between Lebed and Kulikov. In the end, Chernomyrdin dismissed the coup charges, but Lebed admitted to the authorship of the Russian Legion plan. This was enough for Chernomyrdin to accuse him of "crude Bonapartism."

While Lebed tried to arrange an appointment with Yeltsin, his bodyguards arrested four undercover policemen who were tailing him, on Kulikov's orders. By the end of the afternoon the ailing president had had enough. He summoned an ORT TV crew to his residence and signed a decree firing his national security adviser as the cameras broadcast it live. In a voice rife with emotion and barely concealed physical pain, Yeltsin admonished Lebed for sowing discord: "It looks as though some kind of election race is under way. The election won't be held until the year 2000. . . . There has to be a united team; the team should pull together, work like a fist. But . . . Lebed is splitting the team apart. . . . This is totally unacceptable. Korzhakov has been sacked [but Lebed] took him to Tula to present him as though he were his successor. Well, he could have found a better one. They are both birds of a feather."

As Yeltsin wrote in his memoir, he had had enough of generals. From now on, he wanted to work with civilians. Within a week a new national security team was in place, with Ivan Rybkin, a former speaker of the Duma and Yeltsin loyalist, as the NSC secretary and Boris Berezovsky as his deputy in charge of Chechnya.

"Why do you need this, Boris?" I asked, when I heard the news. "Don't you have better things to do than dealing with the Chechens? All of this looks like a comic opera."

"Well, it is a comic opera, but unfortunately they use live ammunition. You see, the Party of War helped us get rid of Lebed, but we cannot let them run away with Chechnya. If the war starts again, this country is doomed. And there is simply no one else to do the job. Believe it or not."

On November 5, 1996, President Yeltsin, now sixty-five years old, underwent open-heart surgery at the Moscow Cardiological Center. After seven and a half hours and five bypasses, the surgery was pronounced a success. Surgeons predicted a full recovery.

Akhmed Zakayev sighed with relief when he learned that Rybkin had replaced Lebed. The former Duma speaker had a solid reputation as a dove. But Berezovsky was a complete enigma to Zakayev. A few days later, when a Russian government plane carrying both men landed at a military airfield near Grozny, Zakayev was pleasantly surprised. Boris was cool-headed, goal-oriented to the point of cynicism, and, most important, not possessed by the usual demon of injured national pride that afflicted all of the Russians who had dealt with Zakayev until now. Their nostalgia for the lost empire had been a slow-acting poison: the Russians all seemed, to Zakayev, to hold the Chechens responsible for their historic misfortunes, from the fall of the Berlin Wall to the emergence of America as the sole superpower, to the declining price of oil. This irrational *ressentiment* was the main obstacle to Zakayev's immediate goals: getting the two remaining Russian brigades out of Chechnya and signing a permanent treaty that would resolve the issue of sovereignty.

"Do you think that Boris's lack of ressentiment had anything to do with his being Jewish?" I asked Zakayev years later.

"Perhaps," Zakayev replied. "But when that became an issue, it did not come from our side."

From the very first day of Boris's appointment to the NSC, the Communists started a fierce campaign against him, claiming that he had obtained Israeli citizenship and so could not be entrusted with a national security job.

"We had nothing against Jews," explained Zakayev. "They did not kill us, the Russians did. Both our peoples have been victims of genocide. And the Israeli connection, if there was any, wouldn't hurt. You know, at one point Dudayev told me about his vision of an alliance between Chechnya, Georgia, Turkey, and Israel, backed by the United States."

"Against whom?" I inquired.

"Russia, of course. And Islamic radicals. But the Americans chose to betray us to the Russians. Anyway, it is all water under the bridge.

"The first thing Boris said to me," he continued, "was, 'You think you are an independent state. We—the Russian government—believe you are part of the Russian Federation. Having said that, let us put aside the issues on which we cannot agree, and then deal with what we can, step by step.' And it was obvious to me that when we started discussing the logistics of troop withdrawals, he was not at all tormented by the vision of the Red Army leaving Eastern Europe."

What immediately impressed Zakayev was that Boris and Rybkin behaved as if they had real clout.

"They were not afraid to tackle difficult issues, and they could make some decisions on the spot, for example, on prisoner exchanges and amnesty. When they could not, they would simply say, 'We have to clear it' or 'We agree, but it will take some lobbying.' They were straight with us. And we trusted them."

Zakayev described the apparent division of labor between Berezovsky and Rybkin: "Boris did the creative stuff, proposed options, invented solutions, and Rybkin was the doubter; he sat there saying 'This can be done, but that will never fly.' Boris was the broker, and Rybkin a spokesman. They had a tremendous asset, ORT TV. Boris was always bringing a crew with him. Whenever we had a breakthrough or faced a problem, Rybkin would go on TV, to cut right through to Yeltsin—he watched the nightly news—and get the facts over to him before our opponents could react."

Nevertheless, the Party of War in Moscow and the rowdy, murderous warlords in the mountains of Chechnya plotted in their separate ways to undermine the negotiations.

"I got some sense of how my counterparts got things done in the Kremlin when I arrived in Moscow at the end of November," recalled Zakayev. The first batch of agreements was ready for signing, defining a legal framework for Chechnya's self-administration until the elections. But the outstanding issue remained the two Russian brigades stationed in Chechnya. The Chechens were adamant to see them go, as was agreed at Khasavyurt.

On Thursday, November 21, Zakayev went to see Boris at the Security Council offices in the Kremlin administration building. He received disappointing news: the withdrawal was blocked by Interior Minister Kulikov, the supreme commander for Chechnya, who had gone on TV to say that the two brigades were to stay for another five years.

"Go talk to Kulikov yourself, so that you can see what we are up against," Boris suggested.

The minister looked at Zakayev "as a soldier at a flea," in the common expression of disdain in the Russian military. "These two brigades are staying there, period. They are there under special presidential decree."

"Then there will be no signing," exploded Zakayev. "As long as there is a single Russian soldier remaining in Chechnya, no further negotiations!"

"So be it!" said Kulikov coldly.

But on Saturday morning, Boris called Zakayev at his hotel: "You have it. The president has signed off on the pullout." Boris also surprised Zakayev with the news that his own prime minister, Aslan Maskhadov, was in Moscow and on his way to the White House for a joint press conference with Chernomyrdin.

Zakayev turned on his TV and learned about a new presidential decree ordering the full and immediate pullout of all Russian forces.

"How did you do it?" Zakayev inquired as he shook hands with Boris at the White House ceremony.

"Well, when I told you to go see Kulikov on Thursday, I already knew that the decree would be signed later that night," explained Boris. "But I wanted to make sure that Kulikov did not suspect as much. Right after seeing you he left for Warsaw for a meeting of East

European police ministers. We used you as a decoy, you see? You were so disappointed. For Kulikov to see you with that face was the best insurance that he would take the trip. Otherwise he might have canceled, rushed to the Kremlin, made a scene, and who knows?

"Sorry for misleading you, my friend."

Years later, Ivan Rybkin, speaking by telephone from his dacha outside Moscow, told me what really happened behind the scenes.

Late on Thursday night, in utmost secrecy, the two NSC planes carrying Boris and Rybkin left for Chechnya. Their major concern was to keep Kulikov's people from learning what was happening for as long as possible. They did not trust telephone communications, so they decided to take the trip to personally inform Maskhadov that Yeltsin had signed off on the withdrawal. As they were approaching Grozny, the pilot informed him that the military had closed down the airport.

"What about Nalchik? Makhackala? Sleptsovsk?" Rybkin inquired.

"No airport in the North Caucasus will let us land."

It was not the weather. It was the military playing tricks, Rybkin thought.

"Do we have fuel?"

"For about an hour," said the pilot.

They turned around in midair and landed in Volgograd (formerly Stalingrad), six hundred miles to the north. It was 4 a.m.

They snatched three hours of sleep in the airport hotel. In the morning, Rybkin's staff worked out landing rights for them in the Ingush airport of Sleptsovsk. Maskhadov and his people drove there from Grozny. They looked at Rybkin and Boris in disbelief when they announced that they were taking them to Moscow because Yeltsin had signed off on the withdrawal.

"Why hasn't it been announced?" the Chechens asked.

"Trust us," said the Russians.

They landed in Moscow, undiscovered, on late Friday afternoon.

On Saturday morning, the two prime ministers gathered at Rybkin's dacha, waiting for Yeltsin to announce the troop withdrawal on TV.

Then, finally, they signed the agreement. Until the last moment Maskhadov did not believe it would happen.

Chechen-Dagestan border, December 14, 1996: Salman Raduyev, the Chechen warlord, is stopped at a border checkpoint on his way to a congress of Chechens living in Dagestan. When the Russian police try to detain him, a backup force of Raduyev's militia moves in, disarms the Russian policemen, and takes twenty-one of them hostage. Defying orders of the Chechen government to release the hostages, Raduyev threatens to kill them unless the Russian command apologizes for impeding his passage.

Boris Berezovsky arrived at Raduyev's stronghold of Novye Gordali on the morning of December 18, the fourth day of the hostage standoff. He was there to make a last-ditch effort to prevent the incident from escalating to a full-scale confrontation. The forces of the Interior Ministry were getting more and more edgy with every hour of captivity of their comrades. Raduyev, the maverick warlord whose oversized beard, dark glasses, and baseball cap concealed a face that had been disfigured in a shootout, had defied all pleas and pressure from the separatist government to free his prisoners. Raduyev did not recognize the Khasavyurt Accord because it did not grant Chechnya full independence. Now, at a minimum, he wanted an apology from the Russians for not letting him travel to Dagestan.

"You have my apology, Salman," said Boris.

"Come on, Boris, you are not the one who I want to apologize," smiled Raduyev.

Suddenly they heard a loud clattering outside. Two unmarked helicopter gunships appeared out of nowhere and showered Raduyev's camp with several bursts of machine-gun fire before disappearing. No one was hurt.

"These are the ones, Boris," said Raduyev. "They know you are here, don't they? I want an apology from *them.*"

After three hours of negotiations they were close to an agreement to exchange the hostages for eleven of Raduyev's men captured a year ago at Pervomaiskoye, a deal they planned to keep secret. But Raduyev still insisted on a Russian apology.

To demonstrate impatience, Boris looked at his watch.

"Nice watch," said Raduyev. "Is it a Rolex?"

"No, Patek Philippe."

"Never heard of it. Is it better than Rolex? How much did it cost you?"

"Fifty thousand dollars," said Boris.

"Nice watch."

"It is yours," said Boris, taking the watch off his wrist.

Raduyev played with the watch for a few minutes.

"Okay, you can have your cops. You can take them today, and I will take your word that you will release my men."

On the same day that Boris was negotiating with Raduyev, in the predawn hours of the morning, masked men broke into the Red Cross compound in the Chechen village of Novye Atagi and, using guns with silencers, killed six foreign relief workers, including five women, in their sleep. On the next night five local ethnic Russians were killed in the same execution style in Grozny. "This is a national catastrophe for us," said Aslan Maskhadov, head of the Chechen government.

As Zakayev later explained, "These murders were completely out of character, even for the renegade Chechens. No claims of responsibility. No political demands. No robbery. To us it was clearly an effort by the Russian secret service to torpedo troop withdrawal and the elections."

Grozny, January 27, 1997: Voters cram the polling stations across Chechnya in what European Union observers call "legitimate, democratic, and free" presidential elections. Fifty-five-year-old former Soviet army officer Aslan Maskhadov, who coordinated military operations against Russia during the war, wins office with an overwhelming majority of 69 percent. The guerrilla leader Shamil Basayev, who had led a terrorist attack on Budyonnovsk, finishes a distant second with 16 percent of the vote. Acting president Zelimkhan Yandarbiyev finishes third, with 15 percent.

One day in late April 1997, Boris Berezovsky summoned me to The Club. "Can you pretend to be a CIA agent?"

"First of all, it is a criminal offense to impersonate a federal officer," I said, with a smile. "Second, knowing you, I hope there will be no gunfire."

"You are a Soros representative, aren't you?" Boris beamed, and added, "Do you have a business card? That's impressive enough. Everyone in Russia thinks the Soros Foundation is a CIA front. Let us go to my dacha. I need you to project American authority. Your job is just to bless us with your presence."

At the dacha I found myself at a dinner for four: Boris, myself, NSC Secretary Rybkin, and Movladi Udugov, the Chechen deputy prime minister, the leader of the Islamist wing in Maskhadov's government. The matter at hand was the wording of the peace treaty that would formally end the war in Chechnya, which was scheduled for signing next month.

It was an improbable scene: Rybkin projected the confidence of a former Soviet apparatchik. Boris sipped his Chateau Latour. Udugov interrupted the discussion for an evening prayer. I simply tried to look important, personifying the clout of the United States as best I could.

The treaty was essentially completed. It began with half a page of lofty phrases declaring reconciliation between the two nations to end their "centuries-long" enmity. What was missing was a legal frame of reference. Rybkin and Boris wanted the agreement to be explicitly derived from the Russian Constitution. Udugov wanted to root it in international law.

They argued for nearly three hours. In the end a compromise was reached as each side added a legal reference of its choosing. In the final version the references were dropped, so the evening's exercise was in vain. Yet I learned something valuable about the process. Both sides were more cagey with their own intransigent members than with each other.

On April 28, 1997, a bomb exploded shortly before 7 p.m. at the railway station in the southern resort city of Pyatigorsk, Russia, killing two and injuring more than forty people. The Chechen peace accord was at risk again. President Yeltsin, vacationing 150 miles away on the Black Sea, immediately imposed tight security measures on the whole southern region of Russia.

Interior Minister Anatoly Kulikov blamed Chechen terrorists, announcing that two Chechen women had been arrested in Pyatigorsk who had confessed to planting the bomb. He claimed that the women were known terrorists who had taken part in the hostage incident in Pervomaiskoye in January 1996. He also disclosed that Chechens had attacked a Russian police station at the Dagestan border the previous night.

"Now everyone can see that the party of war was not in Moscow but in Grozny," Kulikov fumed on TV.

Two days later, however, as Boris and Rybkin flew to Grozny, the Chechens announced that one of the two women named by Kulikov was alive and well and quietly living in that city. The other had been killed a year earlier. Journalists discovered that their stand-ins, the two women who had "confessed" in Pyatigorsk, had been arrested before the bombing, not afterward. Zakayev later said, "We were sure that this was some sort of provocation."

The Chechens promptly gave their evidence to Rybkin and Boris when they landed. Rybkin immediately went on the air to attack Kulikov, using the ever-ready ORT crew that Boris brought along.

"Many people both in Chechnya and in Russia want to destroy the fragile peace, but we will put an end to these attempts . . . regardless of how high a post they occupy or what kind of stars they wear on their shoulder straps," he said in a live interview from the steps of his aircraft.

"And then something really ugly happened," recalled Zakayev, still fuming with rage at the memory. "This idiot, Salman Raduyev, claimed responsibility for the railway bombing." Raduyev was a guerrilla leader who still commanded a militia and was looking for ways to boost his credibility. He announced that the bombing was his way of marking the anniversary of President Dudayev's assassination. "We knew for a fact that he had nothing to do with it," Zakayev said. "Maskhadov was enraged. He ordered him arrested for making false statements. But that was how our own Party of War played off theirs. And it was the first time that I realized that the Russians were prepared to stage terror attacks against their own people so as to blame them on us."

The Moscow apartment bombings were just two years away.

The Kremlin, 12 May 1997

Peace Treaty and Principles of Interrelations between the Russian Federation and the Chechen Republic of Ichkeria

The esteemed parties to the agreement, desiring to end their centuries-long antagonism and striving to establish firm, equal and mutually beneficial relations, hereby agree:

1. To reject forever the use of force or threat of force in resolving all matters of dispute.
2. To develop their relations on generally recognized principles and norms of international law. In doing so, the sides shall interact on the basis of specific concrete agreements.
3. This treaty shall serve as the basis for concluding further agreements and accords on the full range of relations.
4. This treaty is written in two copies and both have equal legal power.
5. This treaty is active from the day of signing.

Boris Yeltsin
Aslan Maskhadov

CHAPTER 6

THE PLOTTERS

Chechnya-Dagestan border, June 6, 1997: Four Russian journalists held by kidnappers are released and flown home to Moscow on Boris Berezovsky's plane. Chechen President Aslan Maskhadov applauds the event. His recent decree imposes the death penalty for kidnappings and launches a special police operation to free any captives still held for ransom by warlords. "Maskhadov's success will bolster his influence," says Ivan Rybkin, the head of the Russian National Security Council. "But not everyone in Grozny and Moscow will clap their hands."

Moscow, summer 1997

The two wars with Chechnya were really a single conflict, with a two-and-a-half-year hiatus in the middle. During that pause, events in Moscow spun out of control for Sasha, as he became entangled in the struggle between FSB top brass and Boris's Kremlin ring. In the meantime, a bitter feud developed among the members of the Davos Pact, undermining the stability of Yeltsin's government. George Soros and I found ourselves sympathizing with the opposing sides of the new divide. I should have seen the split coming when Boris told me in early June that he was trying to take control of Gazprom, the world's largest producer of natural gas, and he once again needed Soros's help.

A board meeting of Gazprom was scheduled for June 28. Boris explained that if George backed him with a major investment this would make it possible for him to become Gazprom's chairman. He had already been assured support from Prime Minister Chernomyrdin. Once in charge, Boris planned to clean up Gazprom operations, modernize its management, and make it a transparent, Western-style company. Future demand for gas in Europe was expected to skyrocket, making Gazprom one of the most powerful companies in the world.

George was then in Budapest, visiting the European headquarters of his foundation. He was interested, he said on the phone. He would see Boris.

We flew to Budapest on the morning of Saturday, June 7, in Boris's Gulfstream jet, which was like a second home to him. I often wondered how he managed to handle his government responsibilities on top of his business deals without showing any signs of fatigue. In the days preceding the Budapest trip he had flown to the Hague, where he took part in a roundtable on Russia-Chechnya relations; to Kiev, to negotiate the division of the Soviet Black Sea fleet with Ukrainian President Leonid Kuchma; to Baku, to discuss the pipeline that would bring Caspian oil to the Russian Black Sea export terminals; and to Dagestan, to pick up the freed Russian journalists.

In the private sector, his investment fund had just signed a deal with General Motors to build Opel cars in northwestern Russia; a team of his managers at Aeroflot was preparing the Russian national airline for privatization; and he had just fought off an attempt by Vladimir Potanin, his fellow oligarch from the Davos Pact, to outbid him in the final auction for 51 percent of Sibneft, the oil company, which Boris held in trust since the days of the loans-for-shares scheme.

Potanin's bid came as a total surprise to Boris. Although it was disqualified on a technicality, it pointed to trouble brewing in the coalition that brought Yeltsin to power one year before. Back in 1995, when Chubais carved up government assets in the loans-for-shares policy and distributed them among a small group of bankers, the agreement among all of them was that those deals could not be revised. In fact, the loans-for-shares policy was Potanin's brainchild, and he was its biggest beneficiary: his Unexim Bank had grabbed Norilsk Nickel, the largest producer of nonferrous metals in Russia, and Sidanko, the oil company, which was even larger than Boris's Sibneft.

"Potanin and Chubais are building a power base for Chubais's presidential campaign in 2000," said Boris as we flew to see Soros.

Potanin was the oligarch closest to Chubais. After the 1996 elections, he became first deputy prime minister for economics. His Unexim Bank received the most lucrative state contracts, including the accounts of the Federal Customs Service. In March 1997 Yeltsin reshuffled his administration, launching what has been dubbed the government of "young reformers." Chubais took Potanin's place as the economic supremo in the cabinet. To beef him up, a new face, not associated with the privatization scandals, was brought in: the thirty-six-year-old Boris Nemtsov. Chubais's previous job as Kremlin chief of staff went to Valentin Yumashev, the journalist friend of Yeltsin's daughter.

After the reshuffle, Potanin returned to his bank but his alliance with Chubais only grew stronger. Unexim people were placed in key economic positions, from the Federal Securities Commission to the Ministry of Finance to the Federal Bankruptcy Commission, among others. Now, as the battle for Gazprom took shape, Potanin and Chubais were pitted against Chernomyrdin and Berezovsky. If Boris could recruit George Soros to his side, it might end the contest in a single blow.

Gazprom was such a prize that George could not resist it. He and Boris shook hands on a partnership. Then George flew to start his planned vacation in the Adriatic. From his yacht he dictated a "Dear Boris" letter: he pledged to invest $1 billion immediately, which at the time would buy him about 3 percent of the company. He also reserved an option to buy $2 billion worth of Gazprom stock within two years, provided that Boris became the gas giant's chairman. The letter also urged the Gazprom board to drop its restrictions on the sale of stock to non-Russian residents. This, Soros wrote, would boost Western confidence in the emerging Russian market as a whole, not to mention create a windfall for current domestic stockholders when stock prices soared.

I got on the telephone to organize a helicopter to airlift George from the Adriatic to the nearest airport in the Balkans, where he would get on a chartered jet that would bring him to Sochi, in the Black Sea, where Prime Minister Chernomyrdin was vacationing. They planned to meet on Saturday, June 14.

———————

Boris's call woke me up in my Moscow apartment in the early morning hours on Thursday, June 12.

"A car will pick you up in fifteen minutes. I have to do an errand en route to Sochi. We are going to Grozny."

A huge military aircraft stood on the tarmac of an airfield outside of Moscow, its motors warming up. It was the airborne headquarters of the Russian National Security Council.

"They would throw a fit if they knew that I brought an American here," said Boris, sitting in the commander's salon with Rybkin. "No one knows who you are except Ivan Petrovich [Rybkin] and Sergei, my bodyguard. So please keep a low profile. And once we start discussing state secrets, you will have to sit with Sergei."

After takeoff, a guard took me to the back of the plane. It was quite something to see. In the communications section a dozen army officers with earphones monitored screens, apparently maintaining contact with the rest of Russia's defense command. Next came a section with two dozen fearsome Spetsnaz paratroopers in full combat gear, with their Kalashnikovs resting in a stack in the corner. Finally I found myself in a tiny compartment with Sergei, whom I had seen at The Club.

"When we land, you stick to me, and ask me if you need anything," he said. "Once these Chechens know who you are, you will be a prime target for kidnapping." We landed. From the window I watched as our paratroopers took up positions in a circle around our aircraft. A van, followed by a Jeep full of armed Chechens, approached. Rybkin, Boris, two other NSC officials, Sergei, and I got into the van, six civilians in a sea of Chechen military. They drove us away, leaving our Spetsnaz escort behind.

"There is no point in taking them with us," explained Sergei. "They are no match for the Chechens, and we do not want them to come in direct contact with their fighters. The Chechen tradition of hospitality, whatever it is worth, is our best protection."

We drove for about fifteen minutes through a countryside ravaged by war, passing bombed-out houses, charred skeletons of trees, and a burned Russian tank.

We arrived at a miraculously untouched building. A caravan of Jeeps and SUVs brought the Chechen delegation: President Maskhadov, dressed in military fatigues, Akhmed Zakayev in a civilian suit—I saw him then for the first time—and Udugov in a traditional Chechen fur hat. Sergei and I remained in the hallway in the company of half a dozen ferocious-looking guerrillas, all dressed in black, armed with automatic weapons of all kinds. We sat in complete silence, staring at each other.

An hour later the negotiations were over. "We are taking Maskhadov to Sochi to see Chernomyrdin," Boris explained, as we drove back to the plane.

As I later learned, these meetings were among the early twists in the new Great Game for control of the flow of North Caspian oil.

An existing pipeline from the Azeri capital of Baku to the Russian Black Sea port of Novorossiysk ran through Chechen territory for ninety miles. The Chechens were insisting that they should be a full sovereign partner to an agreement to reopen the pipe, along with Russia and Azerbaijan. Hardliners in Moscow refused to give the Chechens equal status, complaining that it would be another humiliation for Russia: wasn't control of the pipeline one of the reasons for fighting the war in the first place? But for Boris and Rybkin appearances made no difference; their primary concern was to open the pipeline in order to weaken an American-backed proposal for a new pipeline, from Baku to the Turkish Mediterranean port of Ceyhan, which would bypass Russia.

On June 13, I was virtually the only live audience member for a joint statement of Maskhadov and Chernomyrdin delivered to the ever-present ORT camera at a Russian government dacha in Sochi, which had once been Stalin's summer retreat. Outside were terraced gardens with magnificent cypresses and exotic flower beds. We were less than two hundred miles from Chechnya, but it was another world. Maskhadov and Chernomyrdin announced that they had removed all obstacles to reopening the pipeline, signed a banking agreement, and laid the groundwork for a customs agreement between Russia and Chechnya. The Moscow hawks were unhappy but, at least for now, outmaneuvered.

Soros arrived in the morning, sporting a new tan. He was awed, as I was, by Stalin's famous Black Sea residence. He and Chernomyrdin met as old friends; Chernomyrdin jokingly recalled the anti-Communist sermon he gave Soros at their previous meeting. Now it was George's turn to lecture. Over lunch, he extolled the virtues of open markets and corporate transparency and promised that his investment of $3 billion would change the attitude of others in the West who considered Russia an unsafe place for their money.

Boris beamed. The three of them shook hands on a deal. Then Boris and George took a walk along the beach to talk out the details, after which George took me aside.

"Are you being paid by Boris for arranging this?" he asked.

"Of course not," I said. "I thought I was working for you."

"Good. Are you still a Russian citizen by any chance?"

"No, I lost my citizenship when I left the USSR and I naturalized as a U.S. citizen ten years ago."

"That is a problem," said George. "You see, Boris and I agreed we would set up a vehicle for this, fifty-fifty, and that I should control it, but the law requires that more than half of the ownership be domestic. We need a Russian citizen whom I can trust."

"I have a daughter by my first marriage, in Moscow, who is a Russian citizen, although she is thinking of moving to the United States."

"That's good enough," said George. "Get a copy of her ID to my people as soon as we get to Moscow. We will give her a quarter percent."

Suddenly, I felt a hint of the greed that drove the Borises and

114

Georges of this world. Just by being in the right place at the right time, I stood to gain millions.

Then it all unraveled. The plan to take over Gazprom did not last twenty-four hours after Soros's arrival in Moscow. There he met with Boris Nemtsov, who explained to George that back in March, when he joined the government, it was decided that from now on everything had to be strictly by the book. He strongly advised George against the Gazprom deal, because it had been organized in the old ways of the robber barons. It would be a blow to the government's new attempts at fair play.

George immediately changed his mind, reverting from investor to disinterested helper—or so it seemed. He agreed to lend $1 billion to the Russian budget—to keep it going until the arrival of Eurobond proceeds—and he dropped out of the Gazprom sweepstakes.

George was gloomy as we drove to The Club so he could deliver the news to Boris. He broke his silence only once: "You know, I envy you. You got yourself a ticket in the front row—with my money—and you get to enjoy the show. I cannot afford that. The moment I pop up, I become a player."

In The Club he told Boris that the Gazprom deal was off. Boris could barely control himself. As soon as George left, he exploded: "How could he do it? We shook hands! Did he really believe those clowns? Doesn't he know that Nemtsov's sole role is to act as 'Chubais with a human face' for foreign consumption? I personally recruited him for that role back in March when we still were one team. I was honest with George—I brought him to Sochi so that he could see how the system works. Potanin just puts up smokescreens. George should know better!"

I did not know what to say. Of course I was upset, not least because my own chances of becoming a millionaire had just evaporated. Was George really so naïve? Or did he know something that we did not? George was my boss, but I was beginning to think Boris understood the Kremlin better than he did.

In fact, it turned out that George was still in the game. Boris Jordan, the American-Russian investment banker, soon talked him into backing none other than Vladimir Potanin with a $1 billion pledge for a forthcoming auction of 25 percent of Svyazinvest, the telecom monopoly. In the contest, Soros and Potanin would be pitted against Vladimir Gusinsky, who was backed by a Spanish strategic partner, Telefonica de Espana. Privatization Minister Alfred Koch managed the auction.

On July 26 the winning bid was announced: Soros and Potanin had bought one-fourth of the company for $1.88 billion. It touched off a full-blown scandal. Gusinsky, who had bid $1.71 billion, cried foul. He claimed both that the auction was fixed and, in something of a contradiction, that Chubais had personally promised him that his bid would be uncontested under the Davos Pact rules. Berezovsky backed Gusinsky. Chubais retorted that everything had been honest, and that it was the start of a new era of squeaky-clean capitalism.

That was the end of the Davos Pact. For the three ensuing months the losers, using the full force of their media empires, attacked the winners with charges of cronyism. They painted a picture of a state in the pocket of Potanin, the fat-cat banker, who in turn relied on the patronage of the infamous Wall Street speculator, George Soros. The fight became a national issue, tearing the Yeltsin administration apart, paralyzing the government. Opinion polls indicated a steady decline in the credibility of "the young reformers."

I remember talking to Boris at that time, concerned that the conflict would bring down the government, boosting the Communists and nationalists. Why such a fuss about a phone company for Gusinsky?

He gave me an angry look: "That's not the point. I don't care whether Goose gets it or not. And it's not about fair play: any outcome would have been fixed. It's about whether Tolya [Chubais] can have it his way because he decided that he is the state. Fucking Bolshevik."

As the row deepened, it became obvious that the fight was not between Gusinsky and Potanin. They were just surrogates for the two epic figures of Yeltsin's reign: Chubais and Berezovsky, the ultimate technocrat and the supertycoon. It was a political clash of opposing views on the role of the oligarchs in the new Russia.

According to Boris, the oligarchs who emerged from the Davos

Pact had to remain major players in Russian politics for years to come. It was their historic mission. They are the natural opponents of the Communists and secret services, he said. They are intrinsically pro-democratic and they can get things done. They are the best guarantors of freedom. In other words, what is good for LogoVAZ is good for Russian democracy.

Chubais believed just the opposite: businessmen should stick to business. Oligarchs, who had been created by the state's largesse in the first place, should be tightly controlled and even subordinate to the state. Remarkably, in less than two years, Chubais's views had turned 180 degrees, from sermons of laissez-faire capitalism to praise of state control.

Looking back, this was the point where my disagreement with George Soros took root. I was squarely on Boris's side. George was with the "new" Chubais.

Russia, I tried to explain to George, had no tradition of freedom. Its democratic institutions were still weak. There was no middle class or civil society. For centuries, Russia's troubles came from unrestrained power in the Kremlin. In this context, any alternative center of power that could counterbalance the state, even the self-serving oligarchs, were agents of progress. They substituted for the missing institutional checks and balances.

To George, however, Boris was the incarnation of unrestrained capitalism, the evil he took on in his Western crusades. He looked at Russia through the prism of his article "The Capitalist Threat," published that year in the *Atlantic Monthly,* where he asserted that "the main enemy of the open society . . . is no longer the communist but the capitalist threat."

Moscow, August 19: NTV President Igor Malashenko discloses that his station paid over $1 million to free five journalists kidnapped in Chechnya three months earlier. Deputy NSC Secretary Berezovsky confirms that ransoms were paid for other captives as well. Chechnya's uneasy peace is marked by further hostage takings by warlords' gangs.

While the Kremlin's crony capitalism continued its merry-go-round, there were more sinister changes afoot in the special services. In late August 1997, the career of Sasha Litvinenko took an unexpected turn when he was transferred to a mysterious supersecret department known as the URPO, the Division of Operations against Criminal Organizations. He would now work under a man whom he had been charged with investigating.

It happened after an argument with his boss at ATC, General Volokh. Sasha had just returned from an operation when Volokh called him in.

"I have a report that your people shot and wounded a suspect. Tell me what happened."

Sasha explained that his group was arresting a dangerous criminal, a drug dealer with several murders on his record, who tried to flee. One of his officers fired three warning shots, as prescribed by FSB training, and then hit him in the leg. The suspect was apprehended and brought to a hospital.

Volokh was enraged. He yelled that the last thing he needed was a news story about FSB agents shooting people in downtown Moscow. He ordered Sasha to suspend the officer in question. But Sasha yelled back, slammed the door, and went straight to the office of the FSB director, Nikolai Kovalev.

Kovalev had known Sasha for years. He had a habit of dealing directly with rank-and-file officers, bypassing the layers of command. Sasha was among those whom he would see without notice.

Sasha argued his case to Kovalev. There were no complaints from the prosecutors. Everything had been done by the book. There was no reason for an investigation. He could not let his officers be railroaded. Finally, Sasha threatened to resign.

Kovalev heard him out and did not disagree. He listened to Sasha's praise of his team, agreeing that they were "good people, a strong team," and then dropped a bombshell: "I am transferring you to the URPO. You will report to Colonel Gusak. I already spoke to him, he will take you." Alexander Gusak was a former colleague of Sasha's at the ATC.

Sasha was stunned. How could he work in the URPO, when some months ago he had brought Kovalev a file implicating its commander, Gen. Evgeny Khokholkov?

Back when the war began, in September 1994, Khokholkov, a heavyset man with huge arms who was nicknamed "the Bull," ran a section in the ATC Division of Operations, a position equivalent to Sasha's. But after the war, he was unexpectedly promoted to general and appointed to run the brand-new URPO.

Khokholkov's sudden rise did not please the ATC director of operations, General Vyacheslav Volokh, who was Sasha's—and formerly Khokholkov's—boss. He believed that Khokholkov's new division would compete with his own.

Through the grapevine Sasha had heard about an argument between Volokh and Khokholkov related to the latter's sudden riches, when Khokholkov bought himself a posh restaurant and a dacha. Khokholkov refused to explain himself to Volokh, telling him to keep his nose out of his personal affairs. In midsummer 1996, Volokh had called Sasha in and told him to "dig up everything that there is on Khokholkov."

Sasha started digging. Sure enough, he was able to unearth allegations that Khokholkov might be linked with organized crime figures in Uzbekistan, where he had been stationed before the dissolution of the Soviet Union.

Then a source at the Ministry of Internal Affairs reported that the Organized Crime Unit of the Moscow City Police claimed he had some explosive material on Khokholkov, dating back several years. The allegation was that he had been videotaped in the company of major crime figures. It was no surprise to Sasha that the police might claim to hold such material on Khokholkov without using it. The Moscow police were notoriously corrupt. If it existed, the tape could be useful as an insurance policy to keep the URPO off their backs.

Then came Sasha's September 1996 raid in Moscow and its infamous Lebed files. One of them was a GRU file on Chechnya that contained much about Khokholkov. At some point before the war, Khokholkov spent four months undercover in Germany, posing as an American businessman in an operation personally controlled by the previous FSB director, Mikhail Barsukov. Foreign operations were not part of FSB's charter; it was supposed to deal only with domestic security, while work abroad was normally conducted by the Foreign Intelligence Service (the SVR) or Military Intelligence (the GRU). But this operation had to do with a purely domestic issue: a multimillion-dollar purchase of electronic security equipment for the presidential offices in the Kremlin.

Thanks to this operation, Khokholkov established close ties with Alexander Korzhakov, who at the time was head of Kremlin security. The reason the assignment was top secret was to avoid American export restrictions on the technology that Korzhakov sought. It may also have been kept secret to avoid attention to a second purchase by Khokholkov: the American system that could guide a missile to a land target by homing in on a particular kind of signal, such as that of a satellite telephone. It was the system that was used to assassinate Dzhokhar Dudayev, the Chechen president.

This information, by itself, did not raise any red flags for Sasha. After all, securing the Kremlin and assassinating the leader of a wartime enemy were both well and good, in his eyes. But the report went on to allege that millions of dollars were misappropriated in the operation. Whether it was true or not, this allegation of course was just what Sasha needed as part of his assignment to "dig up anything he could" on Khokholkov.

Backed by his superiors, Generals Volokh and Trofimov, Sasha brought his findings to the FSB director, Nikolai Kovalev. Kovalev thanked him and said that he would take it from there. But nothing happened. Khokholkov continued to build up URPO, his new secret division, and Sasha felt frustrated yet again.

And now Kovalev was ordering him to go to work under Khokholkov's command!

"Don't worry about Khokholkov," said the director, obviously amused at Sasha's bewildered look. "I want my own man in that division. So you will come in and report if you notice anything fishy. That's an order."

———————

Within the FSB, the URPO enjoyed considerable autonomy. It employed about forty opers and had its own car pool, technical support services, a SWAT unit, and agents. It was headquartered in a separate unmarked building away from Lubyanka HQ. Before long Sasha realized that the URPO's mission included carrying extrajudicial actions against suspected criminals.

Most URPO members were veterans of Chechnya, and indeed the very concept of the URPO emerged from the Chechen experience: in extraordinary circumstances, law enforcement must be capable of acting outside of the law. Sasha did not like it. Perhaps in wartime such excesses could be written off as collateral damage, but Russia had not invoked war powers in Chechnya. The army's presence there was always viewed as a law enforcement operation.

Once the law enforcement agencies were allowed to kill and torture Chechens with impunity, it wasn't difficult to use the same approach against organized crime figures back at home.

As Sasha told me, URPO's approach to recruitment was to seek out opers with bloody records. One of its officers, for example, was reinstated in the service after doing time for killing a rape-murder suspect whom he had had to release for insufficient evidence. More senior URPO officers had "wasted" four Dagestan gangsters who had the misfortune of trying to extort money from a store that belonged to the son of an ex-KGB boss.

When he told me about the URPO, Sasha was aware that his revelations cast a measure of suspicion upon himself. As he explained to me, "I don't say I am an angel, but I don't have blood on my hands. I ended up in the URPO because Kovalev planted me there. Khokholkov would never have picked me.

"But one thing is sure: sooner or later all of us would have ended up tainted by blood in the URPO. That was the policy."

He did not deny that he had been told to do illegal things before, but the URPO was a totally different world. Orders were verbal, there were no records, deniability was essential.

Initially he just felt uneasy. His first assignments were against the same types of "objects" he had been targeting at the ATC: gangs, dirty cops, kidnappers. His breaking point was the Trepashkin case. One day in late October, Sasha was told, "There is this guy, Mikhail Trepashkin. He is your new object. Go get his file and make yourself familiar with it."

Sasha studied the file. It turned out that Trepashkin, a lieutenant colonel and ten-year veteran of the KGB, had quarreled with his bosses, gotten kicked out of the service, and then sued the FSB for compensation. He published an open letter to President Yeltsin claiming that the Agency was sunk in corruption. At the time Trepashkin was working as a senior investigator in the tax service. When Sasha was told by a superior that "we should take care of him," he decided to play dumb:

"What do you mean, 'take care'?"

"Well, it's a delicate situation. You know, he is taking the director to court, and giving interviews. We should shut him up, director's personal request."

"How do we shut him up?"

"Let's plant a gun on him."

"No way. He's an oper, he knows all the tricks. It will never stand up in court."

"Well, then, let's just kill him." His superior started to lose patience. "Say that we tried to take away his FSB ID, he resisted, and we knocked him off. Don't play the fool with me, Sasha. Don't you know what we are doing here? We are a special tasks division. We are here to solve problems, not to ask questions."

"Okay, I will need some time to develop the case and figure out our options," said Sasha.

He did not want to do it, so he stalled, hoping to quietly sabotage the assignment by dragging it out for a month or two.

November 4, 1997: Anatoly Chubais and Boris Nemtsov meet with President Yeltsin at his dacha while Prime Minister Chernomyrdin is away on vacation. They present him with a draft decree firing Boris Berezovsky, arguing that the deputy secretary to the National Security Council has been casting himself as "the gray eminence of the Kremlin," undermining the presidency. Yeltsin, fed up with the "oligarch's war," agrees. A week later newspapers disclose that a company owned by Unexim Bank had paid Chubais and four associates $90,000 each on the eve of the Svyazinvest auction, disguised as a "book advance." Yeltsin, enraged, purges the young reformers, including Alfred Koch, from the government and demotes Chubais. A new national security team inherits the Chechen situation.

One day that fall, Sasha was invited to an operational meeting. His superiors were discussing a plan to kidnap Umar Dzhabrailov, a prominent Chechen figure in Moscow, to force his family to pay a ransom, which would then be used to buy the freedom of some of their comrades held in Chechnya. Sasha was invited to the meeting because of his extensive experience with kidnappings.

"I was sitting there, discussing how to take a man hostage," Sasha recalled, "based on my previous experience of freeing hostages. It was like the theater of the absurd. But for the guys there was nothing wrong with it. It was just the continuation of their war in Chechnya. Kidnapping Chechens for ransom was nothing out of the ordinary for them."

By December, the planning of the Dzhabrailov kidnapping was at an advanced stage: URPO opers monitored his movements, tapped his phones, scrutinized his habits, and checked his contacts. The date, time, and place for the operation were set: they would take him when he arrived at a performance by Mahmud Esambaev, the famous Chechen folk dancer.

They even developed a disinformation line, which would be planted in the media in the aftermath of the operation. Dzhabrailov was a co-owner of the Radisson hotel in Moscow, with an American partner, Paul Tatum, who had been gunned down by an assassin near the hotel on November 3, 1996. An "FSB source" planned to plant a story saying that investigators believed that Dzhabrailov's kidnapping was linked to Tatum's murder.

With every passing day of preparation, Sasha became more and more depressed. He knew that after that operation he would be bound to the URPO gang forever. He even asked his old bosses at ATC whether they would take him back. But no one wanted to mess with Khokholkov.

And then, at the last logistical meeting before the hit, the SWAT team that was supposed to snatch the target flatly refused to participate unless they were paid in advance. They had carried out a prior kidnapping on spec, they said, and they were still waiting for their share of the proceeds. Not anymore. They wanted their cut beforehand.

The operation was postponed.

———————

On December 27, Captain Alexander Kamyshnikov, Khokholkov's deputy, called Sasha's department into his office and told them to wrap up their current case, an investigation of mob penetration into a Moscow police precinct.

"This is not the type of case that we should be dealing with," he proclaimed. "We are the department of *special* tasks. Have you read this?" He produced a copy of *Special Tasks*, the recently published memoir of Pavel Sudoplatov, the head of NKVD special tasks under Stalin. He had run the operation to assassinate Leon Trotsky, among other jobs.

"This is our role model!" He waved the book. "Everyone is ordered to read it. We have a new set of objectives ahead of us. There are people, criminals, who cannot be gotten in the normal way. They are tremendously wealthy and can always buy their way out of court. Such people are a grave threat to our country. You, Litvinenko, you know Berezovsky, don't you? You will be the one to take him out."

Sasha did not respond, but his mind was racing. Berezovsky had until recently been a senior national security official and was still a Kremlin adviser. Even discussing the assassination of a person of his caliber was crazy and merited investigation under antiterrorism statutes. As far as Sasha knew no one at URPO had a personal grudge against Boris. The order must have come from the top, or as an outside contract. Or maybe it was a provocation to test him?

He was asked again: "You would bump off Berezovsky, wouldn't you?"

Sasha gestured by shaking his head and pointing at his temple while making a rotating movement with his finger, meaning, "I am not crazy enough to talk about this, because the conversation may be recorded."

Afterward, Sasha's team gathered in his office to try to make sense of what had just happened. They decided to go to their boss, Alexander Gusak, who was on sick leave.

"Why are you so surprised?" Gusak responded when he heard them out. "Khokholkov has already spoken to me about bumping off Berezovsky."

For Sasha, the holidays of early January 1998 were far from joyful. He did not say much to Marina, but she sensed that something was very wrong. He avoided parties. He declined to go to a concert, so she had to return the tickets. When she tried to cheer him up, he sighed, "If you only knew, my darling, how much I don't wish to party."

When he returned to work after the holidays, his superiors did not renew the talk of hitting Berezovsky. Nevertheless, he and his comrades knew that sooner or later, their division would be used for special tasks of a political nature.In several heated discussions, the members of Sasha's team pondered their options: do whatever they were told and hope for the best, or report everything to Kovalev, as Sasha initially suggested. Sasha's second in command, Maj. Andrei Ponkin, a big, ever-smiling fellow, objected: Kovalev surely knew what the URPO was all about. He would back Khokholkov and squash them.

It was Ponkin who first suggested going to Berezovsky. Boris had already managed to get rid of Korzhakov and Barsukov. If he agreed to back them, Ponkin argued, they might have a chance. Everyone concurred, and Sasha was deputized to approach Boris. His superiors, Gusak and Shebalin, were happy for him to take the lead.

It took him a month to get an appointment with Boris. After the 1996 elections they had drifted apart and hadn't seen each other for nearly a year. He started calling his office in mid-February but learned that Boris was in a Swiss clinic recuperating from back surgery after a snowmobile accident. He got through to him only in mid-March, just as Boris was getting busier than ever with Kremlin intrigues.

Although he was no longer with the National Security Council, he was serving Valentin Yumashev, the Kremlin chief of staff, as a special adviser. It gave him tremendous influence over presidential personnel choices. Yeltsin was getting ready to dismiss the entire cabinet, ousting both Chubais and Interior Minister Anatoly Kulikov in one fell swoop.

Sasha got to see Boris in the middle of all this turmoil on March 20. He went straight to the point: "Boris Abramovich, my superiors told me that I should kill you."

Initially Boris did not believe him. He had heard similar warnings before. But when Sasha talked about Khokholkov, Boris became interested. To his multifaceted mind this appeared both as a threat and an opportunity to strike a decisive blow at his enemies in the secret services.

He said he would like to talk to the others in Sasha's division.

After talking to Shebalin and Ponkin, Boris grew even more worried. He went to see Kovalev, the FSB director.

After that, all hell broke loose.

The next day, Kovalev called the whole of Sasha's department into his office. They repeated their allegations. Perhaps all this talk about Berezovsky was nothing but a joke, Kovalev suggested. No joke, they insisted, considering everything else going on in the URPO. The director said he would begin an internal inquiry, swore them all to secrecy, and dismissed them.

A few hours later, Gusak rushed into Sasha's office.

"I had a talk with Khokholkov," he said. "He wants to settle the matter with Berezovsky amicably. He wants to speak with you."

"Why in the world did you go to him?" Sasha fumed. "The director told us to keep our mouths shut, didn't he?"

"Don't be an idiot! The director told him himself."

After he left, Sasha called Kovalev on a secure line: "Nikolai Dmitrievich, you said there would be a secret inquiry, but I have info that Khokholkov knows everything."

The director paused for a moment. Then he said, "It was Gusak who told Khokholkov. Don't go to him."

Sasha went back to Gusak and repeated the director's words. Gusak turned pale.

"You see what they are doing? The director sends me to talk to Khokholkov, and tells you I did it on my own. If we do not settle this, they will make me a scapegoat. You know what Khokholkov said to me? 'If bad comes to worse, you should cover for the director.' They are digging through all my cases. Go to Boris and tell him it was all a joke." Gusak was in a panic.

"No, it's too late," said Sasha. "They are out to get us."

He went home and called Boris on an open line. It was April 14.

"Boris Abramovich, they are covering up. The director told Khokholkov."

"This is what I expected," said Boris. "Tomorrow at ten, you have an appointment in the Kremlin with Evgeny Savostyanov, deputy chief of staff in charge of security services. Bring everyone."

Savostyanov heard them out, saw that they were serious, and told them that the administration would arrange for them to give depositions to a federal prosecutor.

CHAPTER 7

THE WHISTLE-BLOWERS

On the morning of April 19, 1998, Marina and Sasha drove to the house of some friends to celebrate Easter Sunday, a singular traditional holiday that had survived seventy years of Communism. The whole previous day Marina had painted eggs and baked *kulich*, the intense, round-shaped pastry that is usually eaten with sweet raisin-loaded cheese, *paskha*, a particularly gratifying way to break Lent, which, in truth, they did not observe.

It was a beautiful day. The snow was finally gone, and the sun was so unusually warm that they shed coats for the first time in months. Sasha's unhappy mood that Marina had observed since the New Year seemed to have dissipated. He was cheery and confident, and she hoped that whatever problems had tormented him were finally blowing over.

As they finished their meal that afternoon, his cell phone rang. After listening, he became pensive and told her they had to go.

"Where?" she asked.

"You will see." He remained silent throughout the drive, absorbed in thought.

"Perhaps it was his tone, or facial expression," recalled Marina later, "but I instantly realized that I was about to enter a new world, from which he had been trying to shield me all these years." Sure enough, that Easter Sunday turned into a day and night of "big surprises" for her.

They drove to the apartment of Viktor Shebalin, Sasha's colleague. There was another man there whom Marina did not recognize. While she chatted with Shebalin's wife, the three men locked themselves up for about an hour. Then the man left, and Shebalin and Sasha, with Marina at the wheel, drove to Alexander Gusak's home, where another of Sasha's colleagues was already waiting. This was the first time she met Andrei Ponkin, of whom she had heard so much.

The men were edgy. Gusak paced back and forth, smoking nonstop. Marina wanted to leave the room, but Sasha waved her to stay. Then Shebalin made an announcement, the first of Marina's shocks that night.

"They are going to arrest us on Monday, all of us."

The man she had seen at Shebalin's house was a source at the Federal Agency of Government Communications (FAPSI), the equivalent of the National Security Agency in the United States. He reported that he had eavesdropped on an FSB telephone conversation indicating that a group of suspects would be apprehended tomorrow at Lubyanka HQ.

"It all fits," Sasha said. "Kovalev called me yesterday and asked all of us to come to his office at 10 a.m."

Marina distinctly remembered the dynamics of the conversation. Shebalin was calm, but he kept ratcheting up the pressure on everyone else in the room. He insisted that the FAPSI source was reliable. Besides, taking them into custody now would be a reasonable thing for Kovalev to do, because later in the week they were supposed to give their deposition.

Gusak and Sasha argued, both extremely agitated. Ponkin turned his big head from one side to the other, agreeing with each man in turn.

Gusak, pale and panicky, insisted that it was not too late to call the whole thing off. He blamed Sasha for "getting us into this shit." He yelled that going to Berezovsky was "the most stupid of all his stupid ideas." He would never have allowed it had he known beforehand. Sasha yelled back that if Gusak had his way they would be "going around killing everyone Khokholkov wants dead," which would only bring them into even deeper shit. They almost got into a fight and had to be restrained by Shebalin and Ponkin.

Marina listened in complete bewilderment. Although with every phrase the gist of the problem became more and more clear to her, she tried to comfort herself with denial. Perhaps it was just some training exercise they were talking about.

Finally Sasha got everyone to listen to him. Having talked to the Kremlin staff, he argued, they had passed the point of no return. There were two parties to the matter now: the Kremlin administration versus the FSB. "If we backtrack now," he argued, "both will disown us, and we will be done for." They had no choice but to stick with Berezovsky. Besides, he believed in Boris, who, after all, had beaten Korzhakov and Barsukov. He was confident that Boris would do it again.

That sounded convincing. But then again, if they were to be arrested on Monday, they wouldn't be able to testify to the prosecutors on Wednesday. With everyone's consent, Sasha called Boris.

"Come to my dacha right away," said Boris.

It was five minutes to midnight.

By the time they arrived at the dacha—Gusak, Ponkin, Sasha, and Marina, but not Shebalin—Boris had summoned Sergei Dorenko, the ORT star anchor, with a camera crew.

Nine years later, as I watched these recordings in New York, I could not help imagining myself in the shoes of poor Marina, who was the sole audience to the confessions that for the first time opened Sasha's world to her. Boris disappeared after the first half-hour. He knew it all already and preferred to sleep.

In retrospect, Sasha suspected that Shebalin may have been a mole in their group from day one. That night he chose not to go to Boris, saying that he had something else to do. Was it to seek guidance from his handlers at the FSB? In fact, his entire calm speech about the "imminent arrest on Monday" could have been a ploy to scare them into backing out. But if so, it backfired by inspiring the midnight taping, which in the end may have saved their necks.

Sasha later observed that Shebalin never took part in any spontaneous action against the FSB, only those that were planned in advance, and he also never initiated anything.

But Gusak was genuine. The fact that he could not make up his mind testified to that. He was desperately trying to figure out which side would end up winning, and switching his allegiances accordingly. He was not among the initial whistle-blowers and he did not go with them to the Kremlin. He also served as Khokholkov's intermediary in dealing with Sasha. But that night at Boris's dacha he eagerly participated in the marathon taping and he told the whole truth. Yet six months later, in November 1998, when Sasha and his friends staged their famous press conference, Gusak backed out and even left town to be on the safe side.

The three other whistle-blowers, Ponkin, German Scheglov, and Konstantin Latyshenok, were Sasha's loyal crewmembers. In the end they did what he did, and they went down with him.

Remarkably, nine years later, after Sasha's death, Gusak suddenly surfaced in an interview with the BBC, as a lawyer in Moscow. He confirmed that Khokholkov had asked him to kill Berezovsky. But he did not take the order seriously, he said. Only "if the director of the FSB, Kovalev, had personally given me the order, would I have carried it out."

On the Easter Sunday night at Boris's dacha, they were all eloquent, as only confessing sinners can be. By the second hour of the taping Marina could no longer deny the truth: Sasha and his friends, who took turns speaking to a flabbergasted Dorenko, were launching a deadly struggle with their agency. She learned about Trepashkin, who was to be "taken care of," the would-be kidnapping of Dzhabrailov, the talk of killing Boris, and many other things that Sasha called "illegal and criminal." Marina knew that Sasha tended to see the world in black and white, and she assumed his whole profession shared this perspective. Now that he was in opposition to the FSB, Kontora, she feared that he would become its enemy and its target.

Although the initial impulse of the whistle-blowers was to immediately put the tape on TV, by morning they decided otherwise.

Boris agreed. "Films like that are most powerful if they are never seen," he said as they were saying goodbye. "Perhaps we could make an exception for an exclusive screening in the Kremlin, but for the time being it is not necessary. As for your bosses, I suspect they already know what you have been doing all night. You do what you were planning to: go to the prosecutors. And we shall see what happens next."

He looked extremely pleased with himself.

When they arrived at the Lubyanka the next morning, they weren't arrested after all. Kovalev tried to bargain with them, but the discussion went nowhere.

Two days later, they went to the prosecutors. Soon, Khokholkov and Sasha and his friends were suspended pending the outcome of the investigation.

On May 25, *Novaya Gazeta*, the liberal Moscow weekly, printed a story by the journalist Yuri Schekochihin, who was also a Duma deputy and a member of its anticorruption committee. Schekochihin described the questions that he had put to FSB Director Kovalev in a letter as part of his oversight duties including:

Is it true that military prosecutors are investigating the URPO division of the FSB ?

Is it true that the head of the URPO division reports personally to the FSB Director?

Is it true that recruitment of URPO personnel entailed a written pledge to fulfill "any order"?

Is it true that some URPO operatives have committed acts of extortion and attempted murder? Is it true that certain officers of FSB Internal Affairs reported the suspected abuses at URPO to the Kremlin staff?

The Schekochihin article was a bombshell. Years later, in London, I quizzed both Sasha and Boris about whether either of them, or their associates, had organized a leak to the legislator. Both categorically denied it. Schekochihin, an activist member of the social democratic Yabloko Party, was noted for his dislike of the oligarchs, and he particularly hated Berezovsky.

As Boris and Sasha pointed out, Schekochihin's questions to

Kovalev suggest that he had his own source, perhaps in FSB Internal Affairs or in the Kremlin. Schekochihin apparently did not know about the planned kidnapping of Dzhabrailov or the assault on Trepashkin, otherwise he would certainly have mentioned them.

Alas, Schekochihin could not be asked personally; he died of apparent poisoning on July 3, 2003, while investigating yet another FSB scandal.

Chechnya, summer 1998: Amid economic chaos and an influx of militant Muslims from abroad, criminal gangs turn kidnapping into a profitable business. The Maskhadov government estimates that sixty-five people, including two Britons, are being held hostage. Valentin Vlasov, who replaced Ivan Rybkin as Russia's special representative to Chechnya, is kidnapped at gunpoint on the road to Grozny. Maskhadov orders extremist militias to disband, leading to armed clashes in which nine people are killed. On July 23 Maskhadov himself narrowly escapes an assassination attempt when a car bomb explodes as he drives by, killing one of his bodyguards.

In the middle of June, Valentin Yumashev, who often discussed major government appointments with Boris, asked the tycoon for his opinion of one of Yumashev's aides, a man named Vladimir Putin.

Boris knew Putin quite well. He had met him when Putin was deputy mayor of St. Petersburg, Russia's second largest city, and Boris was still involved in the auto business. At the time Putin had the reputation of being uncorrupted, a rarity among officials. More recently, Putin had run an auditing group at the Kremlin administration.

"Why?" Boris inquired.

"We are considering him for the FSB directorship."

Yumashev explained that the principal quality the president was seeking in a new spy chief was loyalty, but he didn't trust any of the existing FSB generals. They were a tightly knit clan. If Putin had one defining feature, it was staunch loyalty. When his former boss, the ardently anti-Communist St. Petersburg mayor Anatoly Sobchak, lost his bid for reelection, Putin preferred unemployment to betrayal. The new mayor had offered to retain Putin, knowing that he knew many of Sobchak's secrets. Putin declined. He then moved to Moscow and found himself a low-level job in the Kremlin.

One particular episode about Putin that favorably impressed the president was the "rescue of Sobchak" that Putin had organized in November 1997, at substantial personal risk. By then, the new mayor of St. Petersburg, in collusion with the prosecutor general Yuri Skuratov, both Communist sympathizers, had finally succeeded in launching a criminal investigation against Sobchak—a clear case of settling scores with one of the key figures of Yeltsin's 1991 revolution. Moscow liberals ran to Yeltsin for help. But Yeltsin was reluctant to lean on government prosecutors to help an old friend.

In the meantime Sobchak suffered a heart attack while under interrogation. He was rushed to the hospital. That very day in Moscow, Skuratov signed his arrest warrant. But two days later Putin went to St. Petersburg and arranged a dramatic escape. Dodging police surveillance, Sobchak's loyalists put the ex-mayor on a stretcher and transported him from the hospital to the airport, where a private jet was waiting. The next day he surfaced in a Paris heart clinic, his wife at his side.

Now, as Yumashev talked to Boris about Putin's candidacy for the FSB, he recited his KGB bio. Putin had served as an intelligence officer in East Germany. After the Wall came down, he ran the KGB station at St. Petersburg University. When the USSR collapsed, he resigned from the service as a lieutenant colonel.

Boris liked the idea of putting a lieutenant colonel over multistar generals; the newcomer would not be a part of the old-boy network, and would in fact be snubbed by the top brass, which should only strengthen his loyalty to the Kremlin.

"I support him 100 percent," Boris said. And so, a process initiated by Sasha's URPO whistle-blowers and steered behind the scenes by Boris plucked their future nemesis from obscurity and placed him in charge of one of the world's most powerful spy services.

"Once upon a time there were two brothers. One was a smart fellow, the other a fool," Sasha once told me. "You know, after I saved him from the Moscow cops, Boris said that from now on we will be like brothers. Between the two of us, I am obviously the fool. But for some reason, the fool turned out to be right. I told him from the very first day that Putin was a snake. But he did not believe me."

When the new director took office on July 25, 1998, Boris said to Sasha, "Go see Putin. Make yourself known. See what a great guy we've installed, with your help."

They did not hit it off. Putin was cold and formal. He listened in silence to Sasha's passionate depiction of corruption in the Agency, but he did not want to meet the other whistle-blowers.

"I know a man by his handshake," Sasha told Marina after that meeting. "His was cold and spongy. I could see it in his eyes that he hated me."

Two years later, as we drove across Turkey together, Sasha gave me his take on the man, the former fellow lieutenant colonel who became the pursuer from whom he was fleeing. Putin, according to Sasha, never really left the service. He was loyal to the KGB all along. He might have lent his loyalty—temporarily—to Sobchak or Yeltsin, but once he returned to the bosom of the Agency, he immediately, and eagerly, fell back into the old fold.

According to Sasha, when Putin suddenly took charge of the Agency, its generals simply pulled Putin's file from the dust and reclaimed him as one of their own, "a prodigal son, if you wish. But to make sure, they staged a little welcoming ceremony. Someone explained that to me before I went to see him."

Three weeks before Putin's appointment was officially announced, amid rumors that his predecessor Kovalev would soon be replaced, a murder occurred. Sasha believed it was an Agency job, arranged as a welcoming gift. In the early morning hours of July 2, retired army general Lev Rokhlin, a member of the Duma, was shot dead as he slept at his dacha. The police immediately announced that his wife, Tamara, confessed to the killing, "on grounds of personal hostility."

Rokhlin was the founder of the movement "In Support of the Army and the Military Industry." He had commanded the troops that took Grozny in 1995 and was an outspoken critic of President Yeltsin. He was one of the leading figures in the Communist-led parliamentary opposition. Indeed, he had openly called for the overthrow of the "hated regime." He was extremely popular in the army and potentially a leader if the army brass ever decided to stage a coup. The Kremlin had good reason to want to be rid of him.

Almost immediately, the press and opposition leaders in the Duma speculated that his death was a political assassination organized by the FSB. On July 7, Rokhlin's daughter and son-in-law appeared on TV to claim that the real killers had sneaked into the dacha, killed the general, and then forced his wife to confess by threatening to hunt down and kill her whole family. Later, Tamara Rokhlina recanted her confession.

After ten thousand people showed up at Rokhlin's funeral, the FSB felt compelled to issue an unusual statement, denying that it had anything to do with the murder. A few days later, three charred bodies were found near Rokhlin's dacha, adding fuel to the conspiracy theory. Were the three perpetrators promptly assassinated, as a cover-up?

Before his appointment with Putin Sasha went to see Gen. Anatoly Trofimov, his old mentor, who was by then retired. They walked through the narrow side streets of Moscow, chatting. Sasha told him all about the URPO scandal: the prosecutors, the Dorenko tape, and Boris's great expectations for the new director.

Trofimov looked doubtful. "I am afraid you've lost, Sasha."

"Why?"

"Don't you see? They killed Rokhlin; surely that was a Kontora job. Now, the guy who came in will have to cover that up. He cannot afford to solve the case. It is like an insurance policy."

Trofimov liked Sasha. He continued meeting him secretly and giving him advice up until he left Russia. On April 10, 2005, Trofimov, who worked as a security consultant, was gunned down, together with his young wife, on a Moscow street in front of their four-year-old daughter.

There is no corroborating evidence for Trofimov's theory of Rokhlin's murder. Tamara Rokhlina was sentenced to eight years imprisonment in November 2000 for murdering her husband, but in the summer of 2001 the Russian Supreme Court overturned her guilty verdict and sent her case for retrial. Later, the European Court of Human Rights in Strasbourg ruled that the Russian government owed her 8,000 euros in damages for unjust imprisonment. On retrial in Moscow she was again found guilty, but given a suspended sentence. She decided not to appeal. To this day she maintains her innocence and claims that three masked strangers killed her husband.

Whether or not Trofimov was correct, there was no doubt in Sasha's mind that the FSB gained a kindred spirit in its new director.

"Putin is Kontora's man, body and soul, and to him I am a traitor," he put it to me, years later. "Never mind that he got there because of me. He had to show them that he had no obligation to me, that's why he had me arrested in the end. He did the same thing to Boris, after Boris made him president."

July 28, 1998: Russian officials collectively known as the Party of Peace, including Chernomyrdin, Lebed, and Berezovsky, call for reconciliation with Chechnya, saying that "recent mistakes and silence have already cost us all much too dearly, and Russia does not need to return to [the violence of] the mid-1990s." Sergei Kiriyenko, Russia's new prime minister, announces that he will meet Chechen President Maskhadov to discuss economic agreements.

By August 1998 clouds were gathering over Russia's economic horizon. Few people predicted a storm more accurately than George Soros. The slide toward financial crisis started with turmoil in Asia. Global investors began pulling out of many emerging markets, including Russia's. This coincided with a major drop in the price of oil—the principal source of Russia's revenue. In January 1998, it dropped to

$15 per barrel, the lowest level since early 1994. By August, it was below $13. The Russian government collected little tax revenue; most of the economy operated off the books. In May, the Communist-dominated Duma dealt a blow to investor confidence by restricting foreign ownership of shares in the major electric utility, UES. Then came another blow: no one bid at the auction for Rosneft, the last big oil company still in state hands. Unpaid wages plagued the government, and coal miners protested by blocking major railways.

To boost revenue, the government relied on short-term ruble-denominated treasury bonds. But as the perceived risk increased, buyers demanded higher and higher interest, which at times reached 150 percent. To pay the interest, the government had to issue more and more bonds, tightening the noose around its neck.

Russia's economic managers were convinced that if bad came to worse, the West would bail them out, as it had Mexico in 1994. Russia was "too nuclear to be allowed to fail," they assumed.

So they kept issuing bonds and nagged the International Monetary Fund for more loans. As Anatoly Chubais, who remained the behind-the-scenes brains of Yeltsin's economic team, put it: we "conned" the international community out of $20 billion in loans because "we had no other way out."

But George Soros knew what was going on, because he himself had been lending Russia money to keep it afloat between infusions of Western cash. In early August, when shortages in liquidity briefly paralyzed the Russian interbank market, he decided it was time to sound an alarm.

On August 13, he published a letter in the *Financial Times* that began, "The meltdown in Russian markets has reached the terminal phase." To avoid catastrophe, he urged the Russian government to "modestly" devalue the ruble by 15 to 25 percent and introduce a "currency board," which in effect meant a new currency linked to the dollar, backed by a $50 billion Western infusion into the Russian treasury.

George simply wanted to offer advice and alert the West to the problem. Instead, his letter acted as a match to a gasoline tank: stocks on the Moscow exchange plunged, the price of dollars soared in the streets, and banks became incapable of paying each other. On August 17, the Central Bank could no longer defend the ruble, so it freed the exchange rate. Prices skyrocketed. People rushed to the streets in search of dollars. Regional authorities reported shortages of supplies due to widespread hoarding. On August 23, Yeltsin sacked the Kiriyenko government. Russians lined up to withdraw their savings. Banks failed. The government defaulted on its short-term bonds.

When the dust settled, several major banks were wiped out, together with the savings of millions of depositors, and foreign investors were left with losses amounting to $33 billion, of which George Soros's share was about $2 billion.

As for Boris Berezovsky, the crisis did not hurt him economically; he did not own a bank, and his oil company took in revenues in dollars and paid most bills in rubles. The devaluation only helped him.

But politically it was a disaster. After two failed attempts in the Duma to reinstall Viktor Chernomyrdin as prime minister, Yeltsin bowed to Communist pressure and accepted the compromise candidate, Evgeny Primakov, the foreign minister and former chief of the Foreign Intelligence Service (the SVR). He was Boris's sworn enemy.

For the first time since the dissolution of the Soviet Union, someone who was neither a democrat nor a reformer headed the government. Primakov, a sixty-eight-year-old veteran of KGB foreign intelligence who was derisively nicknamed "Primus" behind his back, was a staunch ideologue of the Russian empire who viewed the West as a long-term geopolitical threat. From his KGB days, he was a friend of many anti-American dictators, from Saddam Hussein to Slobodan Milosevic.

He leaned toward a state-dominated economic model. In the realm of political reform he preferred law and order to rights and freedoms. As for his attitude toward Russian capitalism, he sent chills through the business community when he announced an amnesty for 100,000 Russian prisoners by saying, "We are freeing up space for those who are about to be jailed—people who committed economic crimes."

For Primakov, no one personified capitalist evil more than Boris Berezovsky. They had an old feud to settle: the contest for the Russian national airline, Aeroflot.

Boris had first become interested in Aeroflot in early 1995, when he was setting up ORT. He quickly discovered that of all the giants of the ex-Soviet economy, Aeroflot was perhaps the most saturated by spy agencies. He knew that to take hold of this prized asset, he would have to confront very powerful and resourceful interests.

But he was not deterred. His moment of opportunity came in the late summer of 1995, when Yeltsin replaced a Communist holdover at the helm of the national airline with Marshal Evgeny Shaposhnikov, Gorbachev's defense minister, who had sided with Yeltsin in the last days of the USSR. Shaposhnikov, a complete novice in business management, asked Boris to help streamline the company, which was losing money. That year it carried 3.5 million passengers to 102 countries on its 110 aircraft. Hoping to eventually privatize the airline, Boris installed his best management team, headed by Nikolai Glushkov, the forty-five-year-old PhD physicist turned financial expert who had been his principal associate in the automobile business. When Glushkov arrived at his new offices in February 1996, he was shocked to discover that the "spy problem" was much greater than anyone could have expected.

The spy agencies were largely left to their own devices during the "shock therapy" of 1991–1993, with little supervision and insufficient funding. What Glushkov discovered was that the spies had turned the national airline into a cash cow to support international spying operations and the livelihood of thousands of operatives around the world.

"The things we found were absolutely mind-boggling," Glushkov told me in a conversation in London ten years later. "Aeroflot finances abroad were managed by mysterious off-shore companies; we could not identify the people behind them."

Proceeds from ticket sales went to 352 foreign bank accounts, but it was impossible to establish who controlled them. All heads of foreign Aeroflot offices were operatives of the SVR or GRU; they were not accountable to the company management.

"To compound the problem, there were secret services personnel on the staff: 3,000 people, out of the total workforce of 14,000! The head of human resources was an FSB officer. The head of security was an FSB officer. And we could not touch them. So you know what I did?" Nikolai smiled. "I sent them a bill. I wrote a letter to the head of the SVR, Mr. Primakov, and the director of the FSB, General Barsukov, asking them to pay for their people's salaries." It was the summer of 1996.

The next thing he knew, he received a phone call from Korzhakov. He screamed and yelled, promising to "destroy" Glushkov if he "continued to violate the rights of the services."

"But that was just the beginning," Glushkov continued. "The real blow to them came when we reorganized our cash flow. We simply closed all of the 352 accounts and channeled all foreign revenue into one financial and accounting center in Switzerland, which we controlled. The company name was Andava. That's what really infuriated them."

Years later, when I was researching this book, I spoke to a Russian defector who lives under an assumed name in a quiet European town. He told me that starting in 1995, the SVR station in Geneva began watching Boris during his visits. They monitored his business in Switzerland, particularly Andava. The SVR information was fed to prosecutors in Moscow and later formed the basis for the so-called Aeroflot case.

My source told me of one SVR station chief who used to freely avail himself of Aeroflot cash for SVR business—that is, before Glushkov took over the company's finances. One day, the local Aeroflot man—an SVR officer as well—told the station chief that he no longer had access to the cash. According to my informant, more that 30 percent of the station's operational funds—hundreds of thousands of dollars—dried up as a result of the Aeroflot cleanup.

"The station chief cursed Boris endlessly and said that if one of the guys took him out, he would do a great service to the Motherland," said my source. He added that when Korzhakov visited, "Much of the time that they spent talking—and drinking—was devoted to the Aeroflot problem, and Boris," my informant recalled.

After the spies were purged, the performance of the airline improved steadily. Glushkov obtained Western insurance coverage for the planes; replaced its aging fleet of Russian aircraft with leased Boeings; hired attractive, bilingual staff; and improved the quality of food. Within three years, the company became profitable; its stock skyrocketed from $7 to $150.

Yet as of early 1998, 51 percent of Aeroflot still belonged to the government. The rest was in the hands of private investors, mostly staff members. Boris's partner, Roma Abramovich, began quietly buying up Aeroflot stock from small shareholders in anticipation of the privatization of the government's majority stake.

In the spring of 1998 I myself got entangled in the Aeroflot saga. I introduced an American strategic investor to Boris. He was a major airline financier, a buyout specialist who had a history of taking on risky projects and turning companies around. It was my second attempt to join the Russian gold rush.

After taking a hard look at the company and the market, the investor offered to join Boris in a deal to take Aeroflot private, adding a huge infusion of cash and talent. When the financial crisis erupted, he still was enthusiastic. He was prepared to go ahead, he said, because he took a long-term view.

A couple of weeks later, the investor was totally bewildered when Boris unexpectedly called off the deal. His reason was simple, but baffling to the American: the "Primakov factor." With the new prime minister in the White House, not only was Boris convinced that there would be no Aeroflot privatization, but he also could not guarantee that the Glushkov team would survive in the company, or that he himself would be around for long.

The American went home disappointed. Once again I had just missed being in the right place at the right time.

August 19, 1998: Armed Islamic fundamentalists from the radical Wahhabi sect take over two villages in the southern Russian province of Dagestan, declare a "separate Islamic territory," and impose Sharia law. The Maskhadov government expects Russia to crack down on the insurgents. Instead, Russian Interior Minister Sergei Stepashin negotiates a formula allowing the Wahhabi to remain in the villages indefinitely. In the meantime, the hostage situation in Chechnya deteriorates. More than one hundred people are held in captivity. Russian Deputy Interior Minister Vladimir Rushailo, assisted by Boris Berezovsky, begins direct negotiations with the hostage-takers, bypassing Maskhadov's officials. He secures release of more than fifty captives. On September 20, Berezovsky flies two Britons, Jon James and Camilla Carr, who have spent fourteen months in captivity, to freedom. Berezovsky denies paying any ransom.

The ascent of Primakov hurt Boris far beyond his plans for Aeroflot. His principal remaining avenues of influence were Chief of Staff Valentin Yumashev and Yeltsin's daughter Tatyana, but they too were weakened. Yeltsin himself went into an apparent depression after having been forced to appoint a government that he did not like. Before the crisis, the Kremlin exercised control of the cabinet through appointments and firings of its ministers. But the newly empowered prime minister did not owe his position to the president, and Yeltsin could not afford to dismiss him, at least for now. If anything, it was the prime minister who was able to pressure the president over high-level appointments. For the sake of restoring stability, Primus argued, it would be much better if there were people in the Kremlin with whom the White House was on the same wavelength.

Boris's influence was visibly in decline. The crowds at The Club were gone. Its bar, with the stuffed crocodile in the corner, stood deserted. Worse, at the beginning of November, Boris found himself the focus of a vicious public debate about Jews and their alleged responsibility for Russia's economic woes. It started with a Communist member of the Duma, Gen. Albert Makashev, who spoke at a rally in the southwestern industrial city of Samara. He claimed that *zhidy*—a Russian slur for Jews—in and around Yeltsin were responsible for the country's mess. The crowd cheered and applauded.

They "drink the blood of the indigenous peoples of the state; they are destroying industry and agriculture," Makashev declared. Journalists immediately rushed to Boris for comment. Boris Berezovsky and his friends in the Kremlin personified a "Zionist conspiracy" to a major swath of the population.

As Boris was digging in his heels, expecting hostile action from the new prime minister, Sasha and his friends were on a collision course with the new FSB director.

After his meeting with Putin in July, Sasha became convinced that his crew of whistle-blowers was under surveillance. Their telephones, he was certain, were tapped. As part of their temporary suspensions, they were made to surrender their weapons and their badges. Internal Affairs combed through their past cases. Someone leaked a fabricated story to the press that Sasha and several other officers from his department were suspected of raiding a Moscow businessman's apartment and seizing a substantial sum of money.

As for URPO, Putin did disband it on a direct order from the Kremlin. However, Khokholkov was transferred to a sinecure position at the tax service. Kamyshnikov was transferred to the ATC. All former URPO opers were reassigned—except the five whistle-blowers. Everyone at the Agency said that their days were numbered.

On September 30, the prosecutors suddenly closed the URPO case without taking any action. During his final visit to the prosecutors' office, Sasha spotted Trepashkin, whom he recognized from the photograph in his file.

"Hey, Misha, I am your would-be killer," he introduced himself.

"And I am your would-be victim. Nice to meet you."

A week later Boris received an official letter.

The investigation focused on two episodes, it said. First, it was confirmed that "on December 27, 1997, [Capt.] A. P. Kamyshnikov, in the presence of Litvinenko, Shebalin, Ponkin and Latyshenok, allowed himself a number of thoughtless statements in reference to you. However, these statements, while discrediting him [Kamyshnikov] as a team leader, did not constitute an intent to commit murder."

Second, the investigators found that, in a separate conversation with Colonel Gusak in November 1997, General "Khokholkov asked whether he [Gusak] would kill you." However, the letter said that "the conversation took place in the absence of other witnesses." Moreover, "when Khokholkov asked him whether he would 'bump' you, [it was] in the context of a subject matter not directly related to you, hence he [Gusak] did not take it as an explicit order to commit murder."

The two other alleged victims, Trepashkin and Dzhabrailov, received similar letters.

This was something that Boris expected. By then he already knew that Prosecutor General Skuratov was secretly cooperating with Primakov in developing several highly political probes that would target the Kremlin inner circle. The URPO investigation was a Kremlin-instigated case. It was not surprising that Skuratov quashed it.

When in mid-October the whistle-blowers met with Boris at The Club to consider their options, Sasha was adamant: they must not give up. This was a cover-up, he said. All the facts had been confirmed. The talk of "bumping" Boris was illegal, whether or not justice would be done. They should go ahead and make the whole thing public. The noose around them was tightening; publicity was their only remaining defense.

Trepashkin, who joined them, backed Sasha. Shebalin, as usual, was silent. Ponkin, Scheglov, and Latyshenok leaned toward Sasha's position. As for Gusak, he had stopped talking to them several weeks ago. He knew which way the wind was blowing.

Boris's first impulse was to talk to Putin, but he thought better of it. At that junction Putin was still an enigma. After his appointment to the FSB, he hid like a hermit crab in his shell. Perhaps it was time to force his hand. If he was committed to reforming the FSB, make him show as much. Boris took a week to think about the best options. By the end of October, he agreed: they should go public.

On November 13, the newspapers published an open letter from Boris to Putin, urging him to pursue the URPO affair. He wrote that the whistle-blowers, after revealing their information to him, had been accused by their superiors of "preventing patriots from killing a Jew who had robbed half of Russia." This charge resounded with the recent scandal about General Makashev's anti-Semitic diatribes.

Four days later Sasha and his friends staged a press conference. Sasha and Trepashkin dressed normally; the other four wore ski masks to hide their faces. The event was a sensation, but not in the way they had hoped. The press focused on only one charge among many that they made: the plot to kill Berezovsky. Boris's notoriety overshadowed their intended message. No one seemed to care about the criminalization of the FSB.

The publicity also failed to support Boris's aim of smoking out Putin. The new FSB chief responded angrily but carefully. He ridiculed the whistle-blowers for not coming up with better evidence and said that they themselves may be rogue agents. He did not say a word about the substance of their allegations.

As General Trofimov explained when they met to review what went wrong, Sasha's major misfortune was bad timing: in a way, the whistle-blowers fell victim to the financial crisis, too. Their main ally, Boris, a formidable force in the beginning of 1998, had lost much of his clout by the end of the year. With Primakov in the White House, he was on the defensive himself.

On December 7, 1998, Yeltsin interrupted his hospital stay to fire his chief of staff, Valentin Yumashev, replacing him with Gen. Nikolai Bordyuzha, the secretary of the National Security Council and formerly the commander of the Border Guards. Apparently the president had had enough of civilians and decided to rely on generals once again.

"Now they will either kill me or put me in jail," predicted Sasha to Marina.

THE MAKING OF A PRESIDENT
(Russian-Style)

Part IV.

THE MAKING OF A PRESIDENT
[Russia-Style]

CHAPTER 8

THE LOYALIST

Chechnya, December 8, 1998: Chechen authorities find the severed heads of four hostages, three Britons and a New Zealander, in a sack outside a village forty miles from Grozny. Their killing was apparently triggered by a rescue attempt staged by President Maskhadov's antiterrorist squad. Chechen officials accuse the leader of a radical Wahhabi group, Arbi Barayev, of the kidnapping and murder. Barayev threatens to unleash a wave of terror in Russia if Maskhadov's forces attack his stronghold of Urus-Martan. Islamist opposition leaders Shamil Basayev and Movladi Udugov demand Maskhadov's resignation.

Sasha's falling out with the FSB coincided with a deadly disintegration of the Russian-Chechen rapport that Boris had helped to build a year earlier. According to Akhmed Zakayev, the fault was squarely on the Russian side. "From the moment Rybkin and Berezovsky were removed from the process, things started deteriorating," he later explained. Zakayev believed that starting in the summer of 1998, the Russian secret service began to systematically destabilize Maskhadov's government by quietly supporting radical Islamists.

"We wanted to build a secular, democratic, pro-Western Muslim state, something along the lines of Turkey, and eventually join NATO," Zakayev explained, "but then all of a sudden, all these Wahhabi appeared, with stacks of money, and started preaching a totally foreign brand of Islam. How do you think they got there? Through Moscow—they all had Russian visas!"

In July 1998, during the crackdown on the militants, the Maskhadov government caught some of them and expelled them to Jordan.

"They were all experienced fighters," Zakayev recalled, "but they had nothing to do with 'the Afghans,' the American-trained jihadists that fought the Soviets in Afghanistan. They were all Arabs who spoke Russian, the old KGB cadre from the Middle East. And we knew that their money came not from Saudi Arabia, but from Moscow."

He pointed out that Khalid Sheikh Mohammed, the eventual mastermind of the September 11 attack, had tried to get into Chechnya in 1997, before he worked with Osama bin Laden. He was not allowed to pass through Azerbaijan. The same was true for at least four of the eventual 9/11 terrorists, including Mohammed Atta. All of them, before going to Afghanistan, tried to enter Chechnya but could not: the place was tightly sealed to outsiders.

"So explain to me, please, how those guys we caught, with their Jordanian passports, not to mention their Arab looks, went to a Russian embassy, got a visa, then flew to Moscow, then to North Caucasus—a trip that required special permission—without the FSB noticing? Impossible!

"And the three Dagestan villages that Stepashin patronized! That was a smart move. We were trying to chase the Wahhabi out of Chechnya, so they gave them refuge in the Russian territory under the FSB's protection!"

Zakayev was particularly indignant about the hostage industry. The Russian practice of paying ransoms only encouraged renegade warlords and provided them with substantial funds, while the Chechen government was strapped. He claimed that the Russians paid $7 million just for Valentin Vlasov, the Yeltsin envoy who had been captured in May 1998 and was released in November. The Russian secret services had their own network for dealing with the kidnappers. Lt. Col. Daud Korigov, the interior minister of the neighboring region of Ingushetia, was Russia's principal intermediary. The overall coordinator of the transactions was Russian Deputy Interior Minister Vladimir Rushailo.

"It was impossible for us to crack these chains," complained Zakayev. "There was a real division of labor there: one criminal gang would specialize in taking hostages, another in keeping them, the third would negotiate with the Russians. They were reselling people down these chains like cattle."

Zakayev complained that there was a high-level conspiracy of silence about ransoms being paid: "The British endorsed it, and the French, too, when their citizens were involved, everybody knew about that. But publicly they denied it."

Initially, the Chechen government quietly pleaded with the Russians to stop. Then Maskhadov went public and accused the Russian government of abetting kidnappers. He even accused the Russian secret services of being in collusion with the hostage-takers. But the industry continued.

Boris, for his part, explained that when he was deputy secretary of the NSC, the policy was to engage the radicals—at Maskhadov's own urging. At one point in 1997, Boris personally delivered $2 million of government money to Basayev, who was then the Chechen deputy prime minister in charge of reconstruction. It was all in cash—there were no banks left in Chechnya.

"Later, when I left the NSC, Deputy Minister Rushailo asked me to continue working with him on hostages, because I had a reputation as someone whom the Chechens could trust. I have no regrets about it, we saved at least fifty people, who otherwise would have been killed; most of them were simple soldiers. And believe me, all of this was strictly official, with the full knowledge and consent of the Kremlin."

Boris refused to confirm that he paid for the release of the two Britons, Jon James and Camilla Carr, in September 1998. He only said, "Sir Andrew Wood, the British ambassador, asked me to help. I checked with Boris Nikolaevich [Yeltsin], and he said, 'Do whatever is necessary to get them out.' So I did."

Boris and Zakayev agreed on one thing: the initial contacts among the FSB, hostage-taking warlords, and Wahhabi radicals later developed into stronger relationships. In the end, the Russian secret services began running some of the renegade Chechen groups. When the FSB wanted to provoke the second Chechen War, it knew where to turn. Exactly how to do it, however, would require a masterstroke by the FSB director turned prime minister, Vladimir Putin.

Putin's ascent from Lubyanka to the White House could be properly traced to the birthday party of Lena Berezovskaya on February 22, 1999. Initially the celebration was intended as a small private event for family and the closest friends. But Putin arrived uninvited, surprising not only Lena and Boris, but much of the Russian political set.

Boris's war with Primus was in full swing, and pundits were taking bets that this time the oligarch might not prevail. Lena and Boris decided against a big party for the first time in years so as not to put people on the spot: for elite Muscovites, Boris was a dangerous liaison.

Two days earlier, they had attended the world premiere of *The Barber of Siberia,* the first Russian Hollywood-style blockbuster, in the Kremlin Palace of Congresses. The building was crammed with five thousand of those elite. When Boris and Lena entered the hall, an empty space formed around them as people instinctively moved away.

Their caution was well founded. In the past several weeks a purge of Boris's empire by Prosecutor General Yuri Skuratov had been the talk of the town.

It started with the tax authority leaning on ORT for back taxes. *Everybody* in the country owed back taxes, but ORT was singled out. Then prosecutors, accompanied by TV cameras and Spetsnaz troops in ski masks, raided twenty-four offices and homes in Moscow, all associated with Boris, including the head office of Sibneft. They were ostensibly looking for evidence of illegal wiretapping by Boris's private security men.

In the beginning of February Glushkov's entire team was purged from Aeroflot. Skuratov's office announced that they were starting a criminal probe into the airline's finances, particularly the role of

Andava, the Swiss company that gathered proceeds from foreign sales of Aeroflot's tickets.

Boris had no doubt that all of this was part of a strategy by Prime Minister Primakov to taint everything associated with Yeltsin as Russia entered an election year. The problem was, the president did not see it that way. He trusted Primus.

At the end of 1998 and into early 1999, Yeltsin, consumed by bouts of sickness and depression, was apathetic and indecisive. He was bitter that his former favorites, "the young reformers" and their banker friends, had let him down by designing enrichment schemes at the time of a critical fight with the Communists. He was wary of relying on the secret services. As he wrote in *Midnight Diaries,* in Primakov he saw a kindred soul, a reform-minded former Soviet boss who saw the light of democracy. His original understanding with Primakov was that they would jointly retire in 2000 after transferring power to a new generation of reform-minded politicians.

Boris, on the other hand, understood Primakov's true colors earlier than many, perhaps because of earlier clashes with him over Aeroflot.

There were precious few around Boris who were determined to stop Primus and still had a fighting spirit, among them, former chief of staff Yumashev, Yeltsin's daughter Tatyana, Roma Abramovich, and Alexander Voloshin, the economic adviser to the president. Collectively, they became known as "the family." Boris was somewhat of a guru in the group; he was at least a decade older than the others.

The influence of "the family" on the president was never as great as pundits believed. Yeltsin did not allow himself to be manipulated, and he always considered his options. To complicate things, he personally disliked Boris, who was the driving force of the group, and he preferred to filter his advice through Tanya-Valya.

Roma Abramovich was the youngest and newest "family" member. In late 1997, he had asked Boris for an introduction to Tanya-Valya, and they immediately hit it off. He became their favorite social companion. Boris was happy about this. At one point he told Roma, "I can work with them, but I cannot live with them, like inviting them for a weekend or going out on a boat. But it is important that you do it." By then, both Boris and Roma had acquired yachts and properties on the Côte d'Azur, retreats from the pressures of Moscow.

"I don't mind living with them at all, if it's good for business," smiled Roma. Boris knew that under the surface of Roma's shy, sympathetic demeanor lurked a calculating, shrewd loner, with a sharp grasp of human weaknesses and a great talent for networking. Both of them knew pretty well that in the internal dynamics of "the family" there were those with clout and those with money; somebody had to pay for the boat trips. They both had money, but Roma was better at taking care of mundane matters. Before long, all monetary and many other "technical" details of "family" life fell under Roma's domain. He got things done.

There was a sixth, aspiring member of "the family," FSB Director Vladimir Putin. Boris saw him several times after his appointment, and Tanya-Valya strongly supported him. After their initial spat over Litvinenko's allegations, Boris and Putin's relationship improved, primarily because they had common enemies. Primus hated Putin and wanted his own man to run Kontora, "a real professional" from the old cadre of KGB intelligence. Every time Primus came to see Yeltsin—often in a hospital—he asked for Putin's head.

Nevertheless, there was no chemistry between Boris and Putin until the day he showed up at Lena Berezovskaya's birthday. His security guard gave Boris twenty minutes' warning that the FSB director was on his way to the dacha. At first, everyone thought there was some kind of emergency, but when Boris went out to meet the guest he saw a huge bouquet of roses emerging from the automobile door ahead of the diminutive spymaster, as his security detail stood in a semicircle.

Boris was surprised.

"Volodya, I am very touched, but why do you need to complicate your relationship with Primakov?"

"I don't care," said Putin. "I am your friend and I want to show it. To third parties, in particular. They want to make you a pariah, but I know that you are clean."

Many years later in London, Boris still believed that Putin was sincere in his birthday gesture. "He did not have any ulterior motive in coming. At the time, I was not among Yeltsin's favorites. Primus was. The last thing Putin needed was to give Primus grounds to say that we were conspiring together."

Our conversation took place after Sasha's death. I found Boris's statement about Putin's sincerity incredible. Boris's views did not match: How could Putin, a selfless friend showing solidarity with Boris in his time of need, also be the instigator of Sasha's murder? One of the two must be false.

"That's the whole point!" Boris exclaimed, with his mathematician's joy of solving a puzzle. "I thought about it a lot. Has anyone betrayed you in your life?"

"Some," I responded.

"Have you wished them dead? Wanted them killed, literally?"

"Why, no!"

"That's the difference! Putin is an exemplary team player, totally dependable. How could he possibly be a murderer? And then I understood. These KGB people, they do have a moral code, but it is different. They are trained to be loyal to the death, and, at the same time, they believe that disloyalty is punishable by death. To him, Sasha was a traitor. Sasha tried to explain this to me, but I did not pay attention before it was too late."

And so from the day of Lena's birthday, Putin became a full-fledged member of "the family," and his skills proved indispensable with the urgent problems at hand: parrying Skuratov's assault and convincing the president that his prime minister was plotting to grab power and steer the country back into the Soviet past.

––––––

Nobody knows for sure how the fateful video originated. Boris said that he learned about it when it was already an open secret in the Kremlin. In *Midnight Diaries* Yeltsin says that a "pornographic tape" appearing to feature his prosecutor general, Yuri Skuratov, "got into the hands" of Chief of Staff General Bordyuzha at the end of January. Yeltsin wrote that Skuratov's "friends . . . among bankers and businessmen" were the ones who "made use of the prosecutor's soft spot."

The Moscow tabloid *Argumenty i Fakti* hypothesized in an editorial that the poor quality of the black-and-white video suggested that it was the work of the secret services, because "they were the only ones who would not have a budget for new equipment."

The insightful journalist-parliamentarian Yuri Schekochihin, in a story in *Novaya Gazeta*, said that the man who made the film was one of the prosecuter's own staff who later surfaced in the Kremlin.

Whoever got the tape to the Kremlin unleashed a chain of events that became Russia's Monicagate.

On February 1, 1999, Yeltsin's chief of staff, General Bordyuzha, confronted Skuratov with the tape and extracted a letter of resignation from him. Late at night on March 16, the tape was shown on Channel 2, with a warning that it was not recommended to viewers under eighteen. The next morning, the Federation Council, the upper chamber of Russia's parliament, gathered to endorse Skuratov's resignation, as required by the Constitution. But the vote turned into a humiliating defeat for Yeltsin. Skuratov said that he had resigned under pressure from the president's staff. In response, the council voted 142–6 to reject his resignation.

Enraged, Yeltsin fired his chief of staff. He called Skuratov, Primakov, and Putin to see him in the hospital, where he was receiving treatment for a bleeding ulcer. He had not been informed about the tape, he said, but under the circumstances he asked Skuratov to go.

Skuratov said that the tape was a fabrication. Yeltsin directed Putin to have the FSB perform forensic analysis to establish its authenticity.

And here Skuratov made a fatal blunder. He told Yeltsin that one of his corruption investigations, involving Yeltsin's daughter, would be taken care of if the president allowed him to stay. Yeltsin says in his memoirs that initially he did not understand what Skuratov was talking about.

A new prosecutor would find it difficult "to dispose of this complex issue," insisted Skuratov. And then, seeking support, he turned to Primakov: "Tell him, Evgeny Maksimovich."

According to Yeltsin, Primakov fell into a long silence, and then said, "If Boris Nikolaevich asked me, I would go instantly. You should go, Yuri Ilyich."

"You betrayed me, Evgeny Maksimovich," retorted Skuratov angrily.

It appeared that the two had a prior agreement of some sort. That was the beginning of the end of Primakov—though, oddly, not of Skuratov, who refused to resign.

For eight months, the Kremlin battled Parliament over Skuratov's resignation. To manage the hostilities, Yeltsin appointed a new chief of staff, Boris's protégé, Alexander Voloshin. In the meantime, Skuratov dug in his heels, continuing his highly publicized probes, which completely destroyed what remained of Yeltsin's credibility. The president's approval ratings fell back into single digits. Russia was slipping into political chaos.

The outside world barely paid attention to the Kremlin soap opera. In the wake of Monica Lewinsky, a sex scandal surrounding a mere state prosecutor was not big news. The only Russian official who made headlines in the West, on March 23, was Primakov, who made a midair turnaround en route to Washington to protest the onset of America's bombing of Serbia. He became an instant hero among nationalists and Communists.

On March 25 military prosecutors arrested Sasha Litvinenko on a street in central Moscow. He was charged with exceeding his official powers, and causing bodily harm to a suspect, back in late 1997.

Grozny: On March 21, President Aslan Maskhadov survives another assassination attempt. The attack comes two days after a devastating bombing at the crowded market in Vladikavkaz, thirty miles from Chechnya, that killed fifty people. In Moscow, FSB chief Vladimir Putin rejects Maskhadov's allegation that the attacks are the result of a conspiracy of "certain forces" in Moscow. On March 29, Putin is named head of Russia's National Security Council, making him responsible for overall Chechnya policy. He retains the FSB director-

ship. By April 15, Russia deploys thousands of extra police and troops along the Chechen border. Speaking on Russian TV, the commander of interior troops says that the aim of Chechen separatists is "to create a single Muslim state out of Chechnya, Ingushetia and Dagestan. This will give [Chechnya] direct access to Turkey, a NATO member."

Even now it cannot be said with certainty who was behind Sasha's arrest. At the time, the two agencies that handled his case were on the opposite sides of a great political divide: Skuratov's Prosecution Service versus Putin's FSB.

Sasha was adamant that it was Putin who delivered him to Skuratov's dogs. He said that the military prosecutor Yuri Bagraev, who was Skuratov's right-hand man, was genuinely surprised to see him in custody. Initially after the arrest, low-level investigators handled him. Then at some point, Bagraev appeared in his general's uniform, walking into the interrogation room. He looked through Sasha's telephone numbers and could not hide his astonishment.

"Oh, I see Berezovsky, Yumashev here," he said. "Do you really know them? Are you the guy on TV? Well, well, we have a VIP here."

"Putin had the power to decide whether to pass my file to the prosecutors or not," Sasha said. "He always hated me. And there was a bonus for him: by throwing me to the wolves he distanced himself from Boris in the eyes of the FSB's generals."

Sasha believed that Putin had initiated his case personally immediately after their press conference back in November.

Putin never made a secret of what he thought of Sasha. In December 1998, he told Elena Tregubova, the Kremlin correspondent for *Kommersant,* "Personally I cannot exclude that these people really frightened Boris Abramovich [Berezovsky}. He had been a target for assassination before. So it was only natural for him to think that another attempt was in the making. I believe that these officers made a scandal simply to develop a job market for themselves. . . . I fired Litvinenko and disbanded his unit . . . because FSB officers should not stage press conferences. This is not their job. And they should not make internal scandals public."

Years later, speaking in the Kremlin on February 5, 2007, Putin gave a slightly different version: Sasha was dismissed from the FSB "for abusing his position of service, namely for beating citizens during arrests . . . and for stealing explosives." These were the charges brought against Sasha after his arrest.

But at that time, everyone believed that Putin had nothing to do with it; Sasha's arrest looked like a subplot of Skuratov's overall assault on Boris.

Boris learned about Sasha's arrest in Paris just as his battle with Skuratov was entering its terminal phase.

On April 2, Putin staged a press conference to announce that the FSB had concluded that the porno tape was authentic. The broadcast was meant to tarnish Skuratov's image, but it had just the opposite effect, perhaps because of Putin's exceedingly pious expression; as one of my law enforcement friends observed, "This guy had never been in a hotel with two girls. Not even with one."

On the same day, Skuratov issued arrest warrants for Berezovsky and Glushkov, alleging that they had siphoned $250 million of Aeroflot money through Andava. Berezovsky responded by saying that the charges were baseless and politically motivated. "The time when the country is run by people with naked behinds is past us," he told the press. For the time being he was stranded in France with Lena.

On April 21 Boris returned to Moscow to face the music and clear his name. He agreed to cooperate with the investigation in exchange for revocation of the arrest warrant. On that day, Yeltsin suffered another setback when the Federation Council rejected his second attempt to oust Skuratov, albeit with a less humiliating vote of 79–61. Prime Minister Primakov pledged his loyalty to the president. The noose of Skuratov's investigation was tightening around Tatyana's neck. The "family" urgently needed Boris's advice.

The first place that Boris visited upon returning to Moscow was Skuratov's den, the state prosecution service. He was questioned for four hours, officially charged with "illegal entrepreneurship" and money laundering, and let go—for the time being. TV crews were waiting outside for a live news feed.

"The case against me was instigated by the prime minister in violation of the law," he said into the camera. "Primakov is in collusion with Skuratov to undermine the president."

As he drove away, his cell phone rang. It was Chernomyrdin, who had been asked by the president to mediate in the scandal. Primus had seen the news. He was expecting Boris at the White House. He wanted to explain himself.

When Boris emerged from an hour-and-a-half meeting with the prime minister, he was tight-lipped: "We did not declare our love for each other," he told the waiting reporters. "We discussed the importance of not confusing politics with criminal justice."

Years later, Boris explained to me what happened inside.

"I give you my word of honor that I have nothing to do with the Aeroflot case," Primakov began. "Here, I have a copy of the official prosecution file. There is no record of any communication from my office. Let us ask Viktor Stepanovich to be a witness."

He rang the bell. Chernomyrdin walked into the room.

Boris reached into his pocket and produced a copy of a letter from Skuratov to Primakov detailing the Aeroflot allegations. (Boris would not tell me where he obtained it. "I had my sources," he said.) Across the page was an inscription in the prime minister's hand: "Initiate criminal proceedings and bring up charges. Primakov."

"I don't believe that I wrote it. Did I really?" Primus was stunned.

"May I go now, Evgeny Maksimovich?" asked Chernomyrdin.

When they were alone, Primakov said, "Boris Abramovich, tell me, what do you want? I have heard that you were interested in the Sber Bank."

"I have not been involved in business for years now, Evgeny Maksimovich. But I would like to be your assistant," said Boris impishly.

The prime minister did not get his sense of humor. He was at a loss. "And what would the Communists say?"

"Just kidding, Evgeny Maksimovich," said Berezovsky, and he left the room.

The next day Boris went to see Putin at his FSB office. He shivered involuntarily as the heavy iron gates closed behind his Mercedes. The car edged into the inner courtyard of the tetragonal Lubyanka building. In the old days, many thousands had passed through this gate and never returned.

A nondescript fellow—a Putin look-alike—ushered him into the elevator and to the brand new director's study on the third floor. Putin's office was renovated to fit his ascetic taste: light wood, strictly functional, apparently influenced by his East German years. The old executive office, where such past masters of the KGB as Beria and Andropov had plotted the cold war, had been converted into an Agency shrine, by the new director's orders.

Putin's small frame looked even smaller behind his huge desk, on which stood a bronze statuette of Felix Dzerzhinsky, the founder of the Soviet secret police. He put his finger to his lips to signal silence and gestured to Boris to follow him through the back door. They passed through a private dining room and exited through another tiny passageway.

Boris looked around. They were in a small windowless anteroom in front of an elevator door, apparently a back exit from the office to the executive elevator.

"This is the safest place to talk," Putin said.

There were two items on Boris's agenda: Primakov and Litvinenko.

It is a peculiar quality of Russian politics that the principal of the Kremlin, be it a tsar, a general secretary, or a president, is endowed with a mystical quality of *vlast*, or "right of power," which instills in the populace a measure of instinctive humility and respect. This regal ingredient of supreme authority links all historical rulers in Russia into a single virtual dynasty from the House of Romanoff through Lenin,

Stalin, Khrushchev, and Brezhnev, down to Gorbachev and Yeltsin. From it flows the concept of heir apparent. In a practical sense, as Putin and Boris—and everyone else—well understood, whomever Yeltsin endorsed as his heir would have an automatic electoral advantage, anywhere from 20 to 40 percent of the vote. It made no difference that Yeltsin himself had negligible approval ratings; the mystique of being the heir to *vlast* worked quite independently from the personality of the incumbent.

The country was just eight months away from the election year of 2000. Obviously, Primus, a seventy-year-old Soviet relic backed by a cabal of Communists, former apparatchiks, and spies, was not what the country needed as it entered the twenty-first century. He had to go; it had been agreed between him and the president from day one. The question was, who would be his replacement, the heir apparent, the next president of Russia?

As they stood in the elevator anteroom in the old KGB building, Boris and Putin understood the responsibility bestowed on them by history. Their joint opinion would probably carry "the family," which in turn would weigh with the president.

Notwithstanding the electoral advantage of the president's endorsement, the candidate should have one essential quality: he should be able to beat the Communist-backed candidate, possibly Primus himself, who had gained popularity in recent weeks. But as Boris and Putin reviewed the list of possible candidates, the landscape was deserted. After the previous year's scandals and crises, reformers of Chubais's school, such as Nemtsov and Kiriyenko, were unelectable. The same was true for Chernomyrdin, with his loser image. Lebed was electable, but he would become something of a military dictator. There were only two people of national standing who seemed minimally acceptable: Sergei Stepashin, minister of the interior, and Nikolai Aksionenko, minister of transportation. Each had his strengths and his weaknesses. Neither was a shoo-in.

"Volodya, what about you?" Boris suddenly asked.

"What about me?" Putin did not understand.

"Could you be president?"

"Me? No, I am not the type. This is not what I want in life."

"Well, then, what? Do you want to stay here forever?"

"I want . . . ," he hesitated. "I want to be Berezovsky."

"No, you don't really." Boris laughed.

They dropped the subject.

Boris's next question was about Sasha.

"Look," Putin said, "I will be straight with you. You know what I think of Litvinenko. He used you. And he is a traitor. But if you ask, I will try to help. The problem is, it's not under my control at all. It is all in the hands of Skuratov's military prosecutors division. Let us first get rid of Skuratov, then we will see what we can do about Litvinenko."

All of this made sense to Boris. But there was something in Putin's expression that he did not like.

"And, Boris," Putin continued, "whatever you think of him, he is not clean. He did some pretty bad things."

"I don't believe you," said Boris. "I know the man."

"I have seen the evidence."

There was an awkward pause. How strange, thought Boris. Putin and Sasha are two men in the FSB who do not take bribes, and they hate each other so much.

"He is a traitor," repeated Putin. "But I will do what I can."

It was getting late. Putin grabbed the door handle. It turned freely without catching the lock mechanism."Fuck," said Putin. "They can't make locks work, and you want me to run the country. To call the elevator, you need a key. We're trapped.

"Hey, someone!" he yelled, banging on the wall that separated the anteroom from the main corridor. "This is Putin here! We are locked out!"

They banged for about ten minutes before someone heard and came to their rescue.

———

In the meantime, in solitary confinement at Lefortovo prison, Sasha was trying to come to grips with his situation.

"Initially, I was in shock," he later wrote in *The Gang from Lubyanka*. "The first night I did not sleep; I stared at the ceiling. On the day I was arrested, the weather was lousy, snow mixed with rain, sludge all over. I don't like this time of the year and by the end of March I live in expectation of the sun. The next day they took me out into a small recreation box, five to six steps across. I looked up—and the sky was blue, with the sun somewhere out there. I was pacing like a beast between those walls. Over me—the iron grid with barbed wire and blue-blue skies. I was in a terrible state: spring had arrived, and I can't see it. I am here, in this damp, cold box. I got so upset that I asked them to bring me back to my cell."

Some years later, on a walk through London, Sasha stopped at the inscription on the statue of Oscar Wilde: "We are all in the gutter but some of us are looking at the stars."

It instantly brought back his memories of prison. "How very right. That was how I felt. In the gutter looking at the stars."

On his third day in solitary, he went on a hunger strike. He demanded to see a human rights representative. He was close to hysterical. They gave him a shot to cool him down. Then the warden, an old man who knew him well from the times when Sasha visited these premises as an oper, came to see him.

"Look, son," he said, "don't destroy yourself, this is not the end of the world. You will need all your strength. Stop it."

That fatherly talk and familiar face from his old life calmed him down. He started eating, and he started thinking.

"I tried to sort out why I was there. Should I consider myself guilty or innocent? Formally I was innocent of course, because the charges were all fabricated. But I had seen people who were imprisoned for nothing, because of an error or a setup, and I was not one of them. I was in for what I'd done: the press conference. I did it, it can't be denied. I'd committed a premeditated press conference. Having a press conference is not a crime. But I cannot say that I did not know that I could go to jail for it. I even discussed it with my wife: would or wouldn't I be arrested? If you ask around, most people would say, 'Serves him right, what business had he staging a press conference?'" And so on, endlessly.

It was during these first weeks at Lefortovo that he realized there was a connection between his revolt and his relationship with Marina. Before he met her, his bond with his service and his adherence to its code of loyalty were absolute. Being disapproved of by his command-ers, or disowned by Kontora, was the worst imaginable thing that could happen to him. But not any more. Losing her would be worse.

"You know, Marina changed the title of ownership," he explained to me later on. "She came and claimed me. Had they put me on a polygraph before I knew her and asked what comes to my mind at the word 'love,' I would have said 'Motherland.' If they said 'faith-ful,' I would have said 'My oath.' If they said 'obey,' I would say 'My orders.' It wouldn't have even crossed my mind to think otherwise. Because I belonged to them. Like a child to his parents, whom I had really never had."

But Marina changed it all in an instant. From the moment he saw her, he belonged to her, and therefore he could not belong to any-body else. It was not like this with Natalia, his first wife. But Marina somehow found the key to the lock even he did not know he had.

"Had I gotten to URPO before her, I would have done whatever I was told, like a robot. But she broke that grip and allowed me to think. Then Boris came along, and he finished the job. Because he explained things. Not like my bosses, who could only bark 'Because I told you so!'"

Lying with his eyes to the ceiling in Lefortovo, he was consumed by guilt about his two families. He did not have any savings. Hopefully Marina would have the good sense to go to Boris and ask for help. But then, surely, they would find a way to present even that request in a bad light, using some dirty trick, like they did with Natalia, his first wife. They had called Natalia in to Internal Affairs, taken away all records of her child support, and made her sign a statement claiming that Sasha was threatening her.

Back in November, at the peak of the scandal, Putin himself had claimed on TV that Sasha was not paying child support: "The wife of one of the press conference participants appealed to me."

"Why did you do it?" Sasha yelled at her at the time. "Do you understand that you are endangering yourself? They will knock you off and pin it on me."

"I didn't know," she cried. "I'm a silly woman. They frightened me."

Such a dirty trick was to be expected from an oper. But for the

FSB director to lower himself to this level! Kovalev or Barsukov would never have done that.

———————

Sasha now had all the time in the world for rumination, but Marina did not have much opportunity to adjust to the shock. She learned about the arrest from Ponkin and the rest of his crew, who came to her workplace in the evening and tried to comfort her. Suddenly she had to take care of a thousand things. In the morning, Boris's office called. Berezovsky is abroad, they said, but we found a lawyer for you. An investigator from the prosecutor's office wanted to see her. Arrangements had to be made for Tolik to stay with his grandparents for a few days.

She went to see the lawyer. He was a veteran of military justice, who said from the outset that he had no experience in political cases.

"But the politics of it will probably not be decided in the courtroom. What I can do is everything that is necessary on the merits of the case, as if it was nonpolitical."

Boris had also arranged for Marina to have a monthly stipend of $1,000, roughly equal to what Sasha had been making.

"Don't worry, we will get him out," he said on the phone from Paris. What else could he say? she wondered.

Then she went to Lefortovo.

"When can I see him?" was her first question to the investigator, Sergei Barsukov.

Barsukov was aloof and formal. He explained the rules: Sasha was entitled to two visits a month, at the investigator's discretion. March was almost over, so she could expect to see him twice in April, unless there was a reason to refuse her visits. But first Barsukov wanted to conduct a search of her home. He presented a warrant.

Why search, she wondered, in view of the charges against Sasha? They were simply on a fishing expedition. They turned her home upside down but did not find anything of interest. Of course, Sasha did have secret files, but he was hiding them elsewhere.

As for the charges, Marina found them laughable. Eighteen months earlier, during the detention of a criminal group, Sasha allegedly beat up a certain Vladimir Kharchenko, the suspect's driver. The bodily harm was in the form of a bruise "the size of a 5 kopeck coin." The lawyer said not to worry; politics aside, on its merits the case would not stand up in court.

In early April she got her first visit. She woke up at 6 to get in line to register by 8. As she listened to the conversation of other women in the line, a fear engulfed her: What if somehow she had exceeded the limit of gifts allowed in the prisoner's package, the allowance for grams of soap and packs of tea, for example, and the whole thing were rejected?

After registering, Marina had to wait for another three hours before she was led into the visitors' room, to a small booth where Sasha sat behind thick glass. They spoke over the telephone while a stone-faced guard listened. The case could not be discussed, nor could anything that might seem like a coded message. They could talk about family, the weather, health, and all the other things important only to them. During the seven months he spent in Lefortovo, she had sixteen visits like that.

———————

Lefortovo is a special prison. It is well funded, clean, efficiently run—and extremely depressing. The worst thing about it, according to Sasha, was the silence. Such devastating stillness he had never heard in his life.

"Lefortovo crushes you spiritually," he later wrote in *The Gang from Lubyanka*. "There is some negative energy coming from those walls. They say that birds avoid flying over it. Perhaps it's the legacy of the old days when Lefortovo was a place of mass executions and torture."

As an FSB prison, Lefortovo was reserved for serious clientele: spies, mob bosses, large-scale economic offenders. Sasha had the distinction of being there for a petty offense: beating someone up. Nonetheless, he was accorded the treatment of a serious customer. They used the full gamut of psychological techniques on him.

From the outset, his investigator let him feel that the outcome of his case was not an issue. There was no point in even talking about it, he said. Just wait for the trial, and you will be sent away, to somewhere in the Urals. There, you will be knocked off. No one will notice or care or have sympathy for you. You are a traitor, and you know how traitors are dealt with.

What Sergei Barsukov really tried to convey to him was that everything could still be reversed. He was the one who had brought it upon himself—and for what? He must admit that siding with Boris was a mistake. If he only faced the truth and admitted that Boris was not worth sacrificing his own life, then they could start thinking together about how to help Sasha out of his predicament.

After thirty-six days of solitary confinement interrupted by such sermons, Sasha was on the verge of going insane. Suddenly he was given a cellmate. He knew it was a plant, but he was still happy to talk to a human being, even though the conversation was surely recorded.

In his seven months in Lefortovo, Sasha changed cellmates five or six times. He saw through them all. Each had been sentenced to a long term and instead of rotting in one of the truly hellish places of the gulag, earned his stay in Lefortovo by reporting on fellow inmates. The method was more or less the same: establishing trust by talking about family and common interests, sharing life stories, and then, gradually, infusing into the "object" the mood of hopelessness, the futility of resisting the system. Or, depending on the need, making the object talk about specific things that the investigator wanted to hear. Sasha knew the routine well enough; "In-Cell Development" had been one of his favorite subjects in counterintelligence school.

He amused himself by playing games with the invisible oper who was running his cellmates. On one occasion he cracked his interlocutor by telling him bluntly that he knew that he was an informer. Once Sasha got out, he threatened, he would check the man's FSB file; there was someone in the Agency who would let him have a peek for a few hundred bucks.

The next day, the Lefortovo oper called him in: "Why are you doing this? Why are you bullshitting my agent?"

"I don't like the man," said Sasha. "He snores. Send me somebody else."

Sasha was perplexed by the direction of the questioning by his

170

investigators and his spy-cellmates: they were all interested in "the Kremlin family": Yumashev, Voloshin, Tatyana, Roma, and Pavel Borodin, the Kremlin's property manager. What were their habits, their relationships with each other, their third-party contacts, spending routines? It was clear that the investigators totally misunderstood Sasha's standing in Boris's circle. Of course he had met all these people, except Borodin, but he was not nearly close enough to provide any answers of that sort, even if he wanted to.

At the time Sasha did not know the politics behind it; he had never heard of "the family" before. But later on, in London, we analyzed his prison experiences. Was he Skuratov's prisoner after all? Or Putin's?

We argued about that for hours. Neither theory made any sense.

Putin would not need to poke into things like the Tatyana-Yumashev relationship; he knew it first-hand. He could not be after Borodin's secrets; he had worked for him for two years. And yet, Sasha was sitting in Putin's prison, under the charge trumped up by Putin's Internal Affairs. So why was he questioned in an essentially anti-Putin investigation?

And then we realized that perhaps both theories were true. Putin, who wanted to see him in jail for his own reasons, was doing it with Skuratov's hands; he knew that Sasha could not tell much of substance, so he threw him to Skuratov like a bone. The prosecutor was after him because he was Boris's friend; Putin, because he was Kontora's traitor.

While Boris and Putin were talking in the elevator anteroom at Lubyanka, the president in the Kremlin was tormented by the same problem: Who should inherit his throne? As he wrote in *Midnight Diaries,* by the end of April, Primakov's fate was sealed. He "regretted it deeply," but Evgeny Maksimovich used "too much of the color red" in his political palette.

Although he did not discuss it with anyone, not even with the man himself, by then Yeltsin had already chosen his crown prince. It was Putin, dependable and uncorrupted. The problem was, it was too early to announce him. He did not want "the society to get used to

Putin during the lazy months of the summer. The mystery, the surprise part must not be wasted. It would be so important in the elections."

But Primakov had to go now, so Yeltsin needed an interim replacement. He chose Stepashin, the softie, who had the best chance of approval by the Duma. The Communists would love to have him in their sights as the opponent to beat in the election. This was Yeltsin's strategy: he would install Stepashin for just a few months and then bring in Putin when the time was ripe. It would throw his opponents off-balance.

On May 12, Primakov was sacked. Sergei Stepashin sailed smoothly through Duma confirmation as the new Russian prime minister. Boris's friend Vladimir Rushailo took over the Interior Ministry. Primus departed for a well-deserved vacation, carrying with him the informal title of the most popular politician in Russia. His approval rating was at 60 percent, compared to Yeltsin's 2.

For the summer months, Russia's political metabolism shifts to the green belt of dachas surrounding the capital. On one steamy night in early June, Igor Malashenko, the president of NTV, greeted a pair of guests at his dacha: the Tanya-Valya team. They came with a mission: to sound out Malashenko regarding Putin. Would NTV support him should he become the heir apparent?

"I was horrified," recalled Malashenko years later. "He was KGB. How can one even think of picking a KGB man? That's a criminal organization."

"But you have not even met him," Tanya-Valya protested. "He is different. He is truly liberal. And loyal. He did not betray Sobchak, and he would not betray us. Papa likes him a lot."

Igor agreed to meet Putin before coming to a final judgment. On Sunday, June 6, a dinner was arranged at the dacha of Peter Aven, one of the original Davos Pact oligarchs, the founder of Alfa Bank. Putin came with his two daughters.

Aven's house, with its over-the-top opulence, must have been a shocker for the teenage daughters of an uncorrupted civil servant.

The dinner was dull. The conversation listlessly eddied around the topic of water shortages in downtown Moscow. Putin kept his silence, acting "like a hero captured by the enemy." Finally Malashenko's wife arrived and livened up the night. She came straight from the airport, seeing their daughter off to her boarding school in England.

That gave them a new subject to discuss: private schools in the United Kingdom. Putin still kept silent, as did his daughters.

A while later, Malashenko's daughter called from Heathrow: nobody was there to meet her. Could Mama contact the school, please? Children were not allowed to travel by themselves.

"Come on, it's Sunday evening, there's no one at school," said Malashenko's wife. "You're a big girl: get a cab, give the address to the driver, and he will take you there."

She hung up. Suddenly Putin spoke for the first time.

"It's a mistake what you just did, you know. You can never tell who could be out there, posing as a cab driver."

Igor's jaw dropped. Was he joking?

But Putin was deadly serious. Igor was an important opinion-maker in Russia, a target for Western intelligence services, he explained. For a man like him it is advisable to be more cautious about the security of his family.

There was not a hint of irony or malice in the remark. Putin was genuinely concerned about the girl's safety.

"That was it, the KGB mind-set," Malashenko explained to me. "The moment I heard it, it was crystal clear. How could we possibly support a man like that to be our president?"

Later on, there were many instances that widened the great divide between Putin and Malashenko's NTV. But the casual remark at that dinner was the start of a chain of events that ended in the storming of NTV studios by Putin's police just one year later.

On July 11, Yeltsin and his family went to Zavidovo, the rural retreat seventy-five miles northwest of Moscow. Four days later Yumashev came back to town and sought out Boris.

"Boris Nikolaevich made up his mind," he said. "It's Putin. Will he accept? What do you think?"

Boris replied that he had already asked and Putin was not interested.

"Well, you are the only one who can make him change his mind," said Valya.

———————

On July 16 Boris's Gulfstream landed in the French resort town of Biarritz on the Bay of Biscay. He found Putin, his wife, and the girls in an inexpensive hotel overlooking the water. The two men went out for lunch.

"Boris Nikolaevich sent me. He wants you to become the prime minister."

There was no need to explain. In all likelihood, it meant Putin would become the next president of Russia, the latest in the regal dynasty of Kremlin rulers.

"I am not sure that I am ready for that," was Putin's immediate response. Boris noted that he had been thinking about it.

"Yes, I know, you would rather be me."

"I was not joking," interrupted Putin. "Why don't you guys give me Gazprom to run? I could handle that."

By then Boris had realized something about Putin's character. He was an officer who could not function outside the chain of command. Once he was at the top, there would be no one to give him orders. This was probably the reason for his insecurity. But Boris also knew that Putin was loyal, a team player, and it was a quality he could make use of.

"Volodya, I understand. Who needs the headache? But consider this: there is no one else. Primus would beat anybody but you. And we will always be around to help. You cannot let us down."

There was a pause. Putin replied, with almost a sigh of resignation, "Yes, that's true. But then I need to hear it from Boris Nikolaevich himself."

"Of course, that's why he sent me, to sound you out. That's part of being presidential, he does not want to hear no for an answer."

Putin accepted.

Makhachkala, Dagestan, August 7, 1999: Russian forces use artillery and air in an assault on Wahhabi militants holding several villages near the border of Chechnya. Eyewitnesses among 2,000 refugees camped at the central square of the Dagestani capital report seeing two Russian helicopters shot down. The 2,000-strong Wahhabi force is led by Shamil Basayev, who is trying to expand the area that has been administered by the militants for nearly a year. On August 8, Russian Prime Minister Sergei Stepashin returns to Moscow from touring the area, only to learn that he and his entire cabinet have been sacked by President Yeltsin, the third change of government within a year.

Prime Minister–designate Vladimir Putin vows to restore order in the south.

CHAPTER 9

THE VICTORS

Buinaksk, Dagestan, September 4, 1999: A car bomb destroys a building housing military families, killing sixty-four and injuring 133. The next day, hundreds of gunmen led by radical warlord Shamil Basayev enter Dagestan from Chechnya, aiming to reclaim several border villages that were taken by Russian forces just two weeks earlier. Thousands of refugees arrive in the provincial capital of Makhachkala. Aslan Maskhadov's government denies involvement in the incursion and disowns the militants. In Moscow, Prime Minister Putin convenes a National Security Council meeting.

Washington, DC, September 1999

The rise of Vladimir Putin was a surprise to many.

On a sunny day in September the Soros Foundation brought to Washington a Russian regional governor, Viktor Kress of Tomsk, Siberia. I took Kress to a luncheon at the State Department, where Russia watchers and policy planners had gathered from all over town.

"Mr. Kress, who will be the next president of Russia?" was the first question.

"Whom do you think?" asked Kress.

"Primakov? Luzhkov? Yavlinsky? Nemtsov? Lebed? Zyuganov?"

"Vladimir Putin," said Kress.

177

There was a murmur at the table. Putin was the new prime minister—the sixth in Yeltsin's presidency—but his approval rating stood at 2 percent. Primakov's was at 22. Nobody had ever heard of Putin until two months ago. Who was this guy?

The man whom Sasha Litvinenko would accuse of his murder was born on October 7, 1952, in Leningrad (presently St. Petersburg), the son of a laborer in a train-car factory. According to *First Person,* a series of interviews with and about Putin hastily compiled and released on the eve of the 2000 presidential elections, his mother was a "kind . . . [but] not highly educated woman." She'd had a series of menial jobs: as a worker in a grocery store, a glassware washer in a laboratory, a night security guard in a secondhand clothing shop. She was a survivor of the famine during the German blockade of Leningrad. When Putin was born, she was forty-one. He was a sickly child.

His father, a veteran of NKVD (wartime KGB) forces, who sustained a severe leg injury in the war, seemed a "serious, solid and angry" man, in the opinion of Putin's schoolteacher Vera Gurevich, who visited the family to discuss the boy's poor performance and unruly behavior. She noted that "there was no kissing and cuddling" in the family; "his father had a tough character" but "was kind in his soul." For major transgressions, he disciplined the young Putin with his leather belt.

The train-car factory allocated the family a 220-square-foot room in a communal apartment on the fifth floor of a dreary walk-up at No. 15, Baskov Street, twenty minutes by foot from Nevsky Prospect, Leningrad's main street. Gurevich recalled that the apartment "did not have any amenities. No hot water, no bathtub. A horrific toilet, cold and depressive, leading to the stairwell. . . . There was practically no kitchen, only a square dark windowless hallway. A gas stove stood on one side and a wash-basin on the other, leaving hardly any space to squeeze through. And behind this so-called kitchen dwelled another family."

As a boy, and later to his friends, Vladimir was known as

Volodya. One of Volodya's early impressions in life was of the hordes of rats that lived in the front entryway. He used to chase them with sticks. "Once I saw a huge rat and went after it, until I got it in a corner. . . . It turned around, and rushed at me. It was unexpected and very scary. Now the rat was chasing me . . . but I was faster, and I slammed the door shut behind me, in its nose." That was how he "learned, once and forever, the meaning of the word 'cornered.'"

By his own admission the young Putin was a *shpana,* the slang term for a juvenile delinquent. Later it became the source of the many street-gang profanities in his public vocabulary. Even though he was small, he was a ferocious fighter. As one of his classmates recalled, in schoolyard fights the preteen Putin was "like a little tiger. He would leap at his enemy, scratch, bite, pull hair." Despite a concerted effort by his teacher and his father, he fell in with bad company: two brothers, who dwelled in the world of the rooftops, garages, and warehouses of the neighborhood. He became fiercely loyal to his friends.

In *First Person* Putin admitted that it was hard to predict "where it would have ended" if, at the age of eleven, he had not taken up martial arts. His judo coach "played a decisive role" in his childhood by "pulling [him] out of the street." His initial motivation to start judo was "to be able to stand up" for himself "in the street and in school." Judo taught him discipline, concentration, and tactical skills. It became his overwhelming passion. According to his coach, he fought like a "snow leopard, determined to win at any cost."

His teacher Vera Gurevich welcomed his new obsession, because it kept him out of trouble. But she noted that from then on he preferred sports to the company of his classmates. He became a black belt and a winner of citywide competitions.

In college he became the all-Leningrad champion for judo, and he continued the sport while learning the tradecraft of espionage. A classmate at School 101 of the KGB's First Chief Directorate (also known as the Red Banner Institute of Yuri Andropov), who now lives in Washington, recalls that whenever he passed the gym, he heard "shrieks and screeches." He knew "even without looking [that] it was Putin, training."

In *First Person* Putin himself makes it clear that he learned lessons in social Darwinism as a street kid and school menace, and his descriptions of several of his judo fights are full of telling details of violence and of his fighting attitude. Years later, as president, these qualities would reappear as subdued aggression, both in word and deed. For example, one of his most quoted remarks as president is this aphorism of power: "We demonstrated weakness, and the weak are beaten."

As Berezovsky explained to me years later, Putin's bellicose image was actively promoted by his campaign managers in 1999. It resounded with the mood of the majority of Russians. Their wounded national pride in the aftermath of the cold war, their yearning for a "strong hand" that would bring about order and stability, and their outrage at the disparity in wealth between a few superrich and the impoverished masses—all were reasons to cheer for an ascetic, introverted, steely little man, the underdog who fights and wins against all odds. Putin was a longed-for conduit of national frustrations.

Unlike American pundits, the political class in Moscow was very much aware that Putin was being groomed as Yeltsin's successor. I remember talking to Masha Slonim, an old friend from my Soviet dissident past who had become a doyenne of Moscow political journalism.

"Tell Boris," she said, "that he is making a big mistake. Putin is KGB, and you don't dance with the KGB—they will outdance you. Surely Primus is also KGB. But at least Primus is old. He won't last long. This one will be with us for a very long time."

Masha and I belong to a class of people who are automatically biased against the KGB. We are not inclined to grant Kontora members the presumption of innocence.

I did speak of this to Boris, but he told me that he trusted Putin. When they disagreed, Putin was straight with him, for example when he called Sasha Litvinenko a traitor. Putin shared Boris's politics. Most important, Putin displayed genuine loyalty. Boris gave me an example.

"I told him, 'Volodya, there is a sure way for you to win the elections. Put me in jail for the duration of the campaign. It will knock Primus's feet out from under him. After the elections, you can let me out.'"

"So what was his response?"

"He agreed with my analysis, but was sure that I would find a better way to win."

A year later, after President Putin had chased Boris out of Russia, I reminded him of this conversation.

"Well, I guess he was saying what I wanted to hear."

"Looking back, was there anything that you noticed, any sign that the man was pulling the wool over your eyes?" I wondered.

"Well, there was a moment when I had second thoughts about him."

It was late August 1999. Boris was on his way to his dacha when Putin called and asked him to come see him right away. Boris made a U-turn and went straight to the White House. Putin received him in Primakov's old study. Everything was much the same, but Boris noted that the bronze statuette of Dzerzhinsky, the KGB founder, which he had seen in Putin's office at the FSB, was now standing on the prime minister's desk.

Putin was white with rage.

"Your friend was here. Goose. He threatened me."

"What with?"

"He said that when Primus becomes president, which is inevitable, all of you will go to jail. Tanya, Valya, you—and I will go too, for covering up for you."

"Volodya, I don't know about Tanya-Valya, but I can assure you that the Aeroflot case is nothing but Primus's grudge . . . "

"I know, I know," he interrupted. "Our service was greatly hurt by you guys, wasn't it? That's not the point. He threatened me."

"Well, Goose is a son of a bitch. He was testing you, that's his style."

"Nobody threatens me. He will live to regret it. I just wanted you to know."

Boris left, not really having understood why Putin wanted to see him.

"That was the second time I saw that emotion in him," Boris recalled later. "It was the same expression as when he talked about Sasha's betrayal. This, and also the Dzerzhinsky statuette, made me wonder."

Boris vacillated for nearly a month. Should he support Yeltsin's chosen successor? Yeltsin's premise was that Putin had left the service eight years earlier once and for all and had joined the reformist brotherhood. But was he a true reformer? Or was he fundamentally a KGB man? Perhaps it was not too late to find a different heir apparent? Boris discussed his doubts with Roma Abramovich and asked him to go to St. Petersburg on October 7 to attend Putin's birthday party. If Kontora still maintained a hold on him, it would surely manifest itself in the spirit of the celebration.

Roma came back reassured.

"You sent me to spy on spies," he said, "but I found no spies there. Normal crowd, his age, wearing denim, someone playing guitar. No KGB types around whatsoever."

"What about his wife?" Boris inquired. "Is she recovering?"

Lyudmila Putina was nearly killed in a car crash in St. Petersburg in 1993. She sustained a serious spine injury, requiring neurosurgery and several years of rehabilitation.

"I found her a little stiff still," reported Roma.

"Any other women?"

"I checked the past five years," said Roma with a wicked smile. "None whatsoever."

———

Elena Tregubova was one of the attractions of the Kremlin in the 1990s. Young, tall, good-looking, and emancipated, she knew how to make her presence felt, and she had no scruples about using her charms to get scoops. She was the Kremlin correspondent for *Kommersant*, Russia's *Financial Times*. She emanated a certain disdain toward ambitious and politicking Kremlin staffers, labeling them "mutants" in her best-selling tell-all, *Tales of a Kremlin Digger*, published in November 2003. Perhaps it was this aura of mystifying superiority that loosened the lips of her highly placed interlocutors. Time and again, they sought interviews with her, even though she usually treated them harshly.

Tregubova claims credit for introducing Vladimir Putin to the world. Her first interview with him was in May 1997, when he had just moved from the Real Estate Office to the Audit Unit at the Kremlin. At the time she found him a "barely noticeable, boring little gray man . . . whose eyes were not merely colorless or disengaged—they were simply absent . . . ; [he] seemed to disappear, artfully merging with the colors of his office."

Apparently she hid those reactions at the time, because Putin granted her an exclusive interview about the role of the secret services in the fight against corruption.

"The FSB, or rather its parent, the KGB, has not been dealing directly with the criminal world," he lectured. "It has focused on intelligence . . . [and] therefore remained relatively clean." The services, he argued, represented the country's last hope to rein in corrupt officials. "If need be, we will put them in jail." Tregubova noted that "the most belligerent words he pronounced with a particularly cool movement of his lower lip, a sort of indulgent half-smile of a juvenile delinquent. Obviously, he imagined himself as someone who could, here and now, without even rising from his desk . . . zap all of Russia's corrupted politicians and anyone else who would stand in the way of his beloved 'services.'"

Seventeen months later, in December 1998, when Putin was the FSB chief, Tregubova again interviewed him, now at his office at Lubyanka. Suddenly he asked her out.

"I managed a casual smile, trying to figure out whether he was recruiting me as an agent or making a pass at me as a woman," she wrote in *Tales*. In the end, the reporter in her won out over the woman, who was "horrified at the very thought." She accepted.

What followed was an intimate meal in a trendy sushi restaurant, cleared of customers by his security detail, where she tried to act like a reporter while he pressed "inept" advances.

"Lenochka," he said at one point, "why do you keep talking about politics and only politics? Wouldn't you rather have a drink?"

Noting that there was no one else in the restaurant, and no agents outside, she asked, "Did you clear the whole block?"

"Come on," protested Putin. "I just booked a table for the two of us, that's all. After all, do I have a right, as a normal man, to have a lunch with an attractive young woman and a talented reporter to boot? Or do you think that as FSB director, this never happens to me?"

"How often does it happen?" she asked teasingly, and immediately regretted it, sensing that he took the question "too personally."

"Well, not often . . . not really."

At that point she felt that she had gone too far, and after declining a thinly veiled invitation to travel together to celebrate New Year's Eve in St. Petersburg, she backpedaled away from him.

As she wrote in *Tales,* she was amazed at Putin's ability to adjust to the wavelength of his interlocutor.

"He is a phenomenal 'reflector'; he copies his counterpart like a mirror, making you believe that he is just like you, a soulmate. Subsequently, I saw this exceptional gift in action during his summits with foreign leaders whom he wanted to win over." He would mimic their body language. Even in official photographs, "one gets a feeling that instead of, say, the Russian and American Presidents, there are two [George] Bushes sitting, smiling at each other. . . . He does it so skillfully that his counterpart does not notice."

The sushi scene sold Tregubova's book. The book earned her many powerful enemies. One day, as *Tales* was nearing the top of Russia's best-seller lists, a small bomb exploded in the hallway next to her apartment, denting her door but failing to harm her. Ever since, Tregubova has spent most of her time abroad, and in April 2007, she applied for asylum in the UK.

By the beginning of September Sasha Litvinenko's case had finally moved through each step of the prosecution process and reached the court. Marina and her lawyer went to see the president of the Moscow district military court, a general.

"Don't worry," he said. "I am an old man and I promise you that you will get a fair hearing." He scheduled the trial for the beginning of October and assigned a judge to the case.

The defense immediately moved to change the "restraining measure," a Russian legal term that resembles a writ of habeas corpus.

Sasha's lawyer was asking that he be released until the trial; as a first offender he was not dangerous to the public and had no reason to flee.

On September 15, Judge Vladimir Karnaukh considered the request. He looked supremely bored. He read the petition, sifted through the case file for a few moments, made faces as he peeked at random pages of the fat volume, and ruled to approve. Marina could not believe it.

"I was doubly shocked," she recalled. "After all these months, I was close to desperation, and now I realized that within this monstrous system there could be normal, reasonable people—that, after all, justice was possible. But then I got so angry. It took this apathetic man just a few moments to nix months of our agony as if it was nothing! It looked almost like an accident. He could have ruled otherwise, or somebody else could have released Sasha months earlier. There must be something wrong with the world if people can be thrown in jail and released with such ease, I thought."

The lawyer interrupted these thoughts. "Come on, let's not lose any time." For some reason he looked worried.

They rushed to Lefortovo.

The duty officer took the court order, checked something in his records, left the room apparently to make a phone call, and then returned to say, "Sorry, this document is no good. It does not have a court stamp."

They rushed back to the court.

"Strange," said Karnaukh. "They know my signature. Why didn't they call me?"

He went to the court president, made him cosign the release order, stamped it, and handed them the paper, saying, "Good luck."

They rushed back to Lefortovo.

The officer took the release and went away. He returned in thirty minutes.

"The release order has not been officially delivered. It should have come here with the court messenger, or through registered delivery or some other official channel. We cannot process it."

"It will take at least two days to arrange that," said the lawyer somberly.

Marina called Boris, who told them to come see him.

Boris heard them out and placed a phone call to his friends in the Kremlin. Within fifteen minutes an FSO officer arrived in a car with lights flashing and siren wailing, retrieved the court order, and delivered it to Lefortovo in an impressive pouch with federal government seals—as official as can be. Marina arrived a half-hour later; she had not been able to keep up with the FSO car.

"Well," said the prison officer, "now it seems all right. We can say that we are officially in receipt. But it is almost the end of the day, and we need at least two hours to process the release, so come tomorrow morning."

The lawyer went to break the bad news to Sasha, who had been waiting in a holding cell since morning.

Sasha met him with a resigned grin. "I did not expect for a minute that they would let me go."

He was right. The next morning the prosecutors protested his release and demanded a hearing. Judge Karnaukh was replaced. The lawyer spent half an hour with the president of the court and then told Marina, "The new judge is Evgeny Kravchenko. I know him, he is a good man. But we should not press him on the restraining measure. There are two decent judges in this court; we've already burned one of them. I do not want to burn the other for the sake of a few weeks of detention. If he rules for release, they will replace him, too. I'd rather have him try the case. So let Sasha stay where he is, it is just one more month."

Sasha's trial approached just as a new war with Chechnya threatened to erupt. For more than a year Boris had been silent on Chechnya. Between the Kremlin intrigues, the president's illnesses, and his fights with Primus and Skuratov, he simply had had no time. But he had closely watched the developments and maintained contact with key Chechens.

Back in the spring, he had had several telephone conversations with former Chechen foreign minister Movladi Udugov, the one-time leader of the Islamist wing whom Maskhadov had kicked out of his government. In early June Udugov came to Moscow to see Boris. From that conversation Boris realized that the Chechens still viewed him—mistakenly—as a prime mover of Chechnya policy. Udugov talked about his plan to replace Maskhadov with an Islamist regime, which he argued would only be to Russia's benefit.

Udugov's rationale was geopolitical. Maskhadov's long-term goal, he said, was to steer Chechnya to full independence and integrate it with the West, eventually joining NATO and the European Union. He viewed pro-American Georgia and Turkey as his key potential partners in the region. In the end, Maskhadov would provide access to the North Caucasus for the Americans, who had been dreaming of a pipeline to the Caspian oil fields. This, naturally, would be bad for Russia.

It would be also bad for Islam, Udugov argued, because America is the Great Satan and the ultimate enemy of all Muslims. From that perspective, the true believers in Allah and the Russian state had a common interest: not to let the West into the Caucasus. An Islamist government in Grozny would automatically be anti-American, that is, by default, pro-Russian.

Udugov's plan was for Basayev's Wahhabi gang to stir up trouble in Dagestan, thus provoking Russia into a limited military action, leading to the fall of Maskhadov. A Basayev-Udugov government would be installed in Grozny. They would compromise on independence, in exchange for religious autonomy. He magnanimously offered to give back to Russia the territories north of the Terek River in Chechnya, populated mostly by ethnic Russians. Udugov was not interested in converting them to Islam.

Boris did not like the idea. There was no proof that Udugov could deliver on any of his promises. Moreover, an Islamic state in Russia's backyard might have unpredictable consequences. On the other hand, from the Kremlin's standpoint, it did not matter whether Chechnya was Muslim or secular as long as it was not pro-American. So Boris told Udugov that he was the wrong man to approach. He no longer had influence on Chechnya policy. He said that he would pass his proposals on to the powers that be. He went to see Stepashin, who was still the prime minister. Stepashin thanked him for the information and said he would take it from there.

Boris repeated all of this to Putin in early September. Basayev's gangs were fighting in Dagestan. The Russian army was mobilizing. Could it be that Putin actually wanted to play out Udugov's gambit?

"Volodya," Boris said, "what's going on? Please be careful. Don't jump into a war with a harebrained scheme. Wars have a tendency not to work out as planned."

"Boris," said Putin, "let's agree on a division of labor: you deal with the elections and I deal with Chechnya. Trust me, I know what I am doing."

"Okay, but let me tell you at least what I think you should do, and then do as you see fit."

"Go ahead."

"Maskhadov is losing control, unfortunately. It is all our doing; we did not keep a single promise we made to him. It may or may not be true that he would sell out to the Americans, but that's water under the bridge now. Basayev and Udugov are powerful, but they are thugs. If they have their way, they will continue making trouble throughout the North Caucasus. We cannot afford to let them run loose, and we cannot ignore them. Our best policy is to pressure them back into a coalition government with Maskhadov. Then they would neutralize each other."

"I will not negotiate with bandits," said Putin.

"Then help Maskhadov."

"You said yourself, he has lost control."

"Than you have to talk to Basayev and Udugov."

"We are going in circles."

"Volodya, don't start a war. This war cannot be won. You will be stuck there forever."

Putin was silent for a moment.

"Boris, I've heard you out. We have not made a decision yet. I promise you, we will take into account what you said. And can you do me a favor?"

"Yes?"

"Stop your contacts with the Chechens. No more phone calls, no messages, no small favors. You cannot imagine what my people are telling me about you. If I believed 1 percent of it, we would not be talking here. But it is becoming a problem for me."

"Okay," Boris said. "I promise."

Moscow: On September 9, 1999, a predawn explosion levels an apartment block on Guryanova Street, killing ninety-four and wounding 249. Four days later another bomb destroys an apartment block on Kashirskoye Highway, killing 119. No one claims responsibility. Chechen extremists are suspected. Prime Minister Putin, using street slang in a nationally televised address, promises to "waste the terrorists in their shithouse." In a last-ditch effort to prevent war, Maskhadov seeks contact with Yeltsin. Russian troops mass on the Chechen border.

The apartment bombings shattered any hope of avoiding a new war. Boris was stunned, as were most observers. The attacks did not make any sense. Basayev and Udugov were bad, but not mad. They wanted power, and eventually they wanted to deal with the Kremlin. If they had ordered the bombings, they were committing suicide.

Putin, of course, stood to benefit from the blasts politically, but it was unthinkable that he would authorize such a thing. That left only two possibilities: rogue elements in the secret services or a foreign interest trying to lure Russia into a war.

On September 10 the whites of Boris's eyes turned yellow, and he was hospitalized with a case of hepatitis. He also faced a new attack: the tabloid *Moscovsky Komsomolets* published a "transcript" of a telephone conversation between him and Udugov, partly true and partly a fabrication, which implied that they had been conspiring to stir up trouble in Dagestan. Putin had warned Boris about ugly rumors, but this one was poisonous. Goose's media immediately picked it up and went so far as to insinuate that the bombings in Moscow were part of a Kremlin election conspiracy, and that Boris was the evil genius behind it all.

After the second explosion in Moscow, Boris decided to hold a press conference to set the record straight. On September 16, as his car pulled up at the Interfax news agency on Mayakovsky Square and camera crews scrambled to get a picture of him, his face and the whites of his eyes were still yellow from hepatitis, a perfect look for a conspiring villain.

In front of the cameras, he began by accusing Luzhkov and Gusinsky of fabricating the transcript and exploiting the bombing tragedy for political ends. He went on to accuse the FSB of "aggravating the situation in Dagestan" by playing games with the Wahhabi. They "could not have been unaware" that the Wahhabi had been building up in Dagestan for two and a half years.

He reminded the public of his own record as a peace negotiator and called for immediate talks with any Chechens who were ready to negotiate, including the terrorists. "I am not afraid of accusations to be poured on me after this statement. I am not after . . . improved political standing, but after saving lives," he said. "The declaration of emergency would make no sense because it will resolve no problems. . . . If we can't kill them all off, we must talk to them."

It was pointless. Whoever bombed the apartment buildings had achieved one result: all across the political spectrum, there were calls for revenge. Even the super-dove Yavlinsky called for "a large-scale action . . . without haste."

The day of the press conference, in the early morning hours, another apartment house exploded, this time in Volgodonsk, in southern Russia, killing seventeen people. Three days after that, on September 19, Putin spoke. The peace accords of 1996–1997 were "a mistake," he declared. "These people must be destroyed. There simply is no other response."

On September 23, 1999, police foil an apparent bombing attempt in an apartment block in Ryazan, 130 miles southeast of Moscow. Putin orders aerial bombardments of Grozny. Two days later, the government suddenly changes its story on the Ryazan incident, say-

ing that it was a training exercise by the FSB, and that the bomb wasn't real.

In retrospect, Boris should have realized that Putin was not playing the limited war gambit developed by Udugov, but chose all-out war as the defining theme of his bid for the presidency. As the Russian army crossed into Chechen territory, Boris still believed that their aim was to go as far as the Terek River. He disagreed with Putin, but he had promised to steer clear of Chechnya. So he decided to leave this aside for a while. They were still part of the same team. They had an election to win, and Boris completely immersed himself in party politics. He was out to promote his new creation, the party of Russian regions called Unity, symbolized by a huge Russian bear, that he had dreamed of while in a fever in the hospital.

A key battle looming in advance of the presidential contest was the elections to the State Duma, the lower chamber of Parliament, scheduled for mid-December. Boris's main concern was how to defeat a powerful coalition led by Primakov: the alliance of Moscow mayor Yuri Luzhkov with many regional governors from across the country.

Ever since the 1993 Constitution granted the provinces the right to elect local governments, provincial leaders had viewed the Kremlin with suspicion: they feared that the center would infringe on their self-rule. All eighty-six governors served on the Federation Council, the upper house of Parliament, and they often opposed the policies of the Kremlin.

However, the governors could not agree on a leader. From their perspective, all provinces of the Federation should be equal. Alliance with the powerful mayor of Moscow strengthened their group, but they were wary of naming Luzhkov to be a first among equals. So it seemed a natural solution to invite Evgeny Primakov, the deposed prime minister, to be the leader of their Fatherland All-Russia Coalition. He did not have his own regional base, yet he was the nation's most popular politician. Primakov brought with him the backing of old-time Soviet apparatchiks and much of the national security and intelligence community. Luzhkov had the support of NTV, Gusinsky's network. The governors controlled the local media and political machines. Altogether it was a formidable political force.

The Duma elections became Boris's obsession. He was running for a Duma seat himself, from the impoverished North Caucasus ethnic republic of Karachayevo-Cherkessia. He and his messengers flew from region to region, talking to apprehensive regional bosses and to their home clans, the provincial mini-oligarchs.

In every provincial capital they repeated the same spiel: "You have been plotting against Yeltsin because he stepped on your toes. But wasn't he the one who gave you your rights in 1993 in the first place? Just wait until Primus gets into the Kremlin! He will bring back his Soviet cohorts, the old-time apparatchiks, the veterans of central planning, the bureaucrats. He will take away your local elections, your rights and privileges. And he will unleash federal cops and prosecutors, hundreds of little Skuratovs, on you. The Yeltsin era will seem like paradise in retrospect. Just look at Primus, the Politburo hack. Is this what you want?"

It was a masterstroke: to turn around the governors' fears of the Kremlin by focusing them on Primus. And it worked. The governors scratched their heads and worried about Primus in the Kremlin. They did not want to go back to the USSR.

On September 22, thirty-nine governors released a document proclaiming a new, pro-Yeltsin political movement, called Unity— Boris's last-minute creation. They would not run for the Duma themselves, but they promised to throw their weight behind Unity's electoral list.

One after another, more governors joined the club. Several members of Fatherland All-Russia defected to Unity. All across the country, Duma candidates from the new party were nominated, supported by regional bosses.

Sasha's trial began in early October. The hearing was closed; Marina had to wait in the hallway. All she could think about was how to catch a glimpse of Sasha as he was led in and out of the courtroom.

The prosecution's claim was that in 1997, in an inexplicable rage, Sasha had beaten the driver of one of his organized-crime targets.

When the victim was called to the witness stand, he said, "All of them beat me with fists and rifle butts, and then they kicked me, taking turns."

"Wait a minute," said the judge. "In your preliminary testimony you said that only Litvinenko beat you. When are you telling the truth, then or now?"

"Now."

"Why did you lie then?"

"Because the investigator told me that he had orders to put Litvinenko in jail. He asked me to single him out."

The prosecution asked for an adjournment. The hearing was postponed several times. A whispering campaign suggested that Judge Kravchenko was under tremendous pressure. The FSB wanted a guilty verdict and the harshest possible sentence of eight years.

The trial resumed on November 26. Journalists and TV cameras packed the court building. The defense made its final argument for acquittal. The judge left the courtroom to deliberate. It took him four hours to reach a verdict. Marina waited in the hallway, "all frozen inside, feeling as if all this was not real."

Finally, the judge returned and announced his decision: "Not guilty. Free to go."

As the guard unlocked the dock cage to let Sasha out, there was a sudden commotion at the door. A squad of armed men in camouflage and masks ran past Marina and stormed into the courtroom, pushing the guards aside.

"Step aside! FSB!" To Sasha they yelled, "You're under arrest!"

They produced an arrest warrant, handcuffed Sasha yet again, and took him away.

As Sasha was led past her, Marina reached out to him. One of the FSB men pushed her away.

"Don't touch her!" Sasha yelled, and in response was hit with a rifle butt, as TV cameras recorded the scene.

The masked agents brought him to a room. His investigator Barsukov appeared, with a new question.

"Where were you on May 30, 1996?"

"I don't remember," said Sasha.

Barsukov read out another set of charges. It was the same offense, but a different episode: on that day, during an operation against a racketeering ring in a Moscow farm produce market, he was alleged to have beaten up a suspect and to have "extorted" a can of sweet peas from one of the vendors.

He refused to answer questions.

This time they took him to Butyrka, the largest criminal prison in Moscow.

The next morning, Boris went to see Putin at the White House. He was angry. The scene of Sasha being rearrested on live TV was grotesque. Putin should never have let it happen, Boris argued. It made their team look impotent. Why did the FSB come up with new charges, trumped up at the last minute?

Putin was apologetic. He simply did not have time to monitor the case, he claimed; after all, he had a war on his hands. He explained to Boris that the new arrest was a low-level initiative at the FSB, among Sasha's many enemies. He needed a few days to correct the situation.

On December 16 the Moscow military court changed the restraining measure for Sasha. He was released, but ordered not to leave town. His passport was taken away.

Three days later, on Sunday, December 19, the Russians went to the polls in the Duma elections. Boris's brainchild, the four-month-old Unity Party, finished in second place with 72 seats, trailing the Communists' 113. Primakov's Fatherland All-Russia Party came in third with 66 seats. Chubais and Nemtsov's Rightist Union, Yavlinsky's social democrats, and Zhirinovsky's nationalists received 29, 21, and 17 seats, respectively. All things considered, it was a triumph for Boris. He became an independent member of the Duma from Karachayevo-Cherkessia. Primus's presidential prospects were greatly damaged. The vote, combined with the war, sealed Putin's position as the leading contender for the presidency in March. His popularity now stood at 45 percent, while Primakov's sank to 11.

On the day the results were announced, Putin invited Boris to the White House. When Boris arrived shortly before midnight, Putin looked solemn. It may well have been the first day that he really believed that he would be Russia's next president.

"I want to tell you, Boris, that what you have done is phenomenal," Putin began, in his monotone. "No one believed you, and I know that you've been ill and worked out of the hospital. I am not given to melodrama, so what I am going to say is particularly significant. I do not have a brother, and neither do you. You should know that in me you have a brother, Boris. Coming from me, these are not empty words."

For a moment, Boris was speechless. He had not expected an emotional outburst from Putin, the most controlled man he had ever met. In the past, albeit rarely, the displays of emotion that Boris had seen were restricted to bursts of aggression. Now, as Putin spoke from his heart, he turned pale, and his voice slightly trembled. Their eyes met. For a split second Boris glimpsed a vulnerable soul, unsure of his sudden success.

"Thank you, Volodya. You should know that I did not do it for you, but for all of us, and—forgive me for melodrama, too—for Russia. Now all eyes are on you. You will beat Primus and Luzhkov and continue the work that Boris Nikolaevich has started. Let's have a drink to that!"

On December 31, 1999, Boris Yeltsin gave a nationally televised address, resigning the presidency and transferring his powers to Vladimir Putin, pending the March elections. He asked for forgiveness for just one mistake: the war in Chechnya.

Grozny, January 24, 2000: Chechen fighters resist the Russian army in hand-to-hand combat throughout the capital. Akhmed Zakayev, now the commander of a thousand-strong force defending the southwestern district, is severely wounded by shrapnel from an artillery shell. For the next ten days he is carried by stretcher from village to village, evading a massive manhunt by the Russian army. Eventually *he is smuggled to Georgia, after his wife bribes her way through the Russian border checkpoint with $5,000.*

The story of the September bomb scare in Ryazan began to emerge only after the New Year. Will Englund of the *Baltimore Sun* and Maura Reynolds of the *Los Angeles Times* were among the first to write about it. They each interviewed residents of the building at 14/16 Novoselova Street and published stories on January 14 and 15, respectively. Their editors found both reports worthy of the front page. Each concluded that the bomb was real, contrary to the "exercise" claims of the FSB.

In Russia, however, the story remained unreported for another month, until the February 14 issue of *Novaya Gazeta*. Pavel Voloshin (no relation to Alexander Voloshin, Kremlin chief of staff), a young disciple of the veteran investigative journalist Yuri Schekochihin, published a detailed explanation of what happened.

On September 22, 1999, at 9:15 p.m., Alexei Kartofelnikov, a tenant of the twelve-story apartment building, called the police to report a white Zhiguli sedan with obscured license plates parked at the front entrance. Two suspicious-looking men were carrying sacks into the basement. By the time the police arrived, the Zhiguli was gone. In the basement the cops found three hundred-pound sacks of white powder. A detonator and a timing device were attached to the sacks. An explosives squad arrived and detected vapors of RDX, a military explosive used in artillery shells, the same substance that was used in the Moscow bombings. The timer was set for 5:30 in the morning.

The building was evacuated for the night and the bomb defused. The sacks were taken away by the FSB. Local law enforcement were put on full alert. Composite sketches of the terrorist suspects, two men and a woman, were distributed to two thousand policemen and shown on TV. By morning, news agencies boasted that a terrorist attack had been foiled in Ryazan. On the national evening news of September 23, Prime Minister Putin praised the vigilance of the Ryazanians and promised full victory in Chechnya.

The next morning brought a stunning shift. FSB Chief Nikolai

Patrushev went on the air to announce that the Ryazan incident was in fact staged by his agency.

"This was not a bomb," he declared. "The exercise may not have been carried out well, but it was only a test, and the so-called explosive was only sacks of sugar."

In their reports a few months later, however, Englund, Reynolds, and Voloshin quoted tenants, the local police, and an explosives expert who contradicted Patrushev. They all believed everything was for real: the yellowish substance in the sacks wasn't sugar, a gas analyzer used by the explosives team had detected RDX, an explosive, and the timer had used a live shotgun cartridge as a detonator.

Voloshin's report challenged the FSB to produce evidence to back up its claim that it was just an exercise: the records, the participants, the sacks with sugar.

After Voloshin's article there were more stories, suggesting possible explanations for why the FSB would make its bizarre claim. Some reports held that the men who planted the bomb, FSB agents all, were about to be arrested, so the Agency needed a cover story. Others claimed that they were in fact arrested, and then released after producing FSB badges. What was established beyond doubt was that late on the night of the incident, Nadezhda Yuhanova, a telephone exchange operator, overheard a suspicious conversation: "There are checkpoints everywhere; split up and leave the city one by one." She alerted the police. They traced the call to Lubyanka, FSB headquarters in Moscow.

On March 13, a second story by Voloshin appeared in *Novaya Gazeta*. He reported an incident at the 137th Airborne Troop Regiment base near Ryazan one night in September. Pvt. Alexei Pinyaev and two of his comrades were on sentry duty guarding the ammunition depot. Perhaps out of curiosity, or to escape the freezing cold, they entered the warehouse and found a pile of ordinary sacks labeled "Sugar." They cut a hole in one of the sacks, removed some of the white powder, and used it to sweeten some tea. The stuff turned their tea foul, not sweet. They called their commanding officer.

The officer had been trained in explosives. He determined that the powder was RDX. Bigwigs from the FSB arrived from Moscow.

Everybody with knowledge of the episode was questioned and sworn to secrecy. Pinyaev and his friends were threatened with a court-martial for poking their nose into something that wasn't their business. In the end all of them were transferred to Chechnya—but not before they talked to Voloshin.

On March 20, by a small margin, the Duma voted down a motion by Yuri Schekochihin to ask the prosecutor general's office to look into the apartment bomb scare in Ryazan for possible violations of the law. By then the flagship NTV show *Independent Investigations* had taped an hour-long town hall discussion about the incident. Among the participants were Ryazanians from the Novoselova Street building, local policemen, explosives experts, and three representatives of the FSB. The verdict of the participants—with the exception of the FSB officers—was unanimous: the bomb was real. The show was scheduled for broadcast on March 24, two days before the presidential elections.

Many years later, in New York, Igor Malashenko, the exiled ex-president of NTV, told me about the agonizing decision he and his boss Goose had to make. On March 23, a messenger came from the Kremlin—none other than Valya, Valentin Yumashev. He brought a warning in no uncertain terms from "you know who": if they dared to broadcast "The Sugar of Ryazan," they should consider themselves finished. Putin's election on March 26 was guaranteed. Should they defy him, he would go after them in force.

"This was a sign of the changing of the guard. Yeltsin would never have resorted to such blunt pressure," said Malashenko.

They decided to go ahead with the broadcast.

––––––––––––

Moscow, spring 2000: Details of events leading to the war in Chechnya emerge in the presidential election campaign. Sergei Stepashin, the former prime minister, discloses that the Kremlin began planning the Chechen campaign in March 1999, six months before the invasion. Speculation that the FSB or GRU could have been involved in the Moscow bombings appears in the liberal press. Putin, in a cam-

paign interview in Kommersant, *dismisses the allegation as "raving madness," saying, "It is immoral even to consider such a possibility."*

On March 26, Vladimir Putin won election to the presidency of Russia by a landslide.

CHAPTER 10

THE FUGITIVES

Geneva, Switzerland, March 17, 2000: Human Rights Watch and Amnesty International urge the UN to investigate massive alleged war crimes in Chechnya. Reports from the war zone depict widespread atrocities by the Russian forces, including more than 120 summary executions and hundreds of cases of arbitrary detention, beatings, and torture. Hundreds of civilians are held for ransom by the military. Refugees report the systematic rape of Chechen women by soldiers. Villages are cut off from food and water, leading to widespread malnutrition and epidemic disease. The area is closed to journalists and international observers.

Later on in London, two schools of thought emerged to explain why Putin, in the words of Berezovsky, "abandoned his mission to preserve and expand Yeltsin's [democratic] policies."

Boris believed, in retrospect, that Putin never understood his mission in political terms in the first place. Putin was "loyal and sincere," but he never had any political philosophy and was an "underdeveloped personality." His identity had always been defined by whichever group he belonged to: his judo team, the FSB, the St. Petersburg liberals, or "the family." His mentality stemmed from the street gangs of his childhood: the "us-ness," rather than the essence, was what counted, "us" against "them," even if "they" are the rest of the world.

When he suddenly found himself at the pinnacle of power—and "the family" dissipated—he had to reinvent himself and find a new gang. He began to see himself as part and parcel of the state. The state became his gang, and he its guardian and protector: *l'état c'est moi.* He was supported in this shift by his two crafty confidantes, Voloshin and Roma. His life took on a new purpose: to prevail over the state's enemies through strength, ruthlessness, and control, just as he had once practiced judo. Those who plotted against him became enemies of the state. How could anybody be against him without aiming at the state, when all he was doing was for the state's sake? They had to be destroyed.

The other view was expressed by Sasha: Putin had never been his own man; he was a Kontora sleeper who was reclaimed as soon as he was returned to the FSB in 1998, or maybe he had never left it in the first place. He had been neither loyal nor sincere, fooling everyone, including Boris. As Boris, the hapless oligarch, maneuvered him to power, Boris empowered his natural enemy, a pawn of the KGB mandarins. Like a secret medieval order, these people had a two-pronged strategy to gain control: overtly, through Primus, or covertly, through Putin.

In support of his theory, Sasha provided lots of argument, starting with the revival of the "KGB cult" at Lubyanka from the day Putin appeared, to his remark at the KGB veterans day on December 18, 1999, when he reported jokingly, "Mission accomplished" in reference to his "undercover penetration of the government."

Sasha discovered that in February 1998, three days after his surprise arrival at Lena Berezovskaya's birthday party with a flower bouquet, Putin had appeared with a similar bouquet at the door of Vladimir Kryuchkov, the last Soviet KGB chief, on *his* birthday.

According to Sasha, the change that Boris observed in Putin in April 2000 was no change at all. Boris was merely discovering the man's essence.

Whichever theory is correct, "Putin's reversal" came as a total surprise to Boris.

In mid-April 2000, shortly after Putin's victory, I stopped in Paris on my way to Moscow. Boris was in town on a long vacation. We had dinner together.

I had not seen much of him during the previous year. He had been busy with his political battles and I had spent much of my time traveling throughout the Siberian Gulag, running my TB project. But I had followed his spectacular successes in the press. He was widely credited with masterminding Putin's victory. He was ranked the richest man in Russia and labeled the most influential among Putin's advisers, outranking even Chief of Staff Voloshin. Little did I know that he would soon be in exile, a dissident, and that Sasha Litvinenko would follow in his wake. The postelection calm was deceptive: the year 2000 would prove to be a turning point for all of us, and for Russia itself.

Boris invited me to visit his electoral district of Karachayevo-Cherkessia, where he was planning to develop a huge ski resort on the slopes of Dombai, in the southern section of the Main Caucasus Range.

"We are planning to build a highway from the Sochi Airport and make it the best winter spot in Europe," he declared.

"I don't see how people will go there with a war raging a hundred miles away," I said.

"That's true," he agreed. "Volodya has to stop that. Chechnya is the one thing that we disagree about."

"Volodya can't stop it," I said. "He is a war criminal. As soon as the war ends, there will be crowds of human rights monitors all over Chechnya, digging out dead bodies, and he will be in big trouble. He has probably outdone Milosevic by now."

"You dissidents, you don't understand politics," Boris retorted. "Russia is not Serbia. I've heard Tony Blair is taking Volodya to tea with the queen this week, isn't he? And if bad comes to worse, he will find some generals to take the blame."

"You oligarchs, you don't understand history," I replied. "When Volodya goes after you, you will run to the dissidents for help."

"Volodya will not go after me," he replied. "He is a team person. And I am part of the same team and we share a mission. For him, going after me would be like going after himself."

While Boris was taking a long vacation, the power configuration in the Kremlin was undergoing momentous change. With Yeltsin gone, the Tanya-Valya team rapidly lost influence. Alexander Voloshin, who had distanced himself from Boris long before, now controlled the Kremlin. Voloshin was even more of a recluse than Putin. The Kremlin became a castle of introverts. A clique of mysterious KGB types appeared on the scene, brought by Putin from St. Petersburg. Boris was already effectively pushed out from the center of power, although he didn't realize it.

One afternoon in mid-May I went for a jog in a birch tree forest surrounding the Holiday Inn in a leafy Moscow suburb. My cell phone, strapped to my belt, suddenly rang; Boris was on the phone from France.

"Tell me, in America, can the president fire a governor?"

"No," I said, "no way. That's the whole point of the federal system."

"Have you heard what they are doing? They want to assume the right to fire governors!"

He was referring to the regional reform package proposed by Putin. It was his first major legislation. He called it strengthening "the vertical axis of power." This was a major reversal of the Yeltsin revolution, which, for the first time in Russian history, had granted the eighty-six provinces the right of self-government.

"I am flying to Moscow tomorrow," said Boris. "Please get me some background info on federalism. I need to explain that to him."

By the time he landed in Moscow, I had compiled a short history of democracy and federalism, from the Magna Carta to the Federalist Papers to the desegregation battles of John F. Kennedy.

For the next several days a hastily assembled team drafted a memorandum to Putin in the back room of The Club. Boris's passionate call for freedom gradually merged with political theory and legalistic arguments. The end result was a six-page document blasting the regional reform for historical, spiritual, economic, legal, and political reasons.

The letter extolled the role of federalism as a safeguard of democracy. It warned that the proposed legislation would "consolidate the powers of the central government, but weaken the feedback" from below, because local authorities would no longer be accountable to the people. It would make the government less, not more efficient. The measures would throw the system back to the old Soviet model.

The memo began, "Dear Volodya." To set the right tone Boris added two epigraphs. One was from Aristotle: "*Amicus Plato, sed amica veritas*" (Plato is dear to me, but dearer still is truth). The other was from the Russian poet Osip Mandelstam, who had been killed in Stalin's Gulag: "I am lawfully wed to Liberty and will never discard this crown."

As we were laboring over the final draft of the letter, the evening news carried reports of another high drama unfolding in the shadows of the Kremlin. On May 11 masked police toting machine guns raided the offices of Gusinsky's Media-MOST, the parent of NTV. Federal prosecutors were investigating Goose's finances. It appeared that the Kremlin's threat to destroy NTV for airing the program on Ryazan had not been an idle one.

"Boris, shall we add a section on free speech to the letter?" someone asked.

"No, no, God forbid, let us not mix apples with oranges. That would antagonize Volodya. You see, for him, I am 'us' and Goose is 'them.' It is important to keep our polemics as an in-house discussion. Let us leave Goose aside."

Some days later Boris called: "We are going public." Earlier that day he had had a meeting with Putin. The president read the letter, he said, but his own advisers were of a totally different opinion.

"Volodya, browbeating is not an argument," Boris said. "Your plan amounts to a major change in the Constitution. This should be explained and discussed not with me, but with the public at large. Instead we hear empty phrases about the 'vertical axis of power.' These are not explanations. There should be a national debate and a referendum, like we had in 1993 when we adopted the Constitution."

"The proposals will be put up for a vote in the Duma."

"Come on, Volodya, I know how things are in the Duma. It's

$5,000 per vote. I can go out and start paying $7,000. This would not be a debate on substance."

"Boris, I don't understand you. We are *vlast*"—the right of power—"and you are supposed to be one of us. But if you go against us, then whom would you represent? Yourself?"

There was a pause. Finally Boris said, "Well, the problem is, I am convinced that you are making a mistake. I have no other option than to start a public discussion. Let us see what other people think."

"You have every right to do so," said Putin coldly.

When he repeated the conversation to me, Boris looked excited. He was gearing up for a new campaign. "Once we've published the letter, we'll sponsor a debate," he said. "An all-Russia conference on federalism. With experts. On prime-time TV. Will you help me?"

"Boris, if you go down this road, I predict in a year from now you will be an exile in your château, or worse, sitting in jail. I must tell you that. This is not politics, this is mafia war, or class struggle, whichever you like to call it. For Putin the substance does not matter—as long as he sees you as one of his gang. But if you go against him publicly, you will cast yourself out of his pack. Then, whatever you do, you are the enemy, like Goose. Of course, I would love to help you, because for me it's like déjà vu. But it's a losing game."

"We shall see about that."

"But why do you need it? I don't get it. Have you suddenly become altruistic?"

"Not at all. It's self-preservation. You are right about Putin. He is going after the governors, he is squeezing Goose because he has cast them as the enemy. Because they supported Primus. He and Voloshin are simply continuing last year's fight, finishing them off. The problem is, he may not realize that, but he is destroying the framework in the process. If he succeeds, my turn will come too, sooner or later, because I cannot be his servant. I have my own interests. But now I still have a chance to persuade them, because Volodya sees me as part of his team. I am not seeking a confrontation. That is why I am not teaming up with anyone—doing it alone. If he sees that I am serious, he will realize he is making a mistake, and he will reverse course."

The publication of Boris's open letter to Putin on May 30, 2000, confused everyone, none more than American Russia watchers who arrived in Moscow in advance of a June summit, the first for Putin and the last for Clinton. Wasn't Berezovsky supposed to be Putin's main backer? Did it mean that Putin was also at odds with Voloshin, a Berezovsky man? Was Putin in collusion with the military? What was the meaning of the crackdown on Gusinsky?

"We Americans are simple people who like to know whom to root for in any competition, political or athletic," wrote David Ignatius in a June 4 *Washington Post* column entitled "A Complicated Kremlin Scorecard." "Putin vs. Berezovsky" appears to be a "most interesting political contest," but "whom should we root for?"

Bill Clinton could not make up his mind either. Before leaving Moscow, he dropped in to say hello to his old friend Boris Yeltsin and to share his reservations about the "new guy," whom he had just seen.

Clinton's aide Strobe Talbott reproduced the conversation in *Russia Hand*. Yeltsin told his "friend Bill" that Putin's main qualifications for the job were twofold. He was "a young man and a strong man." Yeltsin's daughter Tatyana "nodded solemnly": "It really was very hard, getting Putin into the job—one of the hardest things we ever pulled off."

"Boris, you have got democracy in your heart," said Clinton to Yeltsin "You have got the fire in your belly of the real democrat and real reformer. I am not sure Putin has that. Maybe he does. I don't know."

The next shoe to drop was the arrest of Goose himself. He spent three days in mid-June in Butyrka prison and was released with orders not to leave town—just like Sasha. It shook Boris more personally than the federalism fight. The latter might be an honest mistake by a president who wanted an efficient government. The former was clearly an act of revenge.

Goose's arrest happened while Putin was on a state visit in Spain.

As soon as he returned Boris went to see him. He wanted to make one last attempt: perhaps Volodya was not beyond redemption.

"Volodya, why did you put Goose in jail? It served no purpose, and it harmed you internationally."

"Boris, good heavens, of all people! Wasn't he number one on your enemies list? He had threatened us with jail, have you forgotten?"

"Yes, but we've won, this is a senseless vengeance."

"When he threatened me, he should have known better. But he is free now, so what do you want? In any case, go speak to Voloshin. Goose is his favorite project."

"Goose is a traitor," Voloshin told him. "He stabbed us in the back, and he will do it again. He said that we blew up those houses."

"But you didn't, did you?"

"We did not, and he had no right to say that. Anyway, no one will harm him, but he must give up NTV, and he will. He has no way out. He is cornered."

Boris gave a series of interviews comparing Putin's policies to those of Chile's Pinochet: a free economy combined with a lack of political freedom. "This will not work in Russia," he predicted. "Russia is a maximalist country. Once you start on that road you will end up with Stalinist terror."

After that, the Kremlin stopped calling him.

On July 18, the Duma approved Putin's federalism proposals by an overwhelming majority. Boris resigned his Duma seat to protest "the imposition of authoritarian rule." On July 20, threatened with another arrest, Goose signed an agreement to sell his media holdings to Gazprom, which was still controlled by the government. He immediately left for his villa in San Roque, Spain. Later, he announced that he considered the sale of NTV null and void because it had been signed under duress.

And then came *Kursk*, and Boris's exile into the political wilderness.

Kursk was a nuclear submarine armed with cruise missiles, a part of Russia's Northern Fleet, named after the city of Kursk in central Russia. On August 12, it was conducting firing exercises when a huge explosion occurred, apparently resulting from a faulty torpedo launch. *Kursk* sank eighty-five miles off Severomorsk, in the Barents Sea, to a depth of 350 feet. There were 118 sailors aboard. When it hit bottom, another huge explosion occurred. At least twenty-three men survived the blasts, only to face several days of agony on the ocean floor while the world watched a fiasco unfold.

For Putin, the *Kursk* catastrophe turned into a PR disaster. For twenty-four hours after the submarine went down, ORT and NTV showed shots of icy waters and grieving families onshore, alternating with footage of Putin water-skiing and enjoying a barbecue at his dacha in Sochi.

The media coverage made much of the fact that the Russian government, unable to mount a rescue on its own, stalled for four days despite British and Norwegian offers of assistance. After the help was accepted, it took another three days to get the rescue vessels to the site. When British divers finally reached the escape hatch of the *Kursk* it was too late.

When Boris heard about *Kursk* he was in France in his Cap d'Antibes château. He started calling Putin immediately, but could reach him only on August 16, the fifth day of the unfolding tragedy.

"Volodya, why are you in Sochi? You should interrupt your holiday and go to that submarine base, or at least to Moscow. You do not feel the situation and it will damage you."

"And why are you in France? You are on a well-deserved vacation, aren't you?" Putin sounded sarcastic.

"First, I am not the father of the nation, and no one gives a shit where I am. Second, I am flying to Moscow in the morning."

"Okay, Boris, thank you for your advice."

When Boris landed in Moscow on the 17th, Putin was still vacationing. He arrived in Moscow early on Saturday August 19. By then, Voloshin's propaganda masters had woken up to the magnitude of the PR disaster. Putin's press office reported that he immediately went into a series of emergency meetings with senior ministers about *Kursk*.

All Saturday morning Boris was calling the Kremlin, seeking a meeting with the president. He believed that this was the moment when he could get through to Volodya, to make him learn from the lessons of the previous week, to explain how the style of his operation was hurting him. Finally he got through.

"Okay, come over, let's talk," said Putin.

But when he arrived, it was Voloshin who was waiting for him. He went straight to the point.

"Listen, we feel that ORT is working against the president. I am asking you, yield control and we will part amicably."

"Say that again," said Boris.

"Surrender your stock to someone loyal to us. If you don't, you will follow Goose to Butyrka."

Boris tried to find the right words for a response. Voloshin was his own former asset manager, whom he had placed in Yeltsin's Kremlin three years ago, as his best go-getter. Now he was getting him.

"You go fuck yourself," said Boris. "I want to talk to Volodya."

"Okay," said Voloshin, as emotionless as ever. "Come back tomorrow."

In the morning, the three of them met in Voloshin's office. Putin walked into the room holding a folder. He started off in a businesslike manner, as if at an official function: "ORT is the most important channel. It is too important to be left outside of government influence. We made a decision," and so on.

Then he suddenly stopped, looked up with his watery eyes, and said, "Tell me, Boris, I don't understand. Why are you doing this? Why are you attacking me? Have I done anything to hurt you? Believe me, I was more than tolerant with your escapades."

"Volodya, you made a mistake when you stayed in Sochi. Every station in the world . . . "

"I don't give a fuck about every station in the world," interrupted Putin. "Why did *you* do this? You are supposed to be my friend. It was you who talked me into taking this job. And now you are stabbing me in the back. What did I do to deserve it?"

"Deserve what?"

"I have a report here, that your people were hiring some whores to pose as sailors' wives and sisters to bash me."

Alexander ("Sasha") Litvinenko
with his mother in Nalchik, 1966.
(Courtesy of the author)

The wedding of Sasha
and Marina Litvinenko,
October 14, 1994.
(Courtesy of the author)

Sasha, Marina, and Tolik
celebrate their first
New Year's Eve in London.
(Courtesy of the author)

Sasha at Counterintelligence school. *(Courtesy of the author)*

Sasha, right, with Alexander Gusak during the siege of Pervomaisk, during the first Chechen War, 1996. *(Courtesy of the author)*

Negotiations in Chechnya. Yeltsin, Rybkin, Berezovsky, Udugov, Maskhadov, Zakayev.
(Courtesy of the author)

Vladimir Gusinsky and Boris Berezovsky, 1996.
(Aleksander Potapov/ Kommersant)

George Soros at Davos.
(AP Images/Alessandro della Valle)

Vladimir Putin at the Kremlin.
(KLIMENTYEV MIKHAIL/ITAR-TASS/Landov)

Sasha Litvinenko's 1998 press conference, denouncing corruption at the FSB, along with Viktor Shebalin. *(Sergei Kaptilkin/REUTERS/Landov)*

The aftermath of a truck bomb which exploded outside an apartment building in Volgodonsk on Sept 16 1999, killing 18 and injuring 288.

Boris Berezovksy, 2002, denouncing the Russian government and accusing the FSB of blowing up apartment buildings in Moscow in 1999. *(AP Images/Richard Lewis)*

The 2nd Scientific Research Institute (NII-2) of the FSB in Moscow, reputed to be a storehouse for polonium. *(Courtesy of the author)*

The Litvinenkos' home in north London.
(Andrew Stuart/EMPICS/Landov)

Sergei Yushenkov,
member of the Duma
who helped investigate
the 1999 apartment bombings.
He was killed by an unknown
gunman in front of his home
in Moscow, April 17, 2003.
(Associated Press)

Anna Politkovskaya,
crusading Moscow journalist.
(SAEZ PASCAL/SIPA)

Mikhail Trepashkin,
a former colleague of Sasha's,
who denounced the FSB and
was subsequently imprisoned.
(Sergei Karpukhin/REUTERS/Landov)

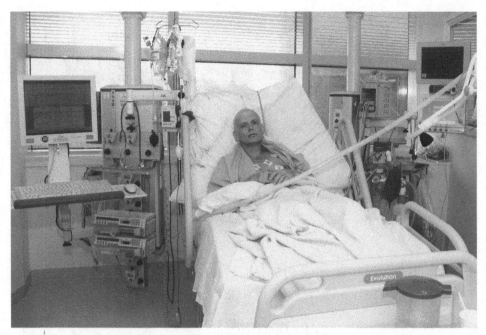

Sasha Litvinenko on his deathbed. *(Natasja Weitsz/Getty Images)*

Dmitri Kovtun and Andrei Lugovoy.
(Mikhail Antonov/REUTERS TV/Landov)

Mario Scaramella.
(CIRO FUSCO/epa/Corbis)

German police taking
radiation samples from
Dmitri Kovtun's car, 2006.
(Sebastian Widmann/dpa/Corbis)

Alex Goldfarb with
toxicologist John Henry.
(AP Images/John Stillwell)

Marina Litvinenko
at Sasha's funeral.
(Dylan Martinez/REUTERS/Landov)

"They are not whores, they are real wives and sisters. Your KGB idiots are feeding you baloney, and if you believe it, you are not any different."

Voloshin froze stiff as a wax doll; his eyes expressed horror.

"You forgot our conversation after the election, Volodya," Boris went on. "I told you that I never swore allegiance to you personally. You promised to continue the Yeltsin way. He would never even think of shutting up a journalist who attacked him. You are destroying Russia."

"Come on, you can't be serious about Russia," interrupted Putin.

"Well, I guess that's the end of it."

"Tell me one thing, Volodya. Sending me the way of Goose, was this your idea or Voloshin's?"

"It makes no difference now." Putin was again his cold closed-up self. "Goodbye, Boris Abramovich."

"Goodbye, Volodya."

They both knew it was their last meeting.

Later that day Boris announced a donation of $1 million for the bereaved *Kursk* families, while ORT and NTV continued to broadcasted interviews with the sailors' mothers and widows, who complained about government inaction. The Kremlin frantically tried to control the coverage, but the two defiant channels used round-the-clock special reports to expose chaos in the navy, indifference in the Kremlin, and human tragedy at the submarine's home base, with aloof, ice-cold Putin presiding over the mess.

_____

When Putin finally arrived at Severomorsk, ten days after the catastrophe, he faced an angry crowd of sailors' families. About five hundred people waited for hours in the rain for the president's arrival, before they were allowed into the hall of an officers' club. They asked sharp questions, wanting to know who was responsible for what everyone believed was a botched government response.

In an attempt to turn the tables, Putin lashed out at the media, without quite naming the two oligarchs, Boris and Goose. "They are liars. The television industry has people who have been destroying the state for ten years. They have been stealing money and buying up absolutely everything," he said. "Now they're trying to discredit the country so that the army gets even worse." In a clear reference to Boris, he said, "There are some who have even given a million dollars. . . . They would have done better to sell their villas on the Mediterranean coast of France and in Spain. Only then could they explain why the property was registered under false names and behind firms. And we would probably ask the question, Where did the money come from?"

We watched the news at Boris's dacha at Rublyovka. Boris pointed at the screen. "This expression," he said. "Note this expression. This is how he is when he loses control. He is like a cornered animal, barking, snapping. This does not happen to him often."

––––––––––

Yuri Felshtinsky, a journalist and historian specializing in the Russian secret services, comes from my cohort of Russian American expatriates. He has lived in Boston since the late 1970s, visiting his old homeland only after the fall of Communism. Like me, in the late 1990s he became a peripheral planet in Boris's solar system, orbiting once every few months, advising him on various matters.

Felshtinsky befriended Sasha Litvinenko after his 1998 press conference. They grew particularly close after Sasha's release from prison in December 1999. Many of Sasha's FSB stories interested Felshtinsky professionally, so he used every opportunity to meet up and talk.

Like me, Felshtinsky was highly skeptical of Boris's relationship with Putin and was happy to learn that there was a disagreement brewing between them. In May 2000, Felshtinsky flew to Moscow to take part in the group that was helping Boris write the federalist memorandum. As he later told me, on one day of that trip he took a break from our labors and went to see Sasha.

He found him in a bad mood.

It was still two weeks before Boris's conflict with Putin would splash across the front pages, but the raid of masked thugs on Media-MOST had already been featured on prime-time television. Sasha was convinced that Kontora had taken over the Kremlin in the person of

Putin and would start cracking down on everyone on its hate list. In general terms, this meant journalists, Chechen lovers, Jews, and oligarchs; more specifically, it meant Berezovsky and Goose, who epitomized all of the above.

As for Sasha, the Kafkaesque investigation of him continued without any end in sight. He was now fighting a third set of charges, after the two previous ones had been thrown out by the courts.

After he had been conditionally released from Butyrka in December, the accusation that he had beaten a suspect and extorted some vegetables at a Moscow market on May 30, 1996, fell apart. As it turned out, on that day in that market, the FSB did indeed beat some people, but Sasha was a thousand miles away in Armenia. He was busy intercepting five truckloads of arms being sent to Chechnya via Georgia. The Armenian Security Ministry provided evidence of his whereabouts. The charges were dropped and two "eyewitnesses" dismissed.

On the day he was cleared, however, he was slapped with new charges. Allegedly, some years earlier, while pursuing a case in the town of Kostroma, five hundred miles northeast of Moscow, Sasha had stolen some explosives from an FSB depot and planted them on a suspect, a local gangster, to frame him. A new criminal case was opened, and Sasha's restraining order not to leave Moscow was extended. This time, however, the charge had an ominous twist: should the case be tried, it would not be in Moscow. It was unlikely that a provincial judge would have the guts to stand up to FSB pressure, as two Moscow judges had managed to do.

After spending an evening with melancholy Sasha and loyal Marina, Felshtinsky came up with an idea: approach the source of the trouble, the Kontora itself, to see what it would take for them to leave Sasha alone. Boris and Putin had not yet publicly split. Felshtinsky figured that he might be able to get access by exploiting Boris's reputation, while it was still worth something.

A couple of days later he sat down for dinner with none other than Gen. Evgeny Khokholkov (Retired) in a classy restaurant on Kutuzovsky Prospect that Khokholkov owned.

Khokholkov not only accepted Felshtinsky's suggestion to meet and talk; he even closed his place to other customers for the night. He clearly viewed his guest as Berezovsky's emissary, and thus two steps removed from Putin.

Years later, Felshtinsky, as meticulous as a historian can be, gave me an account of that conversation. It was on May 22, 2000, from 7:30 to 12:30. Khokholkov was friendly and self-confident. He made no secret that he maintained a close relationship with Kontora. Moreover, it appeared that he had cleared the conversation with his contacts; he kept using "we" to articulate his positions.

Yes, "we" understand that Boris is an important and resourceful man, and agree that there is no reason to continue hostilities between him and the FSB. There is nothing wrong with letting bygones be bygones, although some past injustices could still be reversed. For example, perhaps Boris could help reinstate a certain group of three hundred officers who had been placed on unpaid leave in the aftermath of the URPO scandal.

But as for Litvinenko, sorry, Yuri Georgievich, this is nonnegotiable. He is ours, not yours. He betrayed the system and he has to pay for it. There can be no statute of limitations. I personally would break his neck if I met him in a dark alley, as any of "us" would do—figuratively speaking, of course. I hope you enjoy Moscow, after all these years in America; it must be so pleasant to breathe the air of one's homeland.

A couple of days later, Felshtinsky went to see Sasha again. He did not tell him about the split between Boris and Putin, but he did recap his conversation with Khokholkov.

"I don't believe that Boris will be able to protect you for long, Sasha," he said. "You yourself said that Putin should not be trusted. I suggest you consider leaving the country. Think about it seriously. Emigration is not a picnic, but it is better than sitting in jail, not to mention lying dead in a ditch."

"What am I going to do abroad? I don't speak any languages."

"With your talents . . . you can at least drive a cab . . . or we could write a book together. All your stories, they deserve to be told."

Sasha was hesitant, but they agreed that if and when he was

ready to go, he would let Felshtinsky know, and Felshtinsky would come help him flee on short notice.

Moscow, September 7: At a press conference on the occasion of the first anniversary of the Moscow apartment bombings, the head of antiterrorism at the FSB says that investigators consider the "Chechen version" to be the most likely explanation of the attacks. He names as principal suspects Achemez Gochiyayev, Yusuf Krymshamkhalov, Timur Batchayev, and Adam Dekkushev. All four are believed to be hiding in Chechnya. They are "members of a radical Islamic sect." Their ringleader, Gochiyayev, is named as the man who had rented basement apartments in the buildings where the bombs were planted. He was allegedly paid $500,000 for masterminding the blasts by a Wahhabi warlord named Amir Khattab.

By September 2000 Felshtinsky was deeply absorbed in a new project, hopefully a book, about the role of the FSB in provoking the second Chechen War. He had collected everything that had been printed about it, in English or Russian. The commonly accepted version was that the war had been provoked by the invasion of Dagestan by Wahhabi warlords in August, followed by the apartment bombings in September 1999. Felshtinsky was pretty convinced that the bombings were the work of the FSB. But there were some loose ends in the story that had never been resolved.

First, there was a statement by Prime Minister Stepashin that the planning for the war had begun in March. Second, there was the "transcript" of Berezovsky's conversation with Udugov, in May, about Wahhabi plans to invade Dagestan. Third, there were speculations concerning whether Boris himself could have been involved in the blasts. Most of them appeared in Russian tabloids and could be discounted. However, one such statement came from none other than George Soros, who, in an article in the *New York Review of Books* earlier that year, wrote, "I could not quite believe" Boris was involved in the bombings, but "still, I could not rule it out." Soros referred to a conversation he had with Boris about Chechen terrorists that gave rise to this speculation. Felshtinsky called me, as someone who could shed light on Soros.

His call was not completely unexpected; sooner or later, I figured, I would be dragged into the squabble between George and Boris. I worked for George and yet was a friend of Boris's. I was in an awkward position, but somehow I had managed to avoid loyalty conflicts. Perhaps I should not have introduced them to each other, I thought, but it was too late. Soon I would have to choose between them.

"It is sheer nonsense," I told Felshtinsky, when he asked about Soros's speculation. "The conversation with Boris was in my presence. The only thing Boris told him was how he got some hostages from Raduyev in exchange for his Patek Philippe. He was in the government at the time. But why don't you ask Boris himself? He's in New York."

Felshtinsky flew from Boston to New York to catch Boris, who was giving a talk at the Council on Foreign Relations. It took him two days, chasing Boris between New York and Washington, to grab his attention. On the way to the airport to fly back home, Felshtinsky finally managed to get him to focus on the events of the previous September.

It is true, Boris said, that the war was planned for six months before the Dagestan events, over his objections. It is false that he conspired with Udugov. It is true that Udugov came to see him. It is also true that Udugov and Basayev conspired with Stepashin and Putin to provoke a war to topple Maskhadov and install the Islamist government, but the agreement was for the Russian army to stop at the Terek River. However, Putin double-crossed the Chechens and started an all-out war.

As for the apartment house bombings, Boris said, it is inconceivable that Putin would have done it. It is too convoluted to suggest that some rogue elements did it to help Putin without his knowledge. It is illogical to suggest that Basayev, Udugov, Khattab, or any sane Chechen did it.

"There are Chechens who are insane. Raduyev, for example, or Arbi Barayev," Boris said. "Madmen like them are capable of anything, but I cannot explain irrational behavior. In short, you need some concrete evidence."

"And Ryazan?" Felshtinsky asked.

"What about Ryazan?"

"The FSB 'exercises' in Ryazan."

"It is totally plausible that the FSB would stage drills on civilians without telling them," said Boris. "It perfectly fits their style."

"But the bomb was live."

"What do you mean, 'live'?"

As Felshtinsky later told me, it turned out that Boris, like most Russians, had missed the stories in *Novaya Gazeta* and the NTV report on March 24. He had never heard about Private Pinyaev and his sour tea.

It had never occurred to Boris that it was on September 23, the morning after the Ryazan incident, that the massive bombings of Grozny began. And he had never considered the fact that after the Ryazan episode, the terrorist attacks, which had occurred roughly one per week, had abruptly stopped.

Most important, until that very moment, Boris had tended to discount talk of the bombing conspiracy as a smear directed at him. Now, with a fellow traveler laying out the known facts, he paid attention, and a lightbulb flicked on.

"I am such a fool!" he yelled suddenly. "They did it! Lena, did you hear, I am an idiot!" he cried out to his wife, sitting in the front seat next to the driver. "They did it! That explains everything! What a fool I am!"

By the time they arrived at the airport, Boris had cooled down. He listened intently to Felshtinsky's plan on how to investigate the plot. The problem was that Yuri was an academic, not a detective. He was an amateur in matters of this sort. There was only one man, a professional, who was qualified to do it.

They looked at each other, and said in unison, "Sasha!"

When Felshtinsky took the Boston–New York shuttle to see Boris, he had planned to be away for a day or two. It was now already his fourth day away from home. He called his wife to ask her to retrieve their car from Logan Airport and to explain that he would be away for a few more days. He was going with Boris to Nice, to catch a connecting flight to Moscow.

The next afternoon, he walked with Sasha through the empty alleys of Neskuchny Sad (literally, the Not Boring Gardens), a park that runs along the riverbank in central Moscow. Sasha spoke first. He was ready to flee. He had made up his mind about a month earlier, right after Putin attacked Boris in the aftermath of *Kursk*. He had everything prepared. It was now September 23, exactly one year after the Ryazan incident.

As the autumn leaves crunched under their feet, Sasha gave Yuri his take on the apartment bombings. There was no doubt in his mind that it was a Kontora job.

"It's the signature," he said. "Every crime has a signature. I have worked long enough in ATC to tell you right away, this was not some fringe Chechens. The sophistication, the coordination, the engineering expertise needed for bomb placement—all point to a highly professional team. Have you heard about Max Lazovsky?"

Yuri had not.

"He is the kind of FSB guy who could pull off such a thing. I would start the investigation with him."

The next morning Felshtinsky took a plane to London, to meet up with Boris. As for Sasha's escape, there was nothing more to do but wait for Sasha to call. From London Yuri went back to Boston while Boris flew to Malaga, Spain, for a peace-making meeting with Goose.

Even before Felshtinsky's visit, Sasha had begun preparations for escape. His major concern was surveillance, which he was sure he was under. So, for nearly three months, he painstakingly tried to lull potential watchers and relax their vigilance. He was an ace at surveillance himself, and he found it amusing to be in the role of object to his oper. He had a fairly good idea of who his oper might be at Internal Affairs; he knew them all. He was also pretty sure which one of his friends was reporting to the oper; there was only one who seemed to want to be his guardian, patronizing him about being careful, growing extremely concerned when he came home late or did not call. Marina complained about having a logistical "threesome," but Sasha played along. The suspected scout was his old friend Ponkin, his loyal subordinate who had stood by him at his first trial. Sasha did not hold it against him. In a way, he was happy for Ponkin if it meant he had been able to work things out in this way.

Sasha took special care to make Ponkin's life easy. He fed him accurate information about what he was up to. He also made sure that whatever data were picked up by electronic surveillance— phone monitoring, bugs at his home—matched what Ponkin reported.

Sasha was pretty sure that he was not constantly followed; he could easily spot outdoor surveillance. Tails appeared only when Boris was in town, which was rare. He hoped his oper at Lubyanka was bored to death.

At the end of August, Sasha staged a little rehearsal: his lawyer obtained a court release allowing him to leave town for a one-week vacation. He gave Ponkin and the wiretap listeners advance notice of his vacation plans so that his oper could block the trip if he wished, but nobody objected. When he went with Marina to Sochi for a week on the beach, it appeared that they were not followed. This was all that Sasha needed to know. By the end of September he was fully pre-pared. Marina did not suspect a thing. On the morning of Septem-ber 30, he surprised her with the news that he was leaving, just for a few days, to Nalchik, to help his father sell their house and move closer to Moscow. He had been urging his father to do it, calling him throughout the summer; he had also discussed it with Ponkin, who even helped him research the real estate market.

"I thought I told you. Just for a few days. It's about Papa's house."

"You did not tell me, but never mind."

They drove to the airport. He disappeared for ten minutes, appar-ently to meet someone, and then came back.

"Let's take a walk," he said. "Listen, this is very important. A friend of mine will come to you in a few days. He will tell you what to do. Don't ask any questions; just do exactly as he says. Here is some money, keep it for me."

Marina stared at him. This was the other side of Sasha, the one that she had not seen since he left the FSB, and only two or three times before that. The superconfident, no-nonsense rock of a man. The man who terrified the instructor when she was getting her driver's license. The one who gave her orders without asking nicely, as if she were a soldier in his army without any right to ask questions.

"Okay," she said. "Where are you going?"

"To Nalchik, to see Papa. Don't worry, it will be just a few days."

He left with a small shoulder bag, containing just enough clothes for three or four days. Instead of flying to Nalchik, however, he headed elsewhere. After landing in southern Russia, he took a bus to a small seashore town. Steamboats shuttled from there to an even smaller town in a neighboring ex-Soviet republic, and he planned to take one the next morning. Citizens of both countries could cross the border using internal ID. Foreign travel passports were not required.

He spent the night in a local hotel, paying cash. In the morning he came to the pier twenty minutes before departure.

"You are late, young man," said the woman at the ticket desk. "Do you see the sign? Registration closes three hours before departure, because we have to submit lists to the border control. The next boat is at three o'clock."

Sasha knew the system. But he could not allow his name to be checked against the border control watch list.

"I know, I know I'm late," he said. "But look, I absolutely need to be there by noon. I have a date, you see, she won't wait. What shall I do? Help me."

"Go talk to the crew."

The second mate looked at him sternly: "Don't you know there is a border here? Haven't you heard the USSR ended ten years ago? Okay, it will cost you ten bucks. You will be my crew for the trip. And another ten for the border guard. Put it inside your ID." He nodded to the border guard in the booth nearby.

The sleepy guard glanced at his ID, collected the banknote, and waved him through.

"I walked down the pier. I was wearing the light jacket that I was married in, the only one that I had, and the lucky one. It was the longest walk in my life," Sasha told me later.

220

On October 2, Sasha's friend brought instructions to Marina. She had never met him before, but she had little choice but to listen. He told her to get a new mobile phone, not just a sim-card, turn it on, call a certain number, and then hang up. From then on, he said, keep the phone on at all times, but do not call anybody else from it. When Sasha calls, don't pronounce any last names, use only first names. Don't use the phone at home or in the car.

She did as she was told. The next morning Sasha called.

"Good morning, my darling. Where are you? Driving? Alone? Could you park and take a walk? I will call in three minutes."

While she was parking, she imagined him counting seconds, as she was doing. The phone rang again.

"How are you? How is Tolik? Anyone looking for me? I'm in Nalchik, sure. Listen, this is what I want you to do. Take the money that I left. Go to a travel agent. Not the one you used last time. Anyone but him. Get yourself and Tolya a two-week package to any Western European country, preferably Spain; you always wanted to see it. Or France, or Italy. The sooner the better. This is a surprise, my present for our wedding anniversary. Unfortunately, I can't be with you. There is some work here, but I will be waiting at home when you come back."

"But, Sasha, what will I say at work? Or at Tolya's school?"

"Better to say nothing at all. You can call them after you've left and say that you fell sick. No one should know where you are going, it is very important. Not even your mom. You can tell her later." She knew without asking that it wasn't just a vacation trip.

On October 8, in Boston, Yuri Felshtinsky got Sasha's call.

"I've linked up with my friends whom I told you about," Sasha said. These were the people in a "third country" who could get him a false passport. "Come as soon as you can, please. And bring some cash. Ten grand. Or better, fifteen."

On October 14, Marina and Tolya left for Spain. It was Sasha and Marina's wedding anniversary. He called every half-hour until the plane was on the runway and she had to turn off her phone. When they landed in Malaga, she saw Yuri Felshtinsky waving from behind a barrier.

"Where is Sasha?" was her first question. "He's not in Nalchik, is he?"

Yuri named the third country. "He will call any minute and explain everything."

They got into Felshtinsky's rented car and followed a tour bus. She had signed up with a tour for two weeks in Marbella, a resort on the coast of Andalusia.

"Of course, I realized that something was going on, that Nalchik was a cover. I thought that he wanted to get us out of Moscow because of some danger, you know. Such things happen in his profession," Marina later explained. "But when he called he said that maybe we couldn't go back to Russia at all, ever. I went into total shock. To me, this was unthinkable, like when you are told that you've got cancer or someone close to you was in a car accident."

"What do you mean we might not go back?" she yelled on the phone. "What about my mom, our friends, our home? Where shall we live? Here, in Spain? Without you? How will you get here? You have no passport."

"Marusya, please," he used her nickname, "cool down, talk to Yuri. I will call back in five minutes."

Felshtinsky explained that Sasha was waiting for some friends to get him false documents. When he received them, he would be able to get to a safer place, where Marina and Tolya could join him. This was the best-case scenario. The worst-case scenario was that the documents would not be forthcoming, in which case Sasha would have to go back on the ferry to Russia to face imminent imprisonment. There was no chance that he would be acquitted a third time. The third country where he was waiting was not exactly a safe place, so telephone discussions had to be kept to a minimum. There could be no talk of passports on the phone. For the time being there was nothing they could do but wait.

Finally, she understood. She agreed to defer judgment until the situation cleared up. They checked into the resort, and for the next ten days tried to make the most of their vacation, talking to Sasha about neutral, innocuous things, "like in Lefortovo," she later joked.

On October 23, Sasha called to announce that his friends had delivered on their promise. He was in possession of everything he needed to continue on his journey. Felshtinsky packed up and left to join him. Marina and Tolya stayed in Marbella.

On the morning of the 25th he called again. He was in Turkey, and in relative safety. I had just called him from New York. It was time for Marina to decide: join him in exile, or return to Russia? He would do as she wished. This time he would not decide for both of them. The choice was Marina's.

———

It was the most difficult decision Marina had ever had to make. She loved Sasha with all her heart, but she was not part of his violent and dangerous world; she had never asked for details when he went out to fight his fights. By joining him now, she would become a sort of comrade-in-arms. Perhaps she should return home and let him run alone. She would wait for him. After all, she had waited for him while he was in prison. Why shouldn't he sort out his problems with borders and false passports without her? She had a six-year-old child on her hands, and a mother with a heart condition in Moscow.

In the end, as she explained to me later, it was Boris's call that tipped the balance. She was lying in bed staring at the ceiling while Tolik played outside with a Russian child from their tour. A distant Andalusian rhythm echoed in the background. It was late afternoon. The phone rang.

"Marina," said Boris, "I just spoke to Sasha, and I promised him that whatever happens I will never abandon you and Tolya. That is one thing that I need to tell you. The other is this. I believe that I know what's on your mind. Actually I am now struggling with the same choice right now. The world out there, you know, in Turkey and beyond, must seem scary and cold and unpredictable. The one back in Moscow is warm and familiar, because it's our home. Yet that is why it is so misleading. These people are killers, Marina. I have come to understand it just recently, a month ago to be exact. It's why

I sent Felshtinsky to Moscow to tell Sasha to run. They are really bad news, Marina. If Sasha goes back they will kill him. And I am afraid that if you go back, he will follow you. Maybe not now, maybe in three weeks, or three months, but he will. He is not a loner. You give him the strength to go against Kontora, and he needs this strength now more than ever. That's all."

She lay there for some minutes more. Then she called Sasha to say that she would join him in Turkey.

She lied to her tour leader, saying that she had to urgently return to Moscow. It was late at night when her taxi pulled up at the Malaga Airport. She dragged sleepy Tolik inside the terminal. The departure hall was empty. All flights were gone. No one was waiting for them. Suddenly Felshtinsky appeared.

"We are going to a different terminal," he said. "There are no commercial flights to Turkey, so Boris has sent his plane."

Five days later Sasha was sitting next to me, with Marina and Tolik on the back seat, driving from Ankara to Istanbul, where this story and our friendship began. The fog was thick—as thick, Marina thought, as the uncertainty of exile about which Boris had spoken.

Sasha finished relating his biography, bringing it up to my entrance the previous day and our visit to the American Embassy.

"So what was it that the Americans wanted from you?" I asked.

"Ah," he grinned. "Everyone has his own problems. They wanted to know how we got hold of the missile that hit Dudayev. That homing system was an American toy, you know. For four years, they could not figure out how we got it."

"And you know?"

"Sure I do." He told me about Khokholkov's visit to Germany and Khokholkov's American contact.

"You know the identity of his contact?"

"I found it out just by accident once upon a time in Moscow."

"So you told them the name?"

"Yeah. The FSB has been calling me a traitor for three years, and now I am one. A self-fulfilling prophecy."

"You are not a traitor, Sasha," said Marina. "You did it in self-defense."

"Let me tell you a story," I said. "Once upon a time in Germany, there was this guy in the Foreign Office. He volunteered to spy for the Americans, and was their most important spy during World War II. He warned that the Germans were planning to kill all the Jews in Italy. So tell me, was he a traitor or a hero?"

"For you maybe a hero, and for the Germans, a traitor."

"Okay," I said. "That was then. And now? If you go to Germany now, what do you think the Germans would say?"

"Well, they probably wouldn't know who he was and wouldn't care anyway. And Russia isn't Germany. You can't compare them."

"True," I said. "But didn't Kontora blow up those apartment buildings? Isn't that enough for you not to lose sleep about being a traitor?"

"Well, yes," he sighed, not really convinced by my logic. "But it remains to be proven that they did it."

———

One day in September 2004 in London, after having spent nearly four years investigating the apartment bombings, Sasha came up to me, beaming.

"Have you seen this?" He was holding a copy of *The Independent*. "Remember you told me about that German guy in Turkey? Here is his picture. His name was Fritz Kolbe. There is a story about him. The Germans made him an official hero. Put a plaque on the wall. So maybe you were right. Maybe our time will come too."

PART V

THE RETURN OF THE KGB

CHAPTER 11

THE EXILES

New York, November 7, 2000

As I entered the New York offices of George Soros, I was expecting an unpleasant conversation. George had learned of my Turkish adventures from the newspapers. The story of the Russian FSB agent who sought asylum in Britain had mysteriously gotten into the evening edition of the *Sun* while we were still in Heathrow. By morning my name was next to Sasha's in the Russian press: "Head of Soros Program Smuggles FSB Officer to England."

I had worked with George for almost ten years, managing some $130 million of his money on advancing Russian reforms, and I was probably the longest lasting member of his Russia team. But our relationship had cooled noticeably of late because we differed on the question of who "lost" Russia. George maintained that the reforms fell victim to the excesses of "unrestrained capitalism," that the oligarchs corrupted the weak state and impeded the work of the "young reformers." I, on the contrary, felt that the main problem was the regeneration of the traditional all-powerful Russian bureaucratic police state, and that the only people who could effectively resist this trend were the oligarchs.

Our argument was personified in the figure of Boris Berezovsky. George's and Boris's breakup in the aftermath of the Svyazinvest privatization was like a love affair turned sour. They accused each other of every mortal sin.

"Your friend is an evil genius," George said. "He destroyed Russia single-handedly."

"Soros lost money because the 'young reformers' fooled him," said Boris. "And then he tried to convince the West—out of spite—that the oligarchs were evil and should not be allowed to control the beast."

I listened and said nothing. Both were wrong, but it was useless to argue. George took my contact with Boris personally. He had already stopped inviting me to his summer house in Southampton. The Litvinenko affair would be the last straw, I thought, as I entered his office.

Soros's office is on the thirty-third floor of a building at the corner of Fifty-seventh Street and Seventh Avenue in Manhattan. From the moment you enter, you know you are in a rarefied world. You are immediately treated to a knockout panorama of Central Park to the north and the majestic Hudson sparkling behind the jagged skyline to the west. George's desk sits in the northwest corner. With his back to the Hudson, he can shift his glance from the park to his computer monitor, which is filled with stock index crawlers. The screen's images are a bird's-eye view of global finance.

In the six months since I had last been there, nothing had changed. The same official photographs lined the walls: George with two different presidents in the White House, George with the pope, George with Yeltsin at the Kremlin. My gift, a candle bust of Lenin that I bought at an outdoor market in Moscow, was still on the desk next to the monitor.

"Well, tell me, what happened in Turkey," George demanded as I entered the office. He always has a half smile playing on his lips and a glimmer of curiosity in his eyes. You can never guess his attitude from the expression on his face. After ten years with him, I had learned to guess his mood from the timbre of his voice. This time it reflected absolute calm. His decision had already been made.

He was interested to learn how high up in the U.S. administration my role in Sasha's defection was known. I told him about my contacts in the U.S. administration. The whole thing was extremely unpleasant for him. For the past two years he had been telling anyone who would listen that Russia's reforms collapsed because of the oligarchs and that the worst villain among them was Boris. And now one of his own people had helped Berezovsky's man.

"I understand why your friend needs this." George never used Boris's name when talking about him with me. "That guy in Turkey was a trial balloon. Your friend will soon need to ask for asylum himself, and he has to create a precedent. But why you needed to do this, I cannot understand!"

It was pointless to argue with him about Boris.

"To tell the truth, I didn't expect it to turn out this way. I just planned to bring them to the embassy," I said. "But in the situation I couldn't have acted any differently. I'm sorry about the publicity."

"There," George said animatedly. "Unintended consequences! I've warned you many times not to get involved with your friend. And now you've done it publicly, and that means that you can no longer be associated with me. Not to mention that you'll probably become persona non grata in Moscow. What are your plans?"

"I'm thinking of going back to science."

"That's excellent. There's a hidden plus in all this for me. I'm looking for a way to reduce our presence in Russia. You're giving me a wonderful excuse to shut down the project."

What irony, I thought to myself. Soros is leaving Russia and blames Berezovsky, while Berezovsky is leaving Russia and blames Soros. And neither one of them gets it. Most Russians see no difference between them. Russia rejected them both, and basically for the same reasons: they're both rich, both Jews, both independent characters, confident in their mission to reorder the world. For the gray mediocrity that Putin embodies, each is a threat and a challenge.

As I left the office and merged into the crowd, I pondered an offer Boris had made, to work for him. He wanted me to organize a foundation that would pick up where Soros has stopped short: funding democratic opposition to Putin's regime.

It was a complicated choice for me. I still ran a research lab at the Public Health Institute in New York. At fifty-four I had a pretty successful scientific career, which was already suffering because of my Soros work. If I continued spending a large part of my energy on Russia, I would have to wind that up. But Boris's proposal—an opportunity to get out of my "seat in the front row" and become a player just as the drama was nearing culmination—was too exciting to pass up.

There was also the problem of Boris's reputation. I knew the inside story well enough to discount the horrific allegations made against him, but the fact remained: rightly or wrongly, in the public eye Boris Berezovsky was the embodiment of the dark side of Russian capitalism. Yet, with all his errors and transgressions, he was the only one (except, perhaps, Goose) of the major Russian players who opposed the antihero Putin, and the fact that he did it against his immediate self-interest was also to his credit. Ultimately, I knew that if I wanted to join the fray, there were only two sides to choose from. The choice was obvious. So, in the end, I called Boris at Cap d'Antibes and said, "If you are really serious about the foundation, I am with you."

"Okay, hop on a plane and come over. We'll discuss the details," said Boris.

I landed in Nice on November 12, 2000, eleven days after I'd brought Sasha to London. A driver in a Land Rover was waiting to take me to Château de la Garoupe, Boris's Italianate villa dominating the Cap, with a magnificent view of the Bay of Nice. Although he had owned it for more than three years, he hadn't had the time to renovate it. Much of the decor in the two-story, turn-of-the-century house remained from its previous owners, giving the place an Edwardian flavor.

We spent the evening discussing the would-be foundation over a candlelight dinner in a hall decked with dark, archaic mirrors. The next morning, as I ate breakfast with him and his wife, Lena, Boris shocked us with the news that he was about to leave for Moscow "for a few hours" to answer his summons "as a witness" in the newly reopened Aeroflot case.

It was clear to me that if Boris went, he would be arrested. The summons had been issued ten days earlier, along with one to Goose, who was accused of defrauding Gazprom of $300 million via a loan to NTV. A few days prior to that, Putin had told *Le Figaro* that he had a "cudgel" he planned to use on the two media magnates, "just once, but on the head." Goose announced that he would ignore his summons and remain in Spain. But Boris, in a bout of apparent madness, wanted to go. His plane was waiting at the airport. I literally pulled him out of his car.

"Boris, are you insane? Didn't they tell you that they would put you in jail if you did not give up ORT? Why are you going there? You have nothing to prove!"

"They won't dare. It would be too blatant. If I don't go, it would look like an admission of guilt on Aeroflot."

It didn't make any sense to me. Just a week earlier Sasha had fled, in fear of his life.

"Boris, did not you yourself tell Marina a month ago that they would kill Sasha?"

"With Sasha it is different. Putin considers Sasha one of their own, a traitor."

"You are worse than a traitor to him. You are his ex-brother. He is out to destroy you, Boris, seriously. Putin is your creature, and you have some strange bond to him. If you don't break this bond, you will perish. Lena, will you tell him, please?" I turned to his wife, who was standing helplessly on the steps of the château. "If he goes, you will spend the rest of your life in Tobolsk, Siberia, visiting him once a month in a dungeon."

Lena shook her head. "I don't want to go to Tobolsk."

I got Elena Bonner, the widow of the dissident guru Andrei Sakharov, on the phone.

"Boris," she told him, "Andrei Dmitrievich always said that if you have the choice of leaving the country instead of going to jail, it is prudent to take it."

In the end, we wore him down. He dictated a statement: "They force me to choose between becoming a political prisoner or political émigré, and I am choosing the latter."

The day after we kept him from leaving for Moscow, Boris seemed deeply depressed, the longest period of gloom I have ever observed in his manic personality. At the time I thought that he was coming to grips with the reality of being an exile, something I had had to live with for twenty-five years. But as I learned later, the reason was quite specific: he had left a hostage in Russia, Nikolai (Kolya) Glushkov, his loyal manager of Aeroflot.

Boris was consumed with guilt. Kolya stubbornly refused to leave the country, insisting that he had done nothing wrong and that he looked forward to clearing his name in court should the Aeroflot case go to trial. By refusing to answer the summons, Boris might be forcing the prosecutors to crack down on Kolya. Indeed, three weeks later he was arrested. Then word came from the Kremlin that the price of Kolya's freedom was Boris's 49 percent ownership of ORT.

By then, the battle for control of ORT was already in full swing. According to its bylaws, major decisions in the company, such as appointments and firings of senior editorial staff, required approval by 75 percent of the board of directors. At the time of the *Kursk* incident, Boris's loyalists controlled the network. Among them were Konstantin Ernst, the executive producer; Sergei Dorenko, the anchorman; and Badri Patarkatsishvili, Boris's long-time business partner and ORT's COO. All three were on the board. Because of the 75 percent rule, gaining editorial control entailed turning either Dorenko or Ernst, or both.

If there was any journalist to whom Putin owed a debt, it was Dorenko. During the Duma campaign of 1999, week after week, his Saturday night show mocked and berated Primakov and Luzhkov in the blandest of styles, which earned him the scorn of many members of the journalistic community. Yet his programs were popular, and they did the job for Putin, making him appear to be a stark contrast to his much-ridiculed and degraded opponents. For Putin, Dorenko was unquestionably one of "us," so it was only natural that he would start with him.

"He called me into his office, with a huge double-headed Russian eagle hanging behind his desk, to make me an offer that I could not refuse," recalled Dorenko years later. " 'You are either a member of our team or not. If you are with us, we will pay you well. If you go against us, you cannot continue. As simple as that.' "

Dorenko was in shock. Style is everything, he told me. When Boris wanted something, he would always discuss the substance and ask for objections. If there was a difference of opinion, Boris's would likely prevail, but at least the discussion was civilized. If compromises were to be made, Boris would argue that they were a necessary evil in the context of larger strategies. Dorenko was no purist, but there are limits to everything. What he was facing now pushed him beyond those limits.

"It was the eagle," Dorenko explained. "He was sitting under the eagle, the fucking head of state. I just could not take that. My dad was an officer, you know, I grew up in military towns, and I thought of all those poor bastards for whom the eagle means something. This kind of talk could come from anybody, but I just could not take it from the president."

Dorenko did not take the offer. Later that week, Konstantin Ernst, the long-haired Moscow intellectual whom five years earlier Boris had made the most influential TV executive in the country, called Badri.

"I know that I am a piece of shit, but I will go with the winning side," he said. "It's pointless to resist. Sorry." He hung up.

A few days later, Ernst pulled Dorenko's program off the air and purged senior news editors from ORT. Dorenko was the most handsome face on Russian TV, the Peter Jennings of Russia. He knew that he was finished, but he was determined to have the last word. In an act of unbelievable defiance that brought millions of viewers to the edge of their seats, Dorenko went public on the rival channel, Goose's NTV, which at the time was still under Igor Malashenko's control. He told the national audience about his conversation with Putin, about the eagle, and the offer that he had refused. It was the last time his viewers saw him. A few months later, a navy captain claimed that Dorenko deliberately bumped into him with his motorcycle in the course of a dispute in a Moscow park. Dorenko was slapped with criminal charges, convicted of hooliganism, and given a four-year suspended sentence. He is now hosting a talk show on Radio Echo Moscow, the last remaining outpost of Goose's media empire.

With Dorenko gone and the newsroom under control, the Kremlin turned to ORT's board. By then Boris had announced that he would give his 49 percent in trust to a group of prominent journalists, all of whom were serious men of integrity. But then Glushkov was arrested, on December 7, 2000. With a hostage at Lefortovo, Boris had no choice. He knew he had to compromise.

The Kremlin sent a messenger in mid-December in the person of soft-spoken Roma Abramovich, who flew from Moscow for a weekend on the Côte d'Azur. His villa was a ten-minute drive from Château de la Garoupe. When he drove over for a talk with Boris and Badri, his posture was that of "an honest broker, who was looking out for everyone's best interests," recalled Boris.

"I come with a message from Volodya [Putin] and Sasha [Voloshin, Putin's chief of staff], at their explicit request," said Roma. "You understand, of course, that if they wanted, they could take your share in ORT away and you'd get nothing. But to make it easier for all, we agreed that I would buy you out, on their behalf. I am offering $175 million. It's a good deal."

Boris and Badri looked at each other in shock; it was a fraction of ORT's real value.

"No deal," they said.

"Well, Volodya and Sasha say that they would let Kolya go, as part of the deal."

"Can you guarantee that?"

"Volodya and Sasha say so."

And they accuse me of ransoming hostages, Boris thought. They shook hands on $175 million, and by mid-January 2001 the transaction was complete. Roma allowed the Kremlin to nominate five new board members. Yet Kolya remained in prison.

Grozny, Chechnya, February 24, 2001: A mass grave containing about two hundred bodies is discovered next to Russia's army base of Khankala. According to reports on NTV, many bear signs of tor-

ture. Some of the dead are identified as civilians who had disap-
peared in different regions of Chechnya. In Moscow, Novaya Gazeta
publishes an article by journalist Anna Politkovskaya, claiming that
Russian soldiers were keeping randomly picked civilians as prison-
ers in a pit, demanding $500 ransom for their release. While cover-
ing the story, Politkovskaya is briefly detained by Russian soldiers,
creating a media uproar in Moscow. She is later released.

There are conflicting versions of what exactly happened in Moscow outside the Scientific Hematological Center on April 11, 2001. Niko-lai Glushkov, officially in custody, was hospitalized there for treat-ment of a blood condition. Technically, he was under guard by an FSB detail. But the security was obviously lax: on occasion his guards would allow him to go home for an overnight stay, for a modest mon-etary incentive.

According to the prosecutors, in the early evening of the 11th, Glushkov left the hospital ward wearing his gown and slippers and walked to the gate, where his former Aeroflot associate Vladimir Sko-ropupov waited. As Glushkov was about to get into Skoropupov's car, a squad of FSB plainclothes officers appeared out of nowhere, arrested both men, and charged them with attempted escape from custody. On the next day, the former head of ORT security, Andrei Lugovoy, was detained in connection with the alleged escape attempt. Two months later, former ORT COO Badri Patarkatsishvili fled to Georgia, making use of his Georgian citizenship. The whole group was indicted in the escape plot.

Glushkov, however, offered a different version of the events of April 11 when I interviewed him years later in London. He believed that he had been set up, insisting that he had no intention of escap-ing. He wanted the Aeroflot case to be tried because he knew he was innocent. In fact, he was under the impression that he was about to be released until the trial "through a secret high-level deal," as his lawyers had hinted to him. He was walking in his slippers to the hos-pital gate simply to go home for the night, with his guards' knowl-edge, as he had done a few days earlier.

Glushkov would eventually get his day in court. In March 2004 he was cleared of charges of fraud and money laundering but found guilty of attempted escape from custody and a minor, face-saving charge of "abuse of authority." He was released from Lefortovo. When I asked him whether his stubbornness was worth three years in jail, he said, "Of course, I proved my innocence."

Lugovoy was convicted in the prison escape case, serving a prison term of fourteen months. After his release, he started his own security business.

In 2006 he would become a prime suspect in Sasha's murder.

On April 14, three days after Glushkov's alleged escape attempt, the new Kremlin-friendly management of NTV, backed by armed police, arrived at the network's studios and took control. Goose's journalists were run through a re-interview process, which included a pledge of allegiance to the Kremlin-appointed editors. Some caved in; most did not. Boris immediately invited the unemployed NTV team to join his one remaining media holding, TV-6. Until then, TV-6 had featured sports, music, movies, and comedy shows. Suddenly it became a news channel, the last independent voice in Russian TV broadcasting. Nobody expected it to remain independent for long.

Chechnya and Moscow, May 2001: In one week, Chechen guerrillas carry out more than 140 hit-and-run attacks and Russian sappers defuse 160 explosive devices. Russian defense minister Sergei Ivanov tells reporters that 2,682 Russian soldiers have been killed in Chechnya since the beginning of hostilities in September 1999. His statement is immediately challenged by a prominent nongovernmental organization, the Union of Committees of Soldiers' Mothers, who say that the real losses are nearing ten thousand.

Boris's new role as a sponsor of Russian democracy was announced to the world by Elena Bonner on November 30, 2000, at a press conference in Moscow. Bonner, the seventy-seven-year-old widow of the Nobel Laureate who defied the Soviet system, said that she had accepted a $3 million grant from the New York–based Berezovsky Foundation (which would later become known as the International Foundation for Civil Liberties, or IFCL) as an endowment for the Sakharov Museum and Civic Center in Moscow.

For Boris and me, awarding the first grant to Sakharov was a gesture ripe with symbolism. Elena Bonner had been the first among Russia's human rights activists to say that Putin represented "modernized Stalinism" at the time when Boris was still Putin's "brother." Three decades earlier Sakharov had become an emblematic figure, symbolizing moral resistance to tyranny. The grant to the Sakharov Center was meant to underscore the continuity of Soviet oppression under Putin and the permanence of dissidents' resistance. From the outset it defined the colors of the new foundation.

By May 2001, the IFCL had awarded 160 more grants to NGOs across Russia, which collectively represented, Boris hoped, "crystallization centers" for protest movements: antiwar groups like Soldiers' Mothers, supporters of prisoners' rights, the greens, defenders of ethnic minorities, and local human rights watchdogs. We also announced the Berezovsky legal aid program: we would provide free legal counsel to troubled juveniles and conscripts in litigation with the army, amounting to thousands of cases nationally.

Western pundits took the IFCL with a grain of salt, as a campaign by a cunning oligarch to improve his reputation. But not so the Kremlin. Within days after our wire transfers from New York hit the accounts of NGOs across Russia, Putin's advisers sounded the alarm. The IFCL grants obviously targeted issue-oriented groups, which included some 30 million ethnic minorities who felt like second-class citizens in the increasingly xenophobic atmosphere; the estimated 20 million citizens who had been beaten by the police at least once; 12 million ex-prisoners; and millions of families of would-be army conscripts. Taken together, these groups represented a potential protest electorate. The Kremlin rightly guessed our intent: to develop a grassroots network that could evolve into an antiestablishment political party. Within weeks they launched a counterdrive.

On June 12, Putin met with "representatives of civil society," a handpicked group of some thirty cultural functionaries, which, in the best Soviet tradition, included a cosmonaut, an actor, and a hockey player. The president spoke of his concern that many Russian NGOs were funded by foreign grants. The state must take responsibility for the support of civil society, he said, as was the custom in the USSR. A congress of NGOs would take place in the Kremlin in the fall, where the president would talk to these people's representatives directly, over the heads of the bureaucracy.

But it was too late. The seeds of discontent were sewn. Many NGOs promised to boycott the Kremlin initiative. Soon we received a call from a group of democratic politicians who wanted to meet to talk about setting up a new political party.

Sergei Yushenkov was a veteran of Russia's democratic politics. A former army officer, during the 1991 coup attempt he had organized the "living chain" of civilians around the Parliament to protect Yeltsin from the expected assault by KGB squadrons. An MP since 1989, Yushenkov was a leading proponent of a movement to abolish the draft and a leading critic of the war in Chechnya.

Yushenkov came to Château de la Garoupe in mid-May, along with another dissident Duma member, Vladimir Golovlyov. The meeting had all the hallmarks of a nineteenth-century episode from Russian history: comrades from Moscow travel to Western Europe to see a major émigré figure. Upon return, Yushenkov announced the formation of a new party, Liberal Russia, with Boris and himself as its leaders. Their objective was to run in the 2003 Duma elections on an anti-Putin platform.

The strategy of Liberal Russia was to focus on the protest electorate represented by the grassroots network of civic groups that the IFCL supported. Among other things that Yushenkov and Boris had in common was their suspicion about the 1999 apartment bombings.

They agreed that the matter should be thoroughly pursued and perhaps used as a campaign issue in 2003.

———

Sleptsovskaya, on the Chechen border, July 4, 2001: Hundreds of civilians flee for refugee camps in Ingushetia amid reports of summary executions in Chechen villages. According to one refugee, in the village of Assinovskaya, "They detained all men aged from 15 to 50, over 500 people, and put us down on our knees in a silage pit at the village's edge. . . . They kept us there for the entire day. They ordered us not to move, and beat some people with rifle butts, hunted them with dogs and tortured with electric shockers. In the end, they selected 50 of us and led them away, and let the rest go."

———

The arrival of Yushenkov and the prospect of an opposition party, combined with enthusiastic feedback from our grassroots grant recipients, somewhat lessened my initial pessimism that our battle, though noble, was not winnable. After all, even the Communists, who had had total control of the media and government, had collapsed in 1991. Maybe Boris was right after all: maybe Putin's regime was intrinsically unstable and would collapse at the first challenge.

Shortly after the visit of Yushenkov to the château, I had a chance to share my enthusiasm with Igor Malashenko, who happened to be in New York. We shared a lunch at his hotel overlooking Central Park. Igor was skeptical.

"These kinds of regimes do not fall by themselves," he said. "Communism collapsed not because of brave dissidents, but because the government could not keep up with the arms race. There was consolidated opposition from the West, including a massive anti-Soviet information industry funded by Western governments. Solzhenitsyn wrote a book, and it was immediately trumpeted by the Western support system. Today, try to publish a book about Chechnya! We are completely on our own. Our best strategy is to wait it out until the West wakes up and sees the danger. Then we will have a chance. As for Yushenkov, the moment he becomes a challenge they will whack him, you'll see."

Sadly, if we were to wait for Western help, it appeared we would have to wait for a very long time. On June 16, George Bush met with Putin in Ljubljana, Slovenia. He "looked him in the eye . . . and was able to get a sense of his soul." The U.S. president liked what he saw and announced to the world that Putin was "very straightforward and trustworthy."

"Unfortunately, that tells us more about Bush than about Putin," remarked Boris.

———

Genoa, Italy, July 21: Russian human rights activists appeal to the leaders of the G7 summit of industrial democracies to pressure the Kremlin on Chechnya. The war is "our national disgrace, but also a disgrace for the international community as a whole," says former Soviet dissident and human rights campaigner Sergei Kovalyov on behalf of the Committee for Ending the War.

———

While Boris was reinventing himself in Cap d'Antibes as a leader of émigré opposition, Sasha and Marina slowly adjusted to their new life in London. The IFCL supported them through a resettlement grant, which allowed them to rent a two-bedroom apartment in Kensington. Tolik went to the International School; his school friends' parents became Marina's first social acquaintances. She took English classes. Through the school she found some dance students. Sasha spent a lot of time with his lawyers preparing an asylum request. He also spent hours on the phone with Yuri Felshtinsky as he continued to work on their book, *Blowing Up Russia,* about the bombings of September 1999.

In London Sasha also grew close to two older men who had been legends in the KGB at the time of his recruitment. Negative legends, that is. Vladimir Bukovsky and Oleg Gordievsky personified the two archetypal foes of Kontora. Sasha had first heard of them while studying the "faces of the enemy."

Bukovsky was a quintessential dissident, perhaps the most famous anti-Soviet activist after Sakharov, a veteran of the anti-Communist underground of the 1970s who spent years as a political prisoner in the Gulag and was eventually exchanged for the leader of the Chilean Communists, who had been imprisoned by the Pinochet regime.

Gordievsky was a true spy. For years, as the head of the KGB's London station, he worked as a double agent for the British. Betrayed in 1985 by the CIA mole Aldrich Ames, Gordievsky was recalled to Moscow. He would certainly have been executed, along with other victims of Ames's treachery, if the Brits had not managed to extract him at the last minute. It took a daring operation straight out of a John le Carré novel, involving disguises and decoys and crossing the Finnish border in the false bottom of a tourist automobile.

That these two brave men, icons of anti-Soviet resistance of the previous generation, accepted him as one of their own was a tremendous boost to Sasha's morale. He called Bukovsky almost daily to discuss his writing and seek reaction to his interviews. Whenever I called him from New York, Sasha would quote Bukovsky or Gordievsky. They became his gurus. One day he cited Gordievsky as he talked about our adventures in Turkey: "You know, although I was not extracted by the CIA or MI6, the way I ran—it was a real blow to Kontora. Oleg Antonovich said that it made them a laughing stock in the trade, that Berezovsky and Goldfarb snatched me out from under their noses. They must hate me at Lubyanka as much as they did him."

He sounded happy about it.

On May 14, 2001, George Menzies, Sasha's solicitor, called to give him the good news: the Home Office had granted him political asylum. He should come to the office to sign some papers. Would he please convey George's congratulations to Marina and Tolik?

Seymour Menzies Solicitors are located behind an inconspicuous green door on the top floor of a three-story walk-up in Carter Lane, a narrow, crooked side street not far from St. Paul's Cathedral.

George Menzies, a fair-skinned, athletic, and cheerful Englishman of the sort who once managed the world, opened a bottle of champagne. It was his party, too. For countless days that winter, he had translated into coherent English Sasha's incredible tales of Khokholkov and

Gusak, Kovalyov and Skuratov, Berezovsky and the Party of War, with the aim of persuading an anonymous immigration inspector that Sasha, Marina, and Tolik had a "well-founded fear of persecution" from Putin, the man whom Tony Blair called his dear friend. For six months, that nameless official reader had become a permanent unspoken presence in the Litvinenko household. He was invested with the key attributes of a deity: he (or she?) was invisible, and possessed the power of life and death over them. And now the immigration god had spoken—the incredible was deemed credible. They could stay.

"Now we need to choose a name for you," said George Menzies.

As it turned out, the Home Office gives every new asylum seeker an option to pick a new legal name; this is part of the package. To those who are still sought by the powers from whom they had fled, a new name gives an extra bit of protection, especially when traveling abroad with new British documents.

"You choose a name for me, George," said Sasha. "You, in a way, are responsible for me becoming British, so you have the right to baptize me, so to say."

"Okay, you will be Edwin. He was the first political refugee."

Menzies had studied history. He explained that when the Romans left Britain, it was conquered by the Saxons. At around AD 614 Edwin, the Saxon prince of Northumbria, had to flee for his life from a usurper by the name of Ethelfrith. Edwin sought refuge at the court of King Redwald of East Anglia. But his protection was not secure. Ethelfrith, using a combination of threats and bribes, nearly convinced Redwald to give up Edwin.

Everything would have ended badly had not the queen, who had learned about Edwin's impending extradition, shamed King Redwald for not keeping his word. Should he go ahead and surrender Edwin, he would be punished with guilt and infamy. Redwald changed his mind and decided to put up a fight to protect his guest. He defeated Ethelfrith at a battle on the banks of the River Idel, in Nottinghamshire, at the cost of the life of his beloved son. Thus began the tradition of which Sasha was a beneficiary.

"You will be named Edwin Redwald," said Menzies. "Pauline, please write it down on the form."

"Come on, George, he cannot *possibly* be named that," said Pauline, George's secretary. "It trips off the tongue."

"You're right," sighed George. "Let's pick a less assuming surname. How about Carter, to reflect that we are here, at Carter Lane?"

So Sasha officially became Edwin Redwald Carter, a closely kept secret until the day of his death.

Some time later, Sasha received his refugee travel document from the Home Office. George Menzies assured him that it was now safe for him to travel—at least in the Western world.

"Civis Britannicus sum," he explained. "I am a British subject." It was what Lord Palmerston, Britain's prime minister in 1849, uttered in Parliament to justify sending the navy to help out a single citizen, a Gibraltar-born Jewish merchant by the name of Don Pacifico, stranded halfway around the world. Sasha's new status gave him the protections of a civis Britannicus.

In the meantime, the prosecutor general in Moscow launched an all-out search for Alexander Litvinenko, who had jumped his restraining orders. Once found, he was to be arrested and incarcerated until trial.

In December 2001 his trackers scored a breakthrough. Marina's sixty-five-year-old mother, Zinaida, was returning home after her first visit to London. At Moscow's Sheremetievo Airport she was stopped, brought to a room at Customs, and strip-searched. Initially the elderly lady thought that it was a form of harassment, but then it became clear that they were actually looking for something. They found it: a small piece of paper with her daughter's address in London. Marina had dictated it to her before she took the trip so that she could fill out the UK landing card.

Three months later, two men appeared at the Litvinenkos' flat. Marina, home alone, answered the doorbell.

"We are from the Russian Embassy to see Mr. Litvinenko," the visitor said in broken English through the speakerphone.

"Go away, there is no Litvinenko here," Marina screamed in Russian. "Go, or I'll call the police!" She was terrified. Their address was supposed to be a secret.

The visitors slipped an envelope under the door and left.

It was a summons for Sasha to appear in court for his third case, the one about stolen explosives, the pursuit that refused to go away. Sergei Barsukov, Sasha's old Moscow investigator, had signed it. But this time Sasha was not concerned at all. "Civis Britannicus sum" sounded convincing.

By the end of summer *Blowing Up Russia* was completed. While it was being printed by a small émigré press in New York, Felshtinsky contacted the MP-journalist Yuri Schekochihin to arrange for serialization in *Novaya Gazeta*. The excerpts were published on August 27, filling twenty-two pages of the tabloid-size newspaper.

Alas, the book did not provide any definitive proof of the origin of the 1999 blasts. Nevertheless, it contained a great deal of new circumstantial evidence. It detailed various terrorist operations carried out by groups created by and affiliated with the FSB, suggesting a pattern that fit with the apartment bombings.

First, there was the Lazovsky case. In the fall of 1994, just as the first Chechen War was about to start, Sasha was sharing an office at the FSB with another investigator, Evgeny Makeyev. Makeyev was looking into an explosion that took place on November 18, 1994, on a railway bridge over the Yauza River in central Moscow. It would have been a major terrorist attack if the explosion had occurred while a passenger train crossed the bridge. Apparently the bomb malfunctioned, killing the man who was planting it. A few days later there was another blast in Moscow, in a passenger bus. Due to another apparent mishap by the terrorists, there were no passengers nearby; only the bus driver was wounded. At the time the blasts were blamed on unspecified Chechens. The first Chechen War started within days.

Two years later, the case of the '94 bombings was solved by a Moscow detective named Vladimir Tshai. The man killed on the bridge was Ret. Capt. Andrei Schelenkov, an employee of the oil trading company Lanaco. The owner of Lanaco was Maxim Lazovsky, a longtime FSB agent. The man who planted the bus bomb was apprehended and confessed. He was Lazovsky's driver, Vladimir Akimov.

Tshai arrested Lazovsky and Ret. Lieutenant Colonel Vorobiev, who also turned out to be an FSB agent.

The evidence was overwhelming. In addition to the two bombs, the group carried out several murders, with apparent FSB backing. Lazovsky and Vorobiev were convicted of terrorism, and their FSB connections became part of the record. They never explained who ordered them to plant those bombs, or why. They had no apparent motives themselves. In his last statement in court, Vorobiev called the case "a mockery of the secret services." Lazovsky served three and a half years. He was killed shortly after his release, shot by an assassin on his own doorstep. The man who arrested him, Detective Tshai, died in April 1997 at the age of thirty-nine of sudden, inexplicable organ failure. He was a legend—the best detective in Moscow. Rumors flew that he had been poisoned as FSB revenge for the Lazovsky case.

Then there was the case of a Russian officer in Chechnya who in 1996 launched a massacre in the village of Svobodny and was arrested as a war criminal. According to *Blowing Up Russia,* the officer was told by the Agency that he had two options: he could work as the leader of an undercover hit squad, or go to jail. He chose to form a team of twelve people, all of whom are alleged to have perpetrated atrocities in Chechnya. Beginning in 1998, according to the book, they carried out "liquidations" in Ukraine, Iraq, Yugoslavia, and Moldova. The members of the group started to disappear in 2000, but before going into hiding, their leader left a video confession, which Sasha obtained.

Such stories—there were many in the book—along with a fresh recap of the Ryazan incident, made *Blowing Up Russia* a minor sensation in Moscow that summer. The book did not prove anything, but it made an outlandish theory seem plausible. Was it possible that the secret service was prepared to blow up houses with sleeping innocent citizens?

I was not yet convinced, but Sasha and Boris were excited beyond belief. I sensed the thrill in their voices whenever I spoke with them by phone. I could not quite understand it, based on the evidence uncovered so far.

I began to understand their excitement only when they separately made one nearly identical comment.

"Imagine their faces when they read this in Kontora," said Sasha.

"I'd give a lot to see Volodya's face when he reads it," said Boris.

For them the book was not aimed at the general public; it was not supposed to prove anything. It was a personal message to their nemeses, a declaration of war: We think you did it, and we are out to get you. Indeed, I thought, never mind that the book was hardly a best seller; if the FSB had, in fact, blown up those houses, the book would create havoc in the Kremlin and perhaps provoke a reaction that would become a proof in itself.

It has become a cliché to say that September 11, 2001, changed everything, yet for many things in Russia, which had nothing to do with Osama bin Laden, the cliché held true. In exchange for support of the American war on terror, Putin got what may have ultimately saved his presidency: U.S. acquiescence to his war in Chechnya and the dismantling of Russian democracy. After the attacks, Boris and I went to Washington as soon as we could. The news that Putin had become an American ally was told to us by Tom Graham, the senior Russia hand in the Bush administration, who was then on the Policy Planning Staff of the State Department. It was clear to me that from now on, we would be viewed in Washington as the enemy of a friend.

"Volodya is so fucking lucky," said Boris when we were leaving the State Department building. "If there was no bin Laden, he should have invented him. I wonder whether the Americans understand that he is not their friend at all. He will play them and the Muslims against each other, exploring every weakness to his advantage."

After nearly a year of pleading to the Brits for forgiveness for smuggling Sasha into the UK I was allowed to return. I got to London just in time for the event that I had been planning from my New York exile: the launch of a campaign to remind the Western world about the 1999 apartment block bombings. On December 14, 2001, the Union of Committees of Soldiers' Mothers, the largest NGO in Russia, held a conference in Moscow on the war in Chechnya sponsored by the IFCL. Soldiers' Mothers came from all over Russia. The hall was packed with international journalists, and it was expected that Boris would address the gathering via teleconference from London. It was his first, albeit virtual, appearance in Moscow since he went into exile more than a year earlier.

Boris used the occasion to state that after reading Sasha's book, he had become convinced that the Moscow apartment houses were blown up by the FSB. As a result, the foreign press jumped on the story for the first time. Perhaps it was the audience of soldiers' mothers that did it. Their children were dying in Chechnya, and they seemed to accept the claim as perfectly plausible; no one in the hall raised any objection. Or it could have been the fact that the bombings were retroactively cast as Russia's 9/11. Or maybe it was the drama of a fugitive oligarch accusing a president of mass murder. Whatever the reason, Boris's statement primed a PR avalanche.

The *New York Times*' bureau chief came from Moscow to London to interview Boris, and then traveled to Ryazan to recap the story of the foiled attack there, producing two front-page articles within a week. *Time* magazine compared the Putin-Berezovsky contest to that of Stalin and Trotsky. Then, on March 5, in a packed hall in London, Boris presided over the world premiere of the documentary *Assassination of Russia*. The film was made by two French producers who had initially worked with NTV to expand the "Sugar of Ryazan" program. When NTV was taken over by Gazprom and its journalists defected to TV-6, the project traveled with them. In January 2002, however, the authorities closed TV-6. Boris lost his remaining voice on Russia's airwaves, and the film, 70 percent completed, hung in limbo. The producers came to Boris to finance the remaining work. From that moment Sasha and Felshtinsky became the film's principal consultants.

Leaders of Liberal Russia, Sergey Yushenkov and Yuli Rybakov, flew in from Moscow specifically for the premiere. They said they planned to promote the film around the world "to expose the government cover-up of the horrific crime that led to war." Admittedly, the film did not present any new facts, but in the words of *Kommersant,* "For the first time, the filmmakers collected all the facts and minor details related to the Ryazan case, placed them chronologically," and put them in the context of "some controversial testimony and statements made by the highest officials, including then-Prime Minister Putin."

The London screening was an opening shot in a campaign planned by Yushenkov as a principal theme for the new party.

"The evidence contained in the film is rather persuasive," declared Yushenkov, as he distributed copies among reporters who met him at Sheremetievo Airport upon return from London. "It demonstrates how the secret services deceived Russian citizens." He announced that Liberal Russia would distribute copies of the film around the country. Hopefully, "a television channel can be found that is not afraid to show the film," he told Radio Echo Moscow. He added that screenings at movie theaters were also planned.

From the outset, the FSB mounted a fierce campaign to block the film. Rybakov brought a hundred copies from London to St. Petersburg, but they were confiscated at Customs, in violation of his parliamentary immunity. He later received death threats. His staff members, who organized screenings around St. Petersburg, were harassed and beaten by strangers. Alexander Kostarev, a member of the Liberal Russia governing council, was severely beaten on the street in Perm after he arranged a public screening. No TV station in Russia dared to show the film. However, the main channels in the three former Soviet Baltic republics, Estonia, Latvia, and Lithuania, showed it, under IFCL sponsorship.

In the meantime, Russian video pirates sniffed the money that was to be made; there was a growing demand for the film on the street. The pirates eagerly accepted a couple of master tapes quietly provided by the IFCL and filled the outdoor markets and railway station kiosks with tens of thousands of copies of *Assassination of Russia,* making it an underground best seller. In early April, Liberal Russia deputies distributed copies of the film in the Duma. Everyone wanted to have it, even though the deputies promptly voted down a motion to set up a parliamentary investigation of the 1999 bombings.

On April 14, Agence France-Presse reported the results of a poll by Russia's public opinion research center: 6 percent of the respondents said they were sure that the FSB staged the bombings; 37 percent refused to rule out the possibility; 38 percent did not believe the allegation, but only 16 percent were completely convinced that the bombs were planted by Chechen rebels; 39 percent insisted that the allegations should be thoroughly investigated. Over half said that Berezovsky's film should be broadcast on Russian television.

As paradoxical as these results seemed, we nonetheless counted them as a success beyond our expectations. We had not placed a single ad. The coverage in the government-controlled newscasts was openly hostile. The allegations themselves ascribed an unimaginable monstrosity to the government that, according to the same opinion polls, enjoyed overwhelming popularity. The majority of respondents had neither seen the film nor read the book. Yet everybody had heard of the charges, and almost half accepted Boris's and Sasha's claims as credible.

The Russian national psyche is deeply conflicted at its heart. There is a medieval streak of masochism in Russians' attitude to their *vlast*, which they perceive as divine and fearsome, something that is reflected in the reverence accorded such historical tyrants as Ivan the Terrible ("terrible" is an ambiguous translation of the Russian; a better choice would be the affectionate "awesome").

In a brilliant analysis of this phenomenon in an article about the film in *Time* magazine, Moscow correspondent Yuri Zarakhovich compared the apartment bombings to the famous episode in Russian history when Boris Godunov, the head of the Kremlin's secret police, was voted by the Boyars to succeed the heirless Czar Fyodor, the son of Ivan the Awesome. Godunov's electoral triumph was marred by the allegation that he had cleared his way to the throne by murdering the infant nephew of Fyodor, a grandson of Ivan who might have claimed the throne. The allegation haunted Godunov throughout his reign, in spite of extensive propaganda efforts that he introduced: he "forced Russians to chant a daily prayer to him, while secret police kept hunting for signs of any sedition, and enticed people to squeal." Eventually, the country's economic situation deteriorated, and the fable of the murdered infant became the driving force of a popular uprising.

"Unlike allegations of complicity in one innocent child's murder back in the 17th century, claims of involvement in 247 innocent deaths will hardly bring the regime down now, not after all the millions of such deaths in modern Russian history," wrote Zarakhovich. "Still, the worse things become, the more people will talk. One day, the talk might grow into a roar once again."

The film was the last straw for the Kremlin. On the day of the world premiere in London, the FSB responded by announcing that Berezovsky was "financing terrorist activity" in Chechnya and accused him of taking part in the kidnapping and murder of an Interior Ministry general in 1999. FSB Director Nikolai Patrushev went on TV to state ominously that the FSB would "duly document" Boris's terrorist activities, pass them on "to our partners abroad, and wait for a proper reaction from them." The prosecutor general's office added that "for the safety of investigators, witnesses and the preservation of evidence, we cannot yet make public the documents in our possession about Berezovsky's involvement in the events in Chechnya." But the announcement left no doubt that the Kremlin was gearing up to strike back.

CHAPTER 12

THE SLEUTHS

In the aftermath of Sasha's book and Boris's film, the educated classes of Russia plunged into a bout of soul-searching. Was it possible that their *vlast* was not just a mildly authoritarian regime, which, many argued, was something that Russia needed in order to emerge from oligarchic chaos, but an embodiment of evil itself, rooted in the original sin of killing some three hundred innocent souls in their sleep?

The angst was well reflected in a thoughtful article by Dmitry Furman, a sociologist at the Russian Academy of Sciences, explaining why so many Russians readily accepted the horrific allegation. The theory that the FSB was behind the bombings, he argued, had inner logic: blowing up the apartment houses and blaming it on the Chechens would provoke a war, a response whose assertiveness would boost Putin's popularity on the eve of the elections. The plot appeared rational and successful, except for the disappointing mishap in Ryazan. "The villains in this theory are clever, resourceful and demonic."

The trouble with the official claim that Wahhabi terrorists were behind the attack was "that it is not based on a model of rational behavior of clever villains, but the behavior of idiots, whose motives are impossible to comprehend. . . . There is a striking disparity between the carefully executed plan and the fact that its aim is absolutely incomprehensible." The analogy to 9/11 did not work, argued Furman, because bin Laden had a rational plan: to damage America and provoke anti-Islamic backlash. But why would Wahhabi terrorists want to blow up the working-class apartment houses? Was it to stop the war, or to provoke it? To damage Russia? It didn't make sense. "The second idiocy, implied by the official version, is the idiocy of the FSB. The Ryazan operation (if it was an operation, and not an averted terrorist act) is so ridiculous, that all attempts to explain it fail.

"That the first version implies rational behavior, and the second, idiocy, does not mean that the first is correct, and the second is not. But when people face something very frightening, it's easier for them to believe in a devil's plan, than in the actions of idiots or some absurdity. It's easier to believe that the [young Prince] Dmitry was killed by Boris Godunov, and not the official version, that he stabbed himself to death with a small knife."

Thus, Furman concluded, Russians had a choice: deem their *vlast* criminal or idiotic. Berezovsky had already won, regardless of the truth.

But it was not good enough for me. I needed the truth. Granted, Putin was the quintessential KGB man, a murderous type. But being murderous does not automatically mean being guilty of every murder. And there were other murderous types out there, as I learned while watching the towers go down on 9/11. At heart I was a research scientist trained to treat evidence skeptically. Here I differed with Boris, a mathematician, for whom logic, not evidence, was supreme. For him, Ryazan was sufficiently convincing. For me, Ryazan was impressive but circumstantial. I had no scruples trumpeting the FSB theory in the media because of the obvious official cover-up. But I still wanted to get to the bottom of it.

I was not alone in this. Almost unnoticed among the guests at the London film premiere was Tanya Morozova, a quiet thirty-one-year-old woman with large brown eyes and high Slavic cheekbones. Her mother was killed at the bombing at Guryanova Street on September 9. When introduced to her, those present at the London event tended to become reflective, if only for a moment, reminded of the human stakes that somehow got lost amid the high drama of the Kremlin power intrigue.

Yuri Felshtinsky had discovered Tanya in Milwaukee, Wisconsin, where she lived with her American husband and a four-year-old son. He explained that we were continuing to investigate the bombings. There are two views as to who could have killed her mother. Of all people, she was one who must want to know the truth. We would like her to come to London, hear us out, and decide for herself.

Tanya agreed. In London, she did not say much; she came to listen. But after seeing the film she called her younger sister, Aliona, in Denver to say that the rumor that they had brushed off as sheer madness might actually be true. There were serious grounds for believing that their own government could have planted the bomb that killed their mother and ninety-three of their neighbors. Would Aliona agree to be part of a committee to investigate the allegations?

Aliona was a survivor of the Guryanova Street blast. After Tanya had married and moved to Milwaukee, Aliona, who was twenty-three at the time, stayed with their mother in the one-bedroom apartment in which she had grown up, in a working-class neighborhood of Pechatniki. On the evening of September 8 she was out with her boyfriend, Sergei, who lived in the section next to theirs in the huge apartment block. On the way home they stopped to chat with some friends on the leafy patio with benches and a playground in front of the building.

"Let's have some dinner and watch TV at my place," Sergei said. She agreed. Shortly after midnight Sergei said that he was going to the kitchen to have a cigarette. Those were his last words.

Initially Aliona thought an earthquake had struck. In her shock she heard no noise, as if the sound had been turned off in a movie theater. The wall with Sergei's bookshelf and TV suddenly detached from the rest of the room and slid down, leaving her on the couch at the edge of an abyss. She did not lose consciousness, and her hearing returned within seconds. As the sounds of the street reached her from the outside, she realized that she was looking across the gap that had formed in the middle of the building. Somewhere in that gap lay her boyfriend, his kitchen, her mother, and their entire apartment, which went down with the nine floors that collapsed around the two central entrances.

She was rescued by firefighters. As she wandered distraught through the pandemonium filled with smoke, police, fire trucks, and paramedics, a CNN crew spotted her.

"Were you in the building? Do you need to make a call? You can use my phone," yelled a man with a camera over the noise of the sirens.

"I have no one to call, my sister is in America," she said. "I don't remember the number."

Eventually, courtesy of CNN, she contacted her sister. The next morning Tanya flew to Moscow.

They never found their mother's body. They became frustrated by the nearly inhumane insensitivity of the countless officials whom they had to see because without their mother's body there could be no death record, and all their documents were destroyed. One day, they stood in front of their apartment block with the gaping hole in the middle—four entrances out of six were still intact—amid the crowd of survivors and journalists, separated from their old courtyard by a police line. The powers that be had decided to raze what remained of the block. When the demolition charges boomed, they quivered and burst into tears and clutched each other. Somewhere under that rubble of dust and concrete that bulldozers were about to level lay their mother.

A year later, in the aftermath of 9/11, the contrast to how the Americans handled the consequences struck them.

"The Americans went with a fine-toothed comb over the World Trade Center wreckage, looking for the tiniest clue," Tanya told me. "Why didn't the FSB look for evidence? Why did they bulldoze the place? Did they have something to hide, perhaps?"

It took Aliona three months to restore her papers. As soon as she could, she got on a plane to Chicago. She stayed at Tanya's house for a while. The following fall she enrolled at the University of Denver, majoring in computer design. She had no intention of ever returning home again.

"As for who did it, somehow it did not matter to me initially," recalled Aliona. "They told us it was the Chechens, but I didn't really know much about them. Politics never interested me. They might as well have said 'the Martians.' Eventually I learned all the politics behind it, that someone was playing with us as if we were tin soldiers. But that was much later."

Before going home after the London film premiere, Tanya attended a brainstorming session in Boris's office to decide what to do next. The group included the two Duma members, Yushenkov and Rybakov, Boris, Sasha, Felshtinsky, and myself.

One idea was that Yushenkov set up a commission in Russia to investigate the bombings. He would try to get official Duma support for that. We agreed that Boris should not be a part of it, since he was too controversial. Tanya and Aliona would represent the victims. Felshtinsky and Sasha would continue their investigation, and I would be in charge of the publicity campaign outside Russia.

There was someone in Moscow, Sasha said, who could be very useful to Yushenkov. His name was Mikhail Trepashkin, a former FSB investigator, currently a lawyer. Sasha vouched for him. He offered to call Trepashkin to ask him to see Yushenkov as soon as possible. Also, Sasha noted, Aliona and Tanya were officially considered crime victims. By Russian law, they could get access to the investigation file and participate in court proceedings if anyone were ever to go on trial for the bombing. He suggested that the sisters retain Trepashkin to represent them. Tanya duly signed a power of attorney to Trepashkin.

As we were saying goodbye, I could not help wondering how this newly formed brotherhood would be reflected in the operative report that Russian intelligence would shortly submit to Putin. I tried to look at things through the eyes of the services, as Sasha had taught me in Turkey. Surely all our movements and communications were being watched. Would we be classified as a "subversive émigré organization" in the Soviet style? Or "a terrorist sympathizer cell" in the modern way? How many spies would monitor us?

On April 23, 2002, Sergei Yushenkov arrived in Washington with a large box of copies of *Assassination of Russia*. His schedule, organized by the IFCL, included the usual circuit for an overseas visitor who wanted to make a point to the makers of U.S. foreign policy: the State Department, Congress, key journalists, the expert community. Sergei was not concerned about the absence of direct evidence. He was a politician: he looked at the bombing story from a totally different angle.

"I don't have to prove anything," he explained. "The government has been accused of mass murder of its own citizens, and half of the people believe it; this is enough for me. Presumption of innocence does not apply to governments; it's a device to protect people from the government. Putin has an obligation to dispel the suspicions. Instead, he is covering up. What else is there to prove?"

The meetings in Washington were tough. Tom Graham at the State Department had warned me that barring direct evidence of official complicity in the bombings, the film—and its promoters—would be discounted in Washington.

We brought Aliona from Denver. She and Yushenkov hit it off immediately. They were kindred souls, two Russians on a hopeless mission in the disinterested imperial city.

"The bombings in Moscow? This is like our 9/11, isn't it?" asked a congressional staffer who listened politely to Yushenkov. His expression of deliberate attention could not conceal profound skepticism: these guys are saying that their secret services did it. Well, some people, the lunatic fringe, say that the WTC attacks were the work of the CIA.

Our visit to the State Department was also discouraging. We were received by a junior officer from the Russia desk, who politely took a copy of the film and uttered some platitudes. We were indeed discounted, as Tom Graham had warned.

"This is to be expected," Yushenkov said to cheer up Aliona over lunch in the congressional cafeteria. "Just imagine that we'd come to Washington, say, in 1944, to complain about Stalin. We wouldn't get a sympathetic hearing, would we? Uncle Joe was Roosevelt's favorite ally, so he could get away with anything. It took Americans some time to realize that he was a more serious threat than Hitler. A very similar situation exists now. Still, it's important that we say what we have to say. Some years later they will remember our visit when they realize what Putin is all about."

But some people did take us seriously. After the screening for the staff of the Senate Foreign Relations Committee, our tapes were snatched up like hotcakes.

"Don't be discouraged," an aide to one of the most powerful men on the Hill told us. "We just cannot go out and say that the president of Russia is a mass murderer. But it is important that we know it. Your stuff is serious. I will make sure that the senator sees it."

The most sympathetic hearing we got was from the pundits who packed the conference hall at the Kennan Institute of the Woodrow Wilson Center. It was an act of courage for Blair Ruble, Kennan's director, to let us show the film in his domain; other major venues in Washington had refused.

"Look, we need to protect our operation in Moscow, we have a branch there," another think-tanker had told me when I had called to inquire. "The most important thing for us is access, so we don't want the risk of Russians cutting us off. And they watch."

They watched indeed. The Kennan screening was advertised around town and open to the public. I looked at the registry: there were two guests from the Russian Embassy. I spotted them easily—the KGB stamp was instantly recognizable—in the second row, close enough to the podium to get good-quality audio on their hidden recorders.

"Everyone knows I am not an admirer of Berezovsky," spoke the dean of Kremlinology, Peter Reddaway, after the film. "But the film is convincing and Putin must respond to the allegations to reassure us that he is not what he appears to be." The two embassy types listened with stone faces.

Yushenkov's tour lasted a week and included screenings in New York and Boston, at places like Columbia and Harvard. Invariably he made a strong impression. He was a good speaker, and he projected passion and conviction. Aliona was obviously smitten; she listened to him with her face raised and eyes fixed as if he was a sage, and they spent hours talking when she took him on sightseeing tours.

A year later, Yushenkov was assassinated in Moscow by an unknown gunman. Aliona called me from Denver.

"You know what we talked about during all those hours we spent together?" she said. "It was about Russia. He was in love with Russia. He recited poetry—Yesenin, Lermontov—that I had never known. Actually, he transformed me. After I'd realized that it was the FSB that bombed our house, I had a problem with Russia. Perhaps he sensed that. He said, 'You may never go back, but you should know that that scum that killed your mother, they are not Russia. You and your sister are.' He promised that he would get to the bottom of it. And he knew what he was up against. He was the greatest, the most wonderful man I've ever known."

Tbilisi, February 1, 2002: Russian Security Council Secretary Vladimir Rushailo arrives in the former Soviet republic of Georgia for talks about the situation in Pankisi Gorge, the region bordering Chechnya. The Russians claim that the Gorge is used as a training and staging ground for the Chechen guerrillas. Rushailo demands that the Chechens be ousted from Georgia and threatens military action. Akhmed Zakayev, deputy prime minister of Maskhadov's government, says that there are no Chechen bases in Georgia, only eleven thousand to twelve thousand refugees. Georgia requests U.S. military assistance. On February 28 the Pentagon reveals a plan to send two hundred military advisers to Georgia. Zakayev welcomes the arrival of Americans: "The Chechen side is eager to cooperate with any force waging war on terrorism."

On the day Yushenkov arrived in Washington, Yuri Felshtinsky and Sasha Litvinenko landed in Tbilisi. Sasha, wearing dark glasses, went through passport control as Edwin Redwald Carter, civis Britannicus. Yuri went through separately, and they reunited in a room at the Sheraton Metekhi Palace, where they were joined by the head of a local security company, "the most reliable and best connected in Georgia," according to Boris's security advisers in London. They had come on a secret and dangerous mission: to meet up with the man who claimed to be Achemez Gochiyayev, the FSB's main suspect in the Moscow bombings.

"There is a notion of a 'beacon' in our trade," Sasha explained to me. "After the big splash with the book and the film, we became a beacon. It was only a matter of time before someone contacted us." Sure enough, a few days after the screening, one of Boris's aides received a phone call from Georgia. After that, Felshtinsky handled the negotiations using a clean, pay-as-you-go mobile phone. Yes, of course, he would be interested to talk to Gochiyayev. He agreed to wait on a certain date at a particular street corner in Tbilisi. Felshtinsky would be holding a copy of the *International Herald Tribune*. The man who would meet him would be wearing a green baseball cap. He would take him to see Gochiyayev.

"We can guarantee your security within the perimeter of the capital," said the security man. "But we cannot guarantee anything if you go out of town. So don't. Out of town, the only way to protect you would be to send a platoon in a personnel carrier. As an American you are a prime target for kidnappers."

Equipped with a copy of the *Herald Tribune*, Felshtinsky went to meet the contact. Sasha watched from a distance in case of trouble.

"If you are ready, let's go. I've got a car," said the man in the green baseball cap, a middle-aged Chechen, after they exchanged code words.

"Go where?" inquired Felshtinsky.

"Pankisi Gorge."

"No, I can't. Why don't you bring him here?"

"Impossible, the place is filled with FSB. The Gorge is the only place where they don't go. We've got to go there."

After twenty minutes of arguing, it became clear that a face-to-face meeting with Gochiyayev was impossible. Felshtinsky brought the man to a hotel—not the one where they were staying—where Sasha had rented a room for cash, expecting this kind of contingency. Sasha knocked on the door almost as soon as they entered the room.

"How many cars do you have?" he asked the Chechen.

"One."

"We have one, too," said Sasha. "And I have counted five loitering around. That means that there are at least three from Kontora."

"You see?" said the Chechen. "I told you, the Gorge is the only safe place."

They gave the Chechen a tape recorder, a video camera, and a questionnaire for Gochiyayev that Sasha had prepared. They agreed to meet the next day, when the Chechen would bring Gochiyayev's statement.

The Chechen called Felshtinsky's cell phone three hours later. "I am at home," he said, "but I had company—as far as they could go. You watch out. See you tomorrow."

The meeting never took place. Instead, at six in the morning, the security man appeared.

"You are going home," he declared. "First plane. Leaves in two hours. We cannot guarantee anything, the way things are developing."

They were rushed to the airport in a convoy of Jeeps. A dozen guards surrounded them as they entered the terminal.

"My people will be on the plane until you get off in Frankfurt," their bodyguard said. "From then on you are on your own."

As Felshtinsky and Sasha later learned, the previous night in Tbilisi the car that was assigned to them had been ambushed. The driver was killed.

The Chechen go-between resurfaced two weeks later via e-mail. The tape and the questionnaire were ready, he wrote. He wanted to keep the equipment for further use. He told them how to get in touch with a contact in Paris to get the material.

Tbilisi, Georgia, July 16: Adam Dekkushev, another of the suspects in the 1999 bombings, is extradited to Russia following his arrest by Georgian authorities. Upon arrival in Moscow he is transferred to Lefortovo prison.

On July 25, Felshtinsky and Litvinenko reported their findings to the Public Commission, an unofficial body set up by Yushenkov after the

Duma voted down his motion to formally investigate the matter. That is, the report was virtual: the Commission gathered in Moscow with the press present; the two sleuths were in London, talking by video link. By then, the Commission had acquired a new chairman, the widely respected human rights activist and Duma deputy Sergei Kovalyov, with Yushenkov as his deputy. In the twenty-member group there were five Duma members, including the MP-journalist Yuri Schekochihin. That was about all the parliamentary support Yushenkov could muster after two years of the Kremlin's artful use of carrots and sticks with the legislature. Mikhail Trepashkin was present as an adviser.

That Felshtinsky and Litvinenko were able to find the man who was Number One on the FSB's Most Wanted list was by itself a slap at Kontora. The substance of Gochiyayev's testimony as related by Sasha kept everyone in Moscow spellbound for nearly two hours.

First, Sasha said, there was no doubt that the man who sent the testimony was indeed Gochiyayev. This was confirmed by a top British forensic expert who compared the witness's photographs with the one on the FSB Web site. Should they wish, the authorities could further verify his identity by the extensive personal information, such as his residence and army service details, offered in the testimony, and by an analysis of the handwriting of his six-page statement.

In his statement Gochiyayev admitted that the ground-floor warehouse spaces in the bombed-out buildings had been rented by his construction company using his ID. But he insisted that he did not do it himself. He claimed to have been tricked by a business partner, an ethnic Russian whom he now believed had been working for the FSB.

"He said he discovered a good opportunity of distributing food supplies and offered a joint venture. First I ordered for him a stock of mineral water. . . . He sold it and paid on time. Then he said that he would need to rent warehousing facilities in the southeast [of Moscow], where he had many buyers. I helped him get space at Guryanova St., Kashirskoye Hwy., Borisov Ponds and Kapotnya," Gochiyayev wrote.

On the night of the first explosion, at Guryanova Street, Gochiyayev was not at home. This, he believed, saved him, because the police could not find him that night. His partner called him at 5 a.m. to say that there was a small fire at the Guryanova Street location and that he should go there immediately. Luckily, before leaving a short time later, he turned on the news and heard about the explosion. He went into hiding instead.

For reasons that Sasha and Felshtinsky could not explain, Gochiyayev did not provide the name of his partner. However, he gave another important piece of information. It was he himself, he claimed, who tipped off the authorities about the two other locations in Moscow that were rented by his company. After the second explosion occurred on September 13 and his photograph appeared in the newspapers, he realized that he had been set up. Before leaving town he used his mobile phone to call the police, the fire department, and the emergency service to give them two other addresses that he suspected were part of his partner's plot.

That was an extremely important point, Sasha emphasized. What Gochiyayev said fit with the published reports. Indeed, on September 13 a bomb had been defused in a building in the Kapotnya area. In addition, a warehouse with several tons of explosives and six unused timing devices had been discovered at Borisov Ponds. How the police learned about these sites had never been explained; now Gochiyayev had provided an explanation. If indeed he was the source of the tip, it was easily verifiable because all emergency phone calls are recorded and the telephone companies store all mobile phone calls.

Everyone present at the teleconference knew that it was pointless to ask the authorities to cooperate with the Commission. But Yushenkov's approach was to generate enough public pressure on the official probe so that the findings of the Commission could not be ignored.

"Sergei Nikolaevich," Sasha said to Yushenkov, "I see Mikhail Trepashkin sitting there. I suggest that you charge him with verifying Gochiyayev's claims. If anyone can get to the bottom of it, he will."

Over the summer of 2002 I spent almost five weeks with Sasha working on his second book, *The Gang from Lubyanka*. About half of that time we spent on the beach: two weeks at the Spanish resort of Sitges and a week in Italy. The book was in the form of questions and answers, adopted from a series of interviews that Sasha taped throughout the preceding year in London, which had been transcribed. The book retold Sasha's life from his first visits to the zoo with his grandfather in Nalchik, to the granting of asylum through the good efforts of George Menzies the previous year. Much of the story was devoted to a horrific depiction of the lives and mores of the FSB and to Sasha's take on the epic battle between the oligarchs and security services in the late 1990s. The final section was an update on the bombing investigation, including the Gochiyayev file.

There was one new item: a video and a transcript, which he brought with him to Spain, depicting an odd episode, adding another bizarre twist to the bombing saga.

The material came from Yuli Rybakov, the Duma deputy from St. Petersburg who was one of the members of the Public Commission. He had retrieved something from the official Duma record: a remark by the speaker, Gennady Seleznyov of the Communist Party, on the morning of September 13, 1999, just hours after the second explosion in Moscow. According to the transcript, Seleznyov interrupted the proceedings with a surprising announcement.

"I have just received a report. According to information from Rostov-on-Don, an apartment building in the city of Volgodonsk was blown up last night," he said.

In response, the nationalist Vladimir Zhirinovsky chimed in, "And there is a nuclear power station in Volgodonsk."

Yet there had been no explosion in Volgodonsk on that day. A bomb did indeed destroy an apartment house in that southern town, but three days later. Nineteen people were killed.

When the news of the actual Volgodonsk blast reached the Duma chamber on September 16, Zhirinovsky spoke again: "Mr. Speaker, please explain, how come you told us Monday about the blast that occurred on Thursday?"

"Thank you, I have noted your remark," responded Seleznyov, and promptly turned off Zhirinovsky's microphone. On the video of the Duma session, Zhirinovsky can be seen gesticulating wildly.

Yuli Rybakov sent an official request to the prosecutor general's office asking that Seleznyov be interviewed about the incident. He received no response.

"What do you make of this?" I asked Sasha, as he prepared for a run on the Spanish beach.

"Well, to me it appears that someone had mixed up the order of the blasts, the usual Kontora mess-up. Moscow-2 was on the 13th, and Volgodonsk on the 16th, but they got it to the speaker the other way around. I need to talk to Trepashkin, perhaps he can dig up something on that."

He donned his baseball cap and went out for a run, looking somewhat like Forrest Gump.

Two weeks later, when I met Sasha at the Milan Airport for our final get-together on *The Gang from Lubyanka,* he brought Trepashkin's report.

"The man who gave Seleznyov the note about Volgodonsk was FSB," he announced. "Just as I thought."

It was not the first time that Mikhail Trepashkin had proven himself to be highly capable. For months I had been hearing his name; Sasha had been promoting him relentlessly as "his man" in Moscow. By then Trepashkin was both a consultant to Yushenkov and the attorney for Tanya and Aliona. Sasha argued that there was no one better than Trepashkin to organize the distribution of *The Gang from Lubyanka,* which I planned to print in Riga and then try to bring into Russia across the Latvian border.

Kontora was hardly indifferent to Trepashkin. In January 2002, shortly after Sasha started calling him from London, the FSB showed up at his door with a search warrant. Later on, when his case file became available to his lawyers, a remarkable document was revealed, which had apparently initiated the investigation. In a letter to the Russian prosecutor's office, the FSB claimed that Trepashkin entered into a conspiracy with Litvinenko and Berezovsky, on behalf of the British secret service MI5. The purpose of their conspiracy was "to discredit the FSB through alleging that it had organized the 1999 Moscow bombings." Of course, it was perfectly true that the three men were working together to investigate the FSB's role in the attacks, but it was a typical Agency maneuver to suggest that Trepashkin might be guilty of treason by claiming that he was doing it at the behest of British Intelligence.

The January 2002 search at Trepashkin's home produced nothing, except for one ten-year-old KGB file marked "Classified," unrelated to the bombings, that had apparently been forgotten in his desk, and a few gun cartridges, which he said were planted during the search. He was promptly charged with divulging state secrets, exceeding official powers, and possessing illegal arms. He was not arrested, however, nor even called in for questioning. He was simply ordered not to leave town without the prosecutor's permission. "Just to keep him on the hook," Sasha explained. "They are listening to his telephone so that they know what we are up to, and they will leave him alone for a while."

Sasha was of the same opinion as I: sooner or later Kontora would crack down on Trepashkin. "But don't worry," he said. "He is solid as a rock. He will never break. You can rely on him."

I did not know what to think. I needed to meet the man personally, to look him in the eye, as George Bush would say.

After my adventures in Turkey I could not go to Russia, and it was useless for Trepashkin to ask for permission to go to a Western country. But thanks to the use of a friend's telephone, he managed to tell me he could slip out to Kiev for a day.

Unlike Sasha, who joined the KGB in its waning days, Trepashkin had had ten years of distinguished service as a Lubyanka investigator during the Soviet era. His specialty had been the underground trade in stolen art and antiques. In the post-Soviet period, he moved to Internal Affairs and worked directly for Nikolai Patrushev, who later succeeded Putin as FSB director. He investigated corruption in Kontora and the connections of some of its officers to Chechen criminal groups in Moscow. Once, Trepashkin intercepted a planeload of weapons sold by some rogue FSB officers to the rebels, which won him a medal. Yet he broke with Kontora in 1996, when he made public allegations of corruption. That was how he ended up on the URPO target list. Married for the second time, he had two young children and a teenage boy from his first marriage.

Waiting for him at the President Hotel in Kiev, I recognized him at once: a short, dark-haired man of forty-five, with a perceptive gaze and a reserved smile. He was the complete opposite of Sasha: unemotional, not spontaneous, an introvert. Over several hours of conversation, which continued in a Georgian restaurant, I could not get him to bare his soul, something that had happened instantly with Sasha in Turkey. He avoided reflective talk and ignored all my efforts to draw him into a discussion of the higher reasons behind his self-appointed mission. He would not dwell on politics and did not want to generalize. He behaved as if the apartment bombings were just another crime that he was charged with investigating.

I gave up trying to gauge his deeper motivations. But I wanted to make sure that he understood the limits of what we could do for him if he got into trouble.

"Misha, if I may, do you understand that they will put you in jail if you pursue this?" I asked.

"I am not going to break any laws, Alexander Davidovich. If they jail me, it would be illegal."

"That's my point, Mikhail Ivanovich," I said, acceding to his more formal terms of address. "I have to tell you, I would very much like you to continue, but if you do, you may end up badly, and there is very little that we would be able to do for you."

"I am not doing this for you," he said. "I have my clients, Tatyana Alexandrovna and Aliona Alexandrovna Morozova. And also I am working for Sergei Nikolaevich Yushenkov, the Duma deputy."

The more informal my comments, the more formally he responded. He refused to be initiated into my brotherhood. So be it, I thought. He won't accept the obvious: that he was fighting the system. He preferred to pretend that he was just solving a crime. Perhaps that was his way of avoiding the truth that for all his life he had served the wrong master. One thing was sure, however: I trusted him. He was after the evidence. To keep my conscience clean I warned him for the last time that he was heading straight to prison if he didn't stop, and then we went on to discuss the next matter at hand: getting Sasha's book to Moscow.

Trepashkin insisted that even though the operation was to be secret, it should be strictly legal: the paperwork accompanying the shipment must be in order, it had to be cleared through Customs, and so on. Of course, I agreed, and kept to myself the observation that none of this would protect him. When we said goodbye I did not expect to ever see him again.

On a rainy afternoon in August 2002, Trepashkin met a truck from Riga with ten thousand copies of *The Gang from Lubyanka*, cleared through Customs at a highway border crossing as "printed material." He directed the driver to a secret warehouse that he had rented. The next week, the book appeared in kiosks in central Moscow and became a best seller. The former interior minister Anatoly Kulikov announced that he planned to bring a libel suit against Sasha based on his portrayal in the book. Later on that year, two more shipments went through along the same route.

Moscow, September 2002: Speaking on the third anniversary of the apartment house bombings, Deputy Prosecutor General Sergei Fridinsky says that the alleged ringleader, Achemez Gochiyayev, is hiding in Georgia's Pankisi Gorge. He demands his arrest and extradition. However, Georgian foreign minister Iraklii Menagarishvili denies that Gochiyayev is in the country. The head of the Public Commission on the bombings, Sergei Kovalyov, states that if Gochiyayev is apprehended, he should not be turned over to the FSB.

For about a year after Sasha and Felshtinsky's abortive trip to Georgia, a PR contest between the FSB and the Public Commission was waged on the back pages of Western newspapers and in a few remaining opposition print outlets and Web sites that Boris and Goose supported. For connoisseurs—some eight thousand visitors daily—the IFCL maintained a dedicated Web site at www.terror99.ru. Most Russians, of course, did not use the Internet, and the issue was completely taboo on Russian TV. But Boris was undeterred. He felt that the power of the story would overcome its narrow casting. The bombings had reached a high level of popular awareness. People talked about them, and so the news spread by word of mouth. And he knew, through countless reports from the Kremlin's outer circles, that Putin was very anxious about his doings.

Shortly after Gochiyayev's contact, another middleman approached Sasha and Felshtinsky with a statement from two other alleged perpetrators of the Moscow bombings, Timur Batchayev and Yusuf Krymshamkhalov. They admitted transporting a truckload of the explosive known as RDX to Moscow from a plant in southern Russia, together with a third man, Adam Dekkushev, who was already in Russian custody. Yet, they said, they had never been in touch with Chechen warlords and did not know Gochiyayev. At the time, they believed they were part of a jihadist underground in Moscow. They claimed that someone who posed as a jihad leader had duped them into the operation. They later came to believe he was working for the FSB. He told them that the bomb would be used for attacking "a military or government target," not an apartment house. Whatever that statement was worth, it contained sufficient detail to establish the authors' bona fides. They reported that a manhunt for them was under way in Georgia and claimed that the FSB had put a hefty bounty on their heads. It was only a matter of time before they would be caught or killed. Sasha and Yuri promptly reported all of this to the Kovalyov Commission and released it to *Novaya Gazeta*. Here was more humiliating evidence of FSB ineptitude.

"We do not intend to take part in the PR campaign of some dubious personalities or, all the more, to get engaged in polemics with them," an FSB spokesman responded. "Litvinenko is the man who tarnished the title of a secret services officer, who committed a crime himself."

Moscow, October 23, 2002: A group of about fifty terrorists take about eight hundred people hostage at a Moscow theater, demanding withdrawal of Russian forces from Chechnya. The raid is led by

Movsar Barayev, the nephew of Arbi Barayev, the infamous warlord accused of beheading four Britons in 1998. After a three-day stand-off, FSB commandos take the building, using gas to incapacitate the terrorists; 137 hostages die from exposure to the gas. All hostage-takers are killed execution-style by the commandos, even though they offered no resistance.

Tbilisi, Georgia, December 8, 2002: A suspect in the 1999 Moscow bombings, Yusuf Krymshamkhalov, is apprehended by Georgian security forces after a shootout with a group of rebels. He is extra-dited to Moscow and transferred to Lefortovo prison. His associate, Timur Batchayev, is killed in the operation. President Putin thanks his Georgian counterpart, Eduard Shevardnadze, for his assistance in Krymshamkhalov's capture.

On January 30, 2003, I flew to Strasbourg, France, to meet with Sergei Kovalyov, the chairman of the Public Commission. I had known him for more than thirty years, ever since both of us were members of the small group of dissidents around Andrei Sakharov. A research biologist like myself, Kovalyov was the founder of the first Soviet human rights committee in 1969. When he was arrested by the KGB in December 1974, I passed reports from his trial to Western correspondents in Moscow. Shortly after that, I emigrated, while Kovalyov spent ten years in prison and internal exile for "anti-Soviet agitation and propaganda." Now, at seventy-six, he was one of the few remaining independent voices in the Duma, a former ombuds-man in the Yeltsin administration and a top contender for the Nobel Peace Prize as the founder of Memorial, the human rights group that reported on abuses in Chechnya. Kovalyov was in Strasbourg attend-ing the Parliamentary Assembly of the Council of Europe, where he periodically blasted the Russian government on the war. We met in an empty restaurant not far from the Council HQ, over a late dinner with ample amounts of wine. He was twenty years older and I always treated him with unqualified respect. Kovalyov's dislike of

Boris was widely known. I wanted to see how much we could still cooperate.

"I have absolutely no problem with Berezovsky vintage 2000," he said, sipping his Côtes du Rhône. "I do have a lot of problems with him prior to that time."

He was particularly suspicious about Boris's role at the beginning of the second Chechen War. He wondered if Boris, as a member of the Kremlin "family," could have been involved in a secret deal with Basayev to invade Dagestan in September 1999 as part of a plot to elect Putin.

"This is just one theory, Sergei Adamovich," I said. "Another is that the FSB blew up the apartment houses." I told him what I thought had happened: the Wahhabi were indeed in collusion with the FSB, but the deal was arranged long before Putin. Later it might have evolved into an election-related plot and led to the Moscow bombings. But Boris, I believed, had nothing to do with it.

"But why don't you grill him yourself?" I suggested. "You chair the Commission on the bombing. All of this is relevant. Why don't you go to London and interrogate Boris? Our foundation will pay the costs. Unlike Putin, Boris deserves the benefit of the doubt."

"Putin also deserves the benefit of the doubt," said Kovalyov.

"This is not what Yushenkov thinks."

"If we are not fair, people will not believe us," Kovalyov said.

"There is a paradox here," I observed. "If he did not blow up those apartments, he deserves fairness. But if he did, he will wage total war on us, yourself included. Once at war, one does not strive for fairness, but for victory. As they say in English, all is fair in love and war."

It was a déjà vu conversation, of the kind we had had three decades earlier, sorting out the moral dilemmas of life under the Soviets. In the end we reached the same results this time around: Kovalyov would never compromise his standards under any circumstances; I would change the rules of engagement depending on the behavior of the opposition.

In addition to the Commission's visit to London to interview not just Boris but also Sasha and Felshtinsky, Kovalyov accepted my offer to bring him to Washington to talk to U.S. policymakers. He also promised to look after Trepashkin. I could not expect anything better.

Kovalyov's visit to Washington took place from February 10 to 14. As with Yushenkov, it was an exercise in frustration. Remembering the cold shoulder given to Yushenkov, I urged Kovalyov not to stress the controversial apartment house bombings, but to emphasize Chechnya. Here he had ironclad evidence of massive abuses, including death squads, summary executions, kidnapping, and torture—hundreds of documented cases. Russia was preparing to hold a referendum "at the barrel of a gun," declaring the democratically elected Maskhadov government to be illegitimate and replacing it with a puppet administration led by Akhmad Kadyrov and propped up by the FSB. How could George Bush endorse all of this by calling Putin a democrat and a friend?

I accompanied Kovalyov to the White House to see Tom Graham, who by now had become Bush's senior adviser on Russia at the National Security Council.

"Sergei Adamovich, I have known you for many years, and I will be undiplomatically frank with you," said Tom. "Don't waste your time telling us about Putin. We have no illusions. We know everything you would tell us and maybe more. But we cannot help you. For better or worse, our policy priorities are elsewhere."

For three days and a dozen meetings, Kovalyov tried anyway, stubbornly repeating his moral charge that American "policy calculations sacrifice other people's lives—tens of thousands of lives." His audiences were polite, and uninterested. "This is not a far-sighted policy, it will return to haunt America later on," Kovalyov warned.

He was described by Fred Hiatt in a *Washington Post* editorial as "a frail old Russian, moving like a ghost whom everyone would rather forget . . . in a Washington consumed with hard-headed calculations about Security Council votes and European alliances and intelligence cooperation."

On February 25 Kovalyov and two members of the Public Commission arrived in London to question Boris and his associates. I was not present, but apparently all went well between them. There was not much that Boris and Sasha could add to the bombing case that had not been said already. But they used the occasion to launch another attack on the FSB, this time related to the theater siege in Moscow the previous October. Boris released a statement urging Kovalyov to look into the newest conspiracy theory: that the FSB might have had a hand in *that* attack. He posed five highly provocative questions:

> For years there had been allegations that the FSB maintained relations with the Barayev clan. Could it have known about the planned attack?
>
> How could the police have overlooked the arrival of some fifty terrorists in downtown Moscow, with tons of weapons, ammunition, and explosives?
>
> Why were all the incapacitated terrorists, who offered no resistance and could have provided valuable information, shot execution-style?
>
> Why had the terrorists not set off their waist-belt bombs, even though it took ten minutes for the gas to take effect? Were there any explosives in the building in the first place?
>
> Why was the gas used without any antidote on hand, leading to the death of 137 hostages?

Upon his return to Moscow, Kovalyov announced that the Commission would expand its terms of reference to the controversial aspects of the theater siege. "We will look carefully into Berezovsky's questions, and will perhaps add some of our own," he declared. In the meantime, the IFCL added another NGO to its list of sponsored projects: the association of relatives of victims of the theater siege, who wanted the government to respond to the same set of questions and planned to pursue it in the courts.

Within weeks, new information surfaced that made the circumstances surrounding the theater siege even more suspicious. In the first days of April Yushenkov visited London. He met with Boris to discuss Liberal Russia. He also met with Sasha Litvinenko, who gave him what has later become known as "the Terkibayev file."

The information came from Chechen sources via Akhmed Zakayev, who by then was living in London, fighting a Russian extradition request. It turned out that one of the Moscow theater terrorists had survived. His name was Khanpash Terkibayev; he was mentioned in the list of terrorists published in the media on October 25, the day before FSB commandos stormed the theater. Terkibayev was a known figure in Chechnya, a suspected FSB agent, who had worked in Maskhadov's press office in 2000. In 2001 he went to fight with the rebels. On two documented instances, in April 2001 and March 2002, he had been detained by federal forces and then miraculously released. The report of his presence among the theater terrorists was a surprise to Zakayev, who had assumed that he had gone to work for the Russians. Subsequent inquiries established that shortly after the siege, in November, Terkibayev surfaced in Baku, Azerbaijan, where he tried to infiltrate Chechen émigré groups. He bragged about "being in the theater." He was exposed as an agent provocateur and returned to Moscow. Then, at the end of March, he was spotted in Strasbourg among a group of pro-Russian Chechens whom the Kremlin brought to the Council of Europe to promote the controversial March 23 referendum in Chechnya, ratifying a new constitution. Critics charged that the vote was suspect.

Upon return from London Yushenkov passed the Terkibayev file to Anna Politkovskaya, the Chechnya correspondent for *Novaya Gazeta,* who knew the intricate world of Chechen clans better then anyone. During the hostage crisis, she was in the theater and had interviewed Barayev, the leader of the terrorists. Throughout the crisis she passed their messages to the authorities and later wrote extensively about the episode. She was best suited to investigate the Terkibayev mystery.

Yushenkov was shot on April 17. Ten days later Politkovskaya's article appeared. She managed to find Terkibayev and get an interview from him. When, some months later, I asked Politkovskaya why she thought he agreed to talk, she could only attribute it to his vanity; after all, among Chechens, being interviewed by Politkovskaya was a status symbol.

Terkibayev confirmed that he was in the theater. He said he had guided the terror group through the streets of Moscow, entered the building with them, and left just before the assault. He boasted that he was an agent of the Russian secret service and a consultant for the Kremlin administration. His role was to report on the terrorist group's activities. In the story, Politkovskaya directly alleged that at some level, the authorities must have known of the hostage seizure before it took place.

The story was a bombshell. Although ostracized at home, Politkovskaya was widely respected in the West. Later she told me that Alexander Vershbow, the American ambassador to Moscow, invited her to talk about the article. He "ventured an opinion" that allegations of that sort are so unbelievable that they must be backed by irrefutable evidence to be taken seriously. *Discounted,* I thought, remembering Tom Graham. After the Politkovskaya coup, Terkibayev vanished, despite the best efforts of Moscow journalists to find him. Eight months later he was reported killed in a car crash in Chechnya.

In early March 2003 Trepashkin delivered on his promise. How he got it, no one knew, but one day he brought to Yushenkov and Kovalyov the name, ID number, address, and telephone numbers of Gochiyayev's business partner. Remarkably, he had never been mentioned by the FSB as a suspect in the case. Was he the man who tricked Gochiyayev into renting the spaces where the bombs were planted? Gochiyayev had claimed that his partner called him at 5 a.m. on the morning of the first explosion, shortly before the blast went off. Now this could be easily checked.

Another thing that Trepashkin dug out was Gochiyayev's mobile phone number from which he presumably tipped off the authorities about the two other sites where explosives had been found. This too could now be easily verified. Yushenkov promptly passed the information to the official investigators of the bombing. There was no response—except that Trepashkin was called in to the prosecutor's office and told that he would be indicted for three violations stemming from the search of his home fifteen months earlier. As reporters waited outside to see whether Trepashkin would leave the building,

Yushenkov made a strong statement linking the pressure on Trepashkin to his work for the Public Commission. Trepashkin was released—for the time being.

Then, on March 11, Felshtinsky and Sasha reported that they had reestablished contact with Gochiyayev. He seemed to have left Georgia; most likely he was in Turkey. His middleman suggested a meeting "in a third country" and promised to get back in touch to discuss logistics.

It was clear to all parties that the situation would come to a head when the two suspects held in Lefortovo went on trial. Trepashkin, representing Tanya and Aliona, would be able to raise questions in court, while Yushenkov would do what he could to drum up whatever controversies emerged from the courtroom. So Sasha and Felshtinsky raced the FSB to get to Gochiyayev first, to obtain his full statement before he was killed or caught. To me it looked like we were gaining ground. But then disaster struck.

April 17, 2003: An unknown gunman kills Sergei Yushenkov in front of his home in Moscow. Shocked members of the Duma agree that the killing is political. Most observers link the murder to Yushenkov's role as the deputy chair of the Public Commission. In Denver, Aliona Morozova says in a statement, "I am afraid that to return to Russia would present a threat to my life, and I am asking the U.S. authorities to grant me political asylum." In a message read at the slain deputy's funeral, President Vladimir Putin praises "a brilliant politician who defended democracy and freedom in Russia."

For a long time I was of two minds as to who killed Yushenkov, and why. His murder fit the mounting pattern of conspiracy theories, from the apartment bombings to the Terkibayev revelations. But then again, none of them had been proven, and, as a scientist, I had to consider that they could have been coincidences, however improbable. Intuitively it was logical that the FSB killed Yushenkov, who was the most vocal promoter of anti-FSB allegations. Then, a competing theory about Yushenkov emerged. Two months after the murder, the police caught his assassins. The two perpetrators turned out to be career criminals and drug addicts, who were paid for the hit by a certain Alexander Vinnik, a Liberal Russia functionary from the provincial center of Syktyvkar. Vinnik confessed and said that he had acted on behalf of Mikhail Kodanev, Yushenkov's rival in the Liberal Russia leadership. When the four of them went on trial, Kodanev was the only one who pleaded not guilty. Vinnik was lying, he said.

Yet Kodanev had a motive. In July 2002, a couple of months after Liberal Russia had been formed, Yushenkov had a conversation with a highly placed official at the Justice Ministry. He told him in no uncertain terms that the party would never be registered for the 2003 elections if Berezovsky remained on its candidate list. That was the president's explicit order. Yushenkov had no choice; he agreed to dump Boris. The party split in half, with a Yushenkov wing and a Berezovsky wing. But then Yushenkov came to London, sat down with Boris, and they reconciled: after the party was registered, Boris's wing would return to Yushenkov's fold. Kodanev had been Number Two in Boris's wing, but would have faced a much lesser standing in the reunited party. According to the prosecution, he put out the contract on Yushenkov when he learned about his reconciliation with Boris.

On the testimony of Vinnik, Kodanev was convicted and given a sentence of twenty years. I had met Kodanev a couple of times in London, and I did not like him. But Sasha was adamant that it was all a setup. The two killers were probably recruited by the FSB while in jail, he said. They were promised a few months of freedom and a reduction in their remaining sentences in exchange for the hit and for naming Vinnik as their patron. Vinnik, in turn, was told to name Kodanev or face a life sentence. Sasha had no doubt; he had seen dozens of such cases. With his pledge to make the bombings an election issue Yushenkov was a threat; Kontora would stop at nothing to get rid of him. How could I not see it? Yushenkov was not the first and would not be the last, he predicted. "And there will always be a plausible 'legend.' That's part of the tradecraft."

Indeed, seven months before Yushenkov was killed, his associate, Vladimir Golovlyov, a Duma member who was in charge of Liberal

Russia finances, was shot while walking his dog. His killers were never found. The predominant theory was that it was a business dispute; Golovlyov had been involved in many privatization deals.

Three months after Yushenkov, Yuri Schekochihin, the crusading journalist from *Novaya Gazeta* and a member of the Public Commission, died suddenly from an unexplained "allergic reaction." His medical chart ended up "classified." His colleagues and his family suspected poisoning related to his numerous investigations of the FSB.

"See," said Sasha when we learned of Schekochihin's mysterious death, "I told you, didn't I?"

Sasha was an oper, not a scientist. He did not believe in coincidences. In retrospect, he had a point.

Moscow, April 30, 2003: The prosecutor general's office announces indictments as the result of its now-closed investigation into the apartment house bombings. According to the indictments, nine Islamic fighters carried out the bombings. Five of them were already dead, including the Jordanian-born warlord, Amir Khattab, killed by a poisoned letter delivered to him by an FSB double agent. Two others remained at large, including Achemez Gochiyayev, the mastermind of the attacks. Two men were in custody. Yusuf Krymshamkhalov and Adam Dekkushev would stand trial on charges of terrorism. Boris Berezovsky dismissed the prosecutors' findings as "absolute rubbish."

On May 15 I landed in Istanbul in a last-ditch effort to make contact with Gochiyayev. For some weeks prior to that, the man who called himself his representative had negotiated with Felshtinsky. This time, for the full story, including a personal interview with Gochiyayev, he demanded money. He started at $3 million. He quickly reduced his price to $500,000; a few days later he asked for $100,000, saying that it was his last offer. Felshtinsky could not convince him on the phone that he was saying no because he meant no, not as a way to bring down the price.

We were pretty sure that Gochiyayev was no longer his own master, that he was being handled somehow. First, he could not have gotten into Turkey on his own, without someone providing money and false documents, as he was obviously on Interpol's watch list. Second, the negotiator who called Felshtinsky displayed a level of sophistication indicative of a serious underlying effort, an organization of some sort. When Boris asked my opinion, I was absolutely against any money being paid, as this could be a trap with catastrophic consequences. I volunteered to go on a second unpredictable mission to Turkey to find out.

Akhmed Zakayev, with whom I discussed the trip, supplied me with a bodyguard, an Istanbul-based Chechen, who was waiting for me outside the Hilton Hotel. We got into a yellow Turkish cab. As we approached the walled entrance of the Kempinski Hotel on the bank of the Bosporus, where I was to meet my contact, I felt a bout of nostalgia for my adventures with Sasha three years earlier.

"I can't go in there," said my guard. "I will wait outside. See, I have a weapon here," he slapped himself in the waist, "and they have metal detectors at the entrance."

That's reassuring, I thought. That means that whoever I meet will be metal-free, too.

My interlocutor was about forty-five and spoke an educated version of Russian. He looked like a schoolteacher, not a guerrilla. They were asking for money, he said, because they had to resettle Gochiyayev, who was a hunted man. He suggested we think of it as a witness relocation program.

"We cannot pay you a penny," said I. "We do not know who you are. No offense intended, but you may be a group on some official terrorist list, or a front for the FSB. If we pay you, we expose ourselves. As for Gochiyayev, with Russian charges looming over him, he is doomed anyway. Sooner or later he will be caught. His only chance is to tell the truth and hope that we will help establish his innocence."

"I have to consult my superior," said the schoolteacher. "I will be back in an hour."

While he was gone I had a lonely lunch, watching ships sailing up the Bosporus toward Russian shores. Finally he returned.

"If you are concerned about who we are, my boss says hello. He met you at a dacha near Moscow."

It was his way of telling me that he was speaking for Movladi Udugov, the former Chechen deputy prime minister turned Islamist ideologue. No way could we pay him.

"Look," I said, "your boss, knowing who he is and who I am, knows that there can be no question of money changing hands. The best I can suggest is this: we find a newspaper in London that might be interested in paying for Gochiyayev's interview. For material like this, they might pay a lot of money. If your boss agrees, call me or send me an e-mail." We said goodbye. They never called or e-mailed.

With the Gochiyayev trail running cold, the prospects for our investigation looked bleak. After the death of Yushenkov and Schekochihin, the Public Commission was effectively defunct. Kovalyov was too old and too busy with his Chechnya work to devote much energy to investigating the bombings. In fact, he was about to retire; he had said that he would not run for another term in the December 2003 Duma election. Nobody else on the Commission's roster was all that motivated. Only Trepashkin still continued his lonely pursuit.

Sometime in July, Sasha called: "Come to London, I have something new."

It turned out that Trepashkin had had another breakthrough. He had just sent a courier with a stack of documents to Sasha.

By studying old press clippings, Trepashkin had uncovered the initial composite sketch of the Guryanova Street bomber that the police had released immediately after the attack on September 9. Two days later, the papers had published an image of the prime suspect, a different man; it was a photo of Gochiyayev. The initial sketch was quite elaborate, and Trepashkin thought that he knew the man: Vladimir Romanovich, a suspect in the Chechen-led extortion gang that Trepashkin had investigated seven years earlier when he was still employed by the FSB. At the time he was told by his superiors to leave Romanovich alone because he was working for the FSB.

Trepashkin showed the sketch to a former FSB colleague who

knew the agent's files. The man agreed: it was Romanovich, an undercover agent who specialized in penetrating ethnic Caucasian groups in Moscow's criminal underground. Romanovich had been killed by a hit-and-run driver in Cyprus in the summer of 2000, several months after the Moscow blasts.

In July 2003, Tanya Morozova visited Russia to see her grandparents. While in Moscow, using her status as a crime victim, she visited the official FSB investigator, accompanied by Trepashkin as her attorney. The meeting was inconclusive, but Trepashkin was allowed to look through the case file. There was no Romanovich sketch in it.

Trepashkin then sought the source of the Romanovich sketch that had been released to the press on September 9, 1999. He found a man named Mark Blumenfeld, the former property manager in Tanya's building on Guryanova Street. Yes, said Blumenfeld, on the morning after the bombing he described to local police the man who had rented the ground-floor space. Yet two days later, he said, he was brought to Lefortovo, where FSB officers pressured him to change his story and "recognize" another photograph, that of Gochiyayev.

This was good stuff. Sasha was jubilant: "I told you, Trepashkin is top-notch! Now we will get the bastards."

Trepashkin wrote that he wanted us to keep his discovery quiet until the trial of the two bombing suspects, scheduled to open on October 31, at which he would represent Tanya and Aliona.

Moscow, October 23: Interfax reports that former FSB officer Mikhail Trepashkin has been arrested and charged with illegal weapons possession. Trepashkin is detained in the Moscow area after police find an unlicensed pistol in his car. Trepashkin insists that the weapon was planted.

As it turned out, Trepashkin, every inch the systematic investigator, had planned for contingencies. A few days before his arrest he gave a copy of the Romanovich file to a reporter from *Moscovskiye Novosty,*

Igor Korolkov. After Trepashkin's arrest, Korolkov rushed to Blumenfeld to verify the story. Everything checked out.

"At Lefortovo they showed me a photograph of a certain person," said Blumenfeld in a taped interview, "and they said that this was Gochiyayev and that it was supposedly to him that I had rented out the basement. I answered that I had never seen that man. But they insistently recommended to me that I identify Gochiyayev. I understood what they wanted, did not argue further, and signed the statement."

Korolkov's story ran, but it was the end of 2003 and Putin's media revolution was complete. All television and virtually all print media were under Kremlin control. Korolkov's November 11 story in *Moscovskiye Novosty* was ignored in Russia.

Predictably, it was also discounted in the White House. And yet, among those few who were interested, our conspiracy theories were gradually gaining credence. Speaking on the Senate floor on November 4, 2003, U.S. Senator John McCain declared, "There remain credible allegations that Russia's FSB had a hand in carrying out these attacks."

Moscow, December 30, 2003: Russian police and FSB agents seize a truck and confiscate five thousand copies of Blowing Up Russia *en route from the western city of Pskov to Moscow.*

January 11, 2004: A Moscow judge sentences Adam Dekkushev and Yusuf Krymshamkhalov to life imprisonment for participation in the 1999 Moscow bombings after a two-month-long closed trial, held without a jury.

On a sunny September 15, 2005, I arrived in Kiev, the capital of Ukraine, for a meeting with Mikhail Trepashkin, who had just been released from prison. With me was Andrei Nekrasov, a filmmaker who had made a documentary about Tanya and Aliona Morozova. We had a mission: to convince Trepashkin to flee to the West. I wanted to repeat Sasha's coup. Andrei wanted to film it.

Trepashkin was released as the result of an FSB oversight. Back in 2004 the case against him of illegal gun possession fell apart, and he was acquitted. However, he received a three-and-a-half-year prison sentence for the disclosure of official secrets, a charge stemming from the old KGB file found in his desk in 2002. After serving two-thirds of his sentence in the godforsaken town of Nizhny Tagil in the Urals, he applied for parole. He was a model prisoner, except that he had been a pain in the neck for the prison administration because, as a lawyer, he wrote complaints on behalf of every inmate. The administration supported his parole.

Apparently, no one in Nizhny Tagil knew who Trepashkin was. He was hardly a national celebrity, after all, and he was a first offender, a hapless former FSB officer serving time on an insignificant charge. So they let him go. He arrived in Moscow unannounced and surprised his wife, Tatyana, when he appeared at their doorstep.

By then Goose and Igor Malashenko, backed by an investment from Boris, had launched their new network, Russian TV International. Based in New York, it could be seen on cable in the far-flung Russian diaspora, from California to Kiev to Israel—everywhere except Russia. "We are the only Russian news not subject to Kremlin censorship," boasted an RTVI ad. I saw an interview with Trepashkin on an RTVI dispatch from Moscow. He insisted that he planned to resume his probe into the apartment bombings, and also wanted to look into the theater siege. He added that he planned to start a new human rights group defending the rights of prisoners.

This man is mad, I thought. Sure enough, the next day, the prosecutor general's office appealed his parole.

"Mikhail Ivanovich, let's get together in the same place we met last time," I said on the phone. "And bring your family." Remarkably, his foreign travel passport had never been confiscated.

As he and Tatyana boarded the Kiev-bound plane at Sheremetievo Airport, Nekrasov and I monitored their progress through secure mobile phones. We kept our fingers crossed that they would not be stopped at the last moment.

Tatyana Trepashkina, a pretty blonde of about thirty, was very happy to hear my offer for them to move to the West, to a decent life after their two nightmarish years. But Trepashkin did not want to leave. He considered the Kiev trip nothing but a well-deserved vacation.

"They let you out by mistake. If you return, you are going back to prison, and they will kill you there," we chorused.

I had everything worked out for them. A car was standing by to collect their children, who were visiting with Tatyana's mother in a village in Russia, not far from the Ukrainian border. We would get them tickets to the Seychelles or Barbados, neither of which required visas for Russian citizens. They would jump off at a connection in any airport in Western Europe and request asylum. Boris would underwrite them for a few years. Essentially, it was the same deal as with Sasha.

"If I run, it would undermine my credibility," said Trepashkin. "You may not believe it, but I met a lot of good people in prison. Everyone thinks that I'm right. Particularly the FSB officers. There are many honest officers. If I flee I would be a traitor."

We called Sasha in London.

"Misha, don't be an idiot. Do as Alex says. We will get you a job. People like you are in demand. I have already spoken to some friends in Spain."

Trepashkin was immovable.

I got Boris on the phone. "He wants to be a hero," I reported.

"He is a fucking fool," said Boris. "Let me talk to him. I will make him an offer he can't refuse."

Boris told him to seek asylum in Ukraine if he did not want go to the West. We could give him a job with the Foundation and help him to resettle. Ukraine was a free country now, after the Orange Revolution. The Ukrainians wouldn't give him up.

But Trepashkin refused. Even Elena Bonner, who had helped me with Berezovsky in a similar situation six years earlier, could not convince him. Trepashkin was just not the kind of man who would run. He would stay and fight to the bitter end.

I decided to change tactics: "Why don't we send you out to the Seychelles for two weeks while your parole is being decided. There is nothing illegal in going on vacation. If they leave you alone, you go home. If they announce that you are heading back to prison, then you'll decide."

"I want to go to the Seychelles," said Tatyana.

"No," said Trepashkin. "We are going home."

Tatyana exploded. She had married an FSB officer, she said, not a prisoner. All this time she had assumed that it was Berezovsky's people who were manipulating him, but now she saw that it was he himself who was bent on self-destruction. He was not thinking about the children. If he went back to jail, she promised, she would never visit him, ever. She was nearly hysterical. We had to calm her down.

It was no use. The next morning we put them both on a plane to Moscow.

The next day, a squad of FSB agents converged on their two-bedroom apartment, put Trepashkin in a car, and drove him the thirty-six hours back to Nizhny Tagil. They put him in a cell pending his parole appeal, which he lost some days later.

"He is crazy," I said to Nekrasov as we flew from Kiev to Zurich.

"He is a martyr," said Nekrasov. "All martyrs are nuts. The problem is, he has to get himself killed first. If he does, he will be a real martyr. I am going to make a film about him, *The Hero of Our Time*. But if he gets out, I'm afraid no one will want to see it."

As of this writing, there are still seven months left of Trepashkin's term.

CHAPTER 13

THE QUARRY

One way or another, the war in Chechnya became the defining context for the lives of Sasha and Marina, Boris and Putin, Akhmed Zakayev, myself, and everyone in our collective circles. Chechnya was the graveyard of Russian democracy and the ultimate cause of Russia's drift away from the West. Boris's confrontation with the Party of War and his conflicts with the FSB that dragged Sasha into the whirlwind of Kremlin power struggles started over Chechnya. For Putin, Chechnya became his endless judo match and the glue that cemented his mutual dependence with George Bush, a destructive relationship.

Chechnya inspired those dark Kremlin forces that we presumed to be the villains in our conspiracy theories—from the Moscow bombings to the theater siege to Sasha's own killing. Solidarity with the victims of Chechnya drove Sasha's relationship with Akhmed Zakayev, who in the last year of his life became his closest friend.

Zakayev moved to England in the summer of 2002. His arrival, and his association with the Berezovsky camp, turned London into the center of the Russian antiwar campaign. This alliance also became a major irritant for Putin and the reason the Kremlin eventually declared London a staging ground for "Chechen terrorist activity." Neutralizing the London brotherhood became Russia's top diplomatic priority. First, the Russian government asked nicely for the Brits to give up Boris and Zakayev; when they were refused, the Kremlin decried "British double standards." After the legal options were exhausted, the hit squads began to arrive.

Grozny, Chechnya, August 19, 2002: A rebel missile brings down a huge Mi-26 transport helicopter on its way to Russian military headquarters in Khankala, killing 119. It is the single largest loss of life among the troops fighting in Chechnya in the three-year-old war.

In August 2002, as the death toll in Chechnya mounted, I helped organize a meeting between Zakayev and former NSC secretary Ivan Rybkin, one of the few Russian politicians who stood up to Putin. We wanted to force Putin's hand on the stalemated war.

The conflict was impossible for either side to win. Russian forces controlled most of the country—but only during the day. By night the countryside was in the hands of the rebels, who had an underground cell in every town and village. The guerrillas used road mines and hit-and-run attacks to grind down the Russian forces. Throughout the North Caucasus, the radical followers of Shamil Basayev gained strength with each passing week, an ominous trend that threatened to turn the region into a breeding ground for Islamic extremism. In the meantime, from his mountainous hideout President Aslan Maskhadov urged negotiations and let it be known privately that he no longer insisted on full independence. Within the Russian army and across the broad political spectrum in Moscow, discontent with the war was growing.

The West and the liberal wing in Russia had stubbornly refused to deem Maskhadov a terrorist. His two envoys, Zakayev in Europe and a man named Ilyas Akhmadov in the United States, moved freely through Western capitals, meeting with members of Congress and various European legislators. Western governments, including the United States, quietly pressured Putin to agree to negotiations, concerned that the Chechen crisis was fueling anti-Western passions across the Muslim world.

But Putin's position steadily hardened. It had been his war from

Day One, and he could not bear the political cost of losing it (not to mention the exposure of his generals' war crimes that would inevitably have resulted). A settlement with Maskhadov would mean a humiliating failure for him; he insisted on unconditional surrender. Putin took the war very emotionally, and managed it personally. Journalists who interviewed him knew that Chechnya was the one thing that could make him visibly angry. On occasion, his emotions burst out publicly. When a French journalist asked him at a press conference, "Don't you think that in trying to eradicate terrorism you're going to eradicate the civilian population in Chechnya?," Putin turned pale and lost his composure. "If you want to become an Islamic radical and have a circumcision," he replied, "I invite you to Moscow, because we are a multitalented country and have specialists there. I recommend that you have the operation done in such a way that nothing else will grow there."

On August 16, 2002, wire reports announced that Ivan Rybkin, the former NSC secretary and speaker of the Duma, in defiance of official Kremlin policy, had met in Zurich with Maskhadov's special envoy Akhmed Zakayev to discuss how Russia and Chechnya could jump-start the peace process. Using couriers and coded messages, preparations for the event had been kept hidden from the FSB. I met Rybkin at the Zurich airport and brought him to the Savoy Hotel, where Zakayev was already waiting.

They met as old friends. Back in 1997 the two of them had spent countless hours negotiating the postwar relationship between Chechnya and Russia—several agreements that had never materialized, thanks to the second war. Now Rybkin no longer represented the Kremlin, while Zakayev had full credentials from the rebel government. Their meeting was a slap in Putin's face; it challenged his claim that the rebels were terrorists. Over lunch we drafted a statement: "The two sides should return to the agreement of 12 May 1997 signed by Boris Yeltsin and Aslan Maskhadov."

Over dessert, we placed calls to the Associated Press and Radio Echo Moscow.

"I am confident that peace is possible. I know how it can be reached," declared Rybkin. "As soon as I get back to Moscow I will seek a meeting with President Putin to tell him how this can be done."

"Our side is in full agreement," added Zakayev. "President Maskhadov is ready for peace. The ball is in the Kremlin's court."

Of course Putin refused to meet with Rybkin. The Union of Committees of Soldiers' Mothers endorsed Rybkin's initiative, however, and the pressure on the Kremlin increased, from Russian elites and foreign leaders, to stop the war. Rybkin later told me that when he returned to Moscow people of all persuasions, from liberals to Communists to the military, called to congratulate him.

On August 30 it was announced that several Russian politicians, including another former Duma speaker, Ruslan Khasbulatov, and the MP-journalist Yuri Schekochihin, had met with Zakayev in Lichtenstein in the aftermath of the Zurich meeting. Next, none other than former prime minister Primakov, who was still very influential within the intelligence community, came out publicly in support of negotiations with the Chechens.

In early September Rybkin traveled to Tbilisi to meet with Georgian president Eduard Shevardnadze, who endorsed his peace initiative. The Georgian trip must have particularly irritated the Kremlin: that same week, Putin sent a letter to UN Secretary-General Kofi Annan, threatening a military strike on Georgia over the Chechen presence in Pankisi Gorge.

With Boris's support, Rybkin was planning to run in Russia's 2004 presidential elections. His peace initiatives were a prelude to his campaign.

On October 23, I shepherded Rybkin in Washington from a meeting with Senator Richard Lugar to a lunch with the former U.S. national security adviser Zbigniew Brzezinski. En route, we heard shocking news: a gang of Chechens led by Movsar Barayev had taken seven hundred people hostage in a Moscow theater. So much for any hope of peace.

Copenhagen, October 30, 2002: Police arrest Akhmed Zakayev, the envoy of separatist president Aslan Maskhadov, after his arrival in the Danish capital for the opening of the World Chechen Congress. Zakayev is detained under an Interpol warrant filed by Russia, naming him as a suspect in the theater siege of the previous week. A court in Copenhagen remands Zakayev for two weeks, to give the Danish Justice Ministry time to consider the extradition request. On the same day, Russia discloses the nature of the incapacitating gas the FSB had used in the botched rescue mission. It was a secret, nonlethal weapon, an aerosol version of Valium, which was not supposed to kill anyone.

Sasha was certain that the theater siege was another FSB conspiracy aimed at boosting Putin's war policy and labeling the Maskhadov government as terrorists, "a new version of the apartment house bombings." When Sasha pronounced his theory I was dismissive. But he offered a spirited argument.

"Look," he said, "imagine you are an FSB agent named Movsar Barayev. Your oper comes to you and offers a foolproof deal. Your gang will drive to Moscow with no police interference, guaranteed; then you'll take over the theater and mine it with dummy explosives. The Russians will negotiate and agree to a cease-fire in Chechnya. You'll return home a hero, and get well paid for it, too. Being a dumb mountain thug, you don't see any hidden traps. You think they really will negotiate for peace. You don't realize they are luring your gang into their sights. So you go along with it. After all, you have done business with the FSB before.

"Then the FSB uses gas that is supposed to be nonlethal and shoots all the hostage-takers. But they screw up the gas, and lots of people die. And by the way, they pin it on Zakayev and Maskhadov; that's their response to Rybkin and Zakayev's meeting in Zurich."

It was true that the terrorists did not harm the hostages. Those poor souls died mostly from suffocating on their own vomit, because no one bothered to tell the rescue teams how to handle the inhalation of a tranquilizer. Still, I wasn't convinced.

"A typical FSB mishap, something akin to Ryazan," Sasha

observed. "Good planning, bad execution. Otherwise it would've been a brilliant operation: all hostages alive, all terrorists dead."

"One thing does not fit in your scheme," I said. "Basayev took responsibility for the theater."

"Basayev is bullshitting," said Sasha. "The terrorists are dead now; for Chechens they are heroes—*shahids*. So Basayev jumped on the bandwagon."

The theater siege greatly hurt the Chechen cause and the opponents of the war in Russia and became a PR bonanza for the Kremlin. By design or accident, it gave Putin leverage in his dialogue with the West: now, he was able to say, the Chechens had finally qualified as real terrorists, and Russia had to be viewed as a true victim of terror. The war in Chechnya should be certified as just and honorable.

Immediately after the siege, the Kremlin embarked on a concerted propaganda effort to blame the Maskhadov government for the attack. At a press conference in Moscow on October 31, Putin's spokesman, Sergei Yastrzhembsky, played an FSB tape of a telephone conversation between the terrorists' leader, Movsar Barayev, and one of his accomplices. On the tape the name "Aslan" can be heard; this was supposed to demonstrate that the terrorists were acting with Maskhadov's knowledge.

Maskhadov's government denied any role and disowned both Basayev and Barayev. Nonetheless, attacks on Maskhadov dominated the Russian message.

"We can see that the image of Maskhadov—even in the eyes of those who pushed Moscow toward negotiations—has seriously paled," declared Yastrzhembsky. "Name one leader [in Chechnya] with whom we could negotiate. I don't know of any such person."

Next, they moved against Zakayev. The warrant for his arrest cited no evidence, simply the charge that he was connected to the siege. The Danish government had to decide whether or not to turn him over to Russian authorities.

An unlikely coalition rose to defend him. From Washington, a bipartisan duo of seasoned cold warriors, former national security adviser Zbigniew Brzezinski and former secretary of state Alexander

Haig, appealed to the Danish government not to extradite Zakayev. In Britain a "Save Zakayev" campaign was championed by such politically diverse personalities as the leftist actress Vanessa Redgrave and the ultraconservative author Lord Nicholas Bethel. Human Rights Watch and Amnesty International issued statements in support of Zakayev.

If there was one Chechen who consistently opposed terror, it was Zakayev. But his case became a test of different things for different people: the legitimacy of Russian actions in Chechnya, the notion that Russia had failed as a democracy, the extent to which the war on terror justified compromises on human rights. For Chechens in the mountains and throughout their far-flung diaspora in Europe—and, indeed, for moderate Muslims around the world—the Zakayev case became a test of Western fairness. For Putin, it was a way to assess the reciprocity of his Western partners: in Afghanistan, we helped you fight *your* terrorists, now you have to help us to fight *ours*.

"The Danes will not send an innocent man to his death," said Boris with his usual optimism. We were in London, discussing what to do for Zakayev. I wanted to get involved.

"When Russia slaughtered two hundred thousand civilians in Chechnya the West looked the other way. Why would they stand up to Putin over Zakayev?" I said. "He needs all the help he can get."

For Boris, this was a serious dilemma. His asylum application was pending. Russian officials had ominously hinted that they could bring up terrorism charges against him, related to his Chechen connections. The last thing he needed was to associate himself with a man accused of terrorism. His lawyers strongly advised him to steer clear of Zakayev. His PR adviser, Lord Timothy Bell, who took it upon himself to explain what the British *really* meant, was extremely concerned: "You can't imagine how vicious Whitehall may become if it believes that its real interests are at stake."

But Boris sided with me: we had to put up a fight for Zakayev, both on principle and for pragmatic reasons. If we let Putin get him, Putin would come for us next.

On November 1, we announced that the IFCL would assist

Zakayev's defense and pay for his legal expenses. Four days after our announcement Russia submitted to the United Kingdom a request to extradite Boris—on fraud charges involving his auto business.

November 4, 2002: Russia demands that Qatar extradite former Chechen president Zelimkhan Yandarbiyev, claiming that he was in contact with the Moscow theater attackers. A Russian foreign ministry spokesman hails the cooperation of other Arab countries in fighting terrorism, saying, "Not a single Arab country supports the rebels in Chechnya."

On November 9 I returned from Copenhagen to London and went to stay with Sasha and Marina in their Kensington apartment. The previous day I had accompanied Ivan Rybkin to the Danish Parliament, where he campaigned in defense of Zakayev. After the meeting, we visited Zakayev in jail. Rybkin was also putting his political reputation on the line by providing moral support to someone in custody on terrorism charges.

"They will kill Rybkin," said Sasha over lunch. "Tell him he should come to London and ask for asylum. I know a good lawyer."

I spent that night on the telephone, trying to add signatures on a petition to the Danish government not to give up Zakayev. Vanessa Redgrave originated the appeal, so it had an impressive list of names from the international left, from the Danish film director Lars von Trier to the American intellectual Susan Sontag. I was trying to rally a Russian constituency. It was easy for me to enlist dissidents: Elena Bonner, Vladimir Bukovsky, Boris Berezovsky, and Sergei Kovalyov. Then came a surprise.

As I was talking to Bukovsky in his home in Cambridge, England, he passed the phone to a visitor, Vladimir Kara-Murza Jr., a functionary in the Union of Right Forces (SPS), the centrist party of Chubais and Nemtsov.

"Have you tried Nemtsov?" asked Kara-Murza.

"He would never sign," I said. "He's in Putin's pocket."

"Why don't we try? He is highly supportive of Rybkin and even wanted to join the negotiations."

Twenty minutes later he called back: "We reached Nemtsov in Moscow. He is signing."

Surprised, and pleased that I was wrong about Nemtsov, I faxed the list of Russian signatories to Vanessa Redgrave and went to see a movie.

When we walked out of the movie theater I had three messages from Kara-Murza to call as soon as possible.

"Nemtsov has recalled his signature," he said. "They leaned on him, full force."

Kara-Murza reported that within an hour after talking to Bukovsky, Nemtsov had received a call from Chubais, who yelled at him, "Borya, what do you think you are doing? They will cut the oxygen to SPS. We can forget about staying in the Duma after the next elections. Are you out of your mind?"

Chubais said that Vladislav Surkov, the Kremlin deputy chief of staff, had just contacted him to warn that if Nemtsov signed the appeal, the president would consider the SPS an enemy party. The consequences were obvious.

"It's Saturday, past midnight in Moscow," observed Sasha. "Do you understand what happened? Surkov is not sitting in the Kremlin eavesdropping on Nemtsov's conversations. That means the FSB monitors his phone in real time, not through a recording. It took only an hour between Nemtsov talking to London and Chubais calling him. Just imagine: an analyst must be on hand all the time to assess the contents of our phone calls, with enough brains to know what to report. Then it goes up the chain of command to a liaison officer in the FSB, then it's passed to the duty officer in the Kremlin, who alerts Surkov. All via secure lines. All verbally, because there was no time for transcribing and filing. That means there is a whole team working, with standing orders to report all contacts with us as a top priority. I wouldn't be surprised if Putin runs the operation personally."

Indeed, some time later, Nemtsov told a mutual friend in Moscow that Putin scolded him for the Zakayev appeal, saying he should be "vigilant against Berezovsky's provocations."

Weeks passed. The uncertainty over Zakayev dragged on, with the Danish court twice extending his remand. Finally, the gallant Danes came through. On December 3, citing "insufficient evidence," the Danish Justice Ministry released him. A litany of protests came out of Moscow. "It seems Denmark has its own interpretation of how one fights international terrorism," said a spokesman for the Russian prosecutor's office.

"A Free Man in Copenhagen," extolled the *Wall Street Journal* in an editorial. "The Kremlin warmongers, who have unleashed an inhuman war against the Chechen people, today are doing everything to neutralize those politicians who seek an end to the conflict," said a triumphant Zakayev on the steps of the Danish jail before going back to London. But the Russians weren't ready to let him remain free, not yet.

London, December 11, 2002: Akhmed Zakayev, facing another extradition charge—this time in Britain—is released on £50,000 ($80,000) bail posted by actress Vanessa Redgrave. Russia's charges include kidnapping, torture, mass murder, and armed rebellion. Russian Foreign Minister Igor Ivanov sharply criticizes the decision not to take Zakayev into custody, comparing him to Osama bin Laden.

It had been two years since the Litvinenkos had arrived in England. Their life had gradually taken on a rhythm and a routine. The rhythm came from Tolik's school, to which Marina took him every morning. Sasha usually slept late after staying up in front of his computer or watching Russian videos. There was a peculiar difference between them. Marina did not miss Russia at all, except for her mother of course, and did not tend to cling to things Russian; she was wholly absorbed by her new surroundings. Sasha, by contrast, needed a daily fix of Russica: the latest news from the Internet, Russian

DVDs, and Russian books. It was not that he suffered from nostalgia; the remembrance of the old country did not haunt him. But thanks to the wonders of the information age, a part of him simply kept on living in the old country. One of the reasons, of course, was that he continued to be a public figure back in Moscow. His fans and detractors argued about his books on the Internet. The Moscow bureaus of Reuters, the Associated Press, and Radio Echo Moscow kept calling for his comment. But in London, even his neighbors had no idea who he was.

Within the marriage, he and Marina gave each other room. Just as it had been in Moscow, Marina did not care that she was not a part of the world he shared with Felshtinsky and Trepashkin, Boris and Putin, the FSB and the Chechens.

His work was not entirely confined to the Kremlin's wars, however. Toward the end of 2002 he told me that he became "involved" with a large security company specializing in risk analysis and overseas operations, run by ex-British secret service officers. He did not go into much detail, but I understood that it had to do with his old area of expertise: Russian organized crime. Only after his death did I learn that this side of his life kept expanding and that he ended up consulting with law enforcement agencies in several European countries, from Estonia to Georgia to Spain. Among other things, he took part in efforts to free the British banker Peter Shaw, who had been kidnapped in Georgia in 2002, and was instrumental in the arrests of Russian mafia suspects in Spain in 2006. By Marina's estimates, in 2006 roughly half of his income came from security consulting. It was like in the old days in Moscow: he would just disappear for a few days and then reappear, cheerful as ever.

What they both longed for during the first two years in London was more stability. They had rented a furnished flat that never quite felt like a home. Marina wanted to have her own things to arrange the way she liked: a home to decorate, a kitchen to equip. Sasha, the most domestic man I have ever known, was even more keen to build a nest. One day he made a calculation: their Kensington rent was more than a mortgage payment on a decent home in the suburbs. They started to look for a new home.

Every Saturday morning Marina took Tolik to a Russian-language school in Finchley, in the north of London, because they were determined that he not forget the mother tongue. She used those Saturday mornings while he was in class to explore the area. She talked to real estate agents and toured houses. Finally, on the fourth or fifth Saturday, she discovered a new development of single-family homes in Muswell Hill, with some units still under construction. One of Boris's companies bought the house and rented it to Sasha and Marina.

They moved into their new home in February 2003. It was a two-story, three-bedroom unit, with a huge kitchen for Marina and a basement that Sasha converted into a gym. He was a fitness freak who spent a fortune on all kinds of exercise equipment. They bought new furniture, kitchen equipment, and linens. It was the happiest time of their life together. He was extremely proud of the new home and invited everybody to see it.

Among the guests at their housewarming party was Akhmed Zakayev. He was looking for a permanent place as well, after spending a year in an exceedingly expensive rental in Chelsea. Zakayev needed a much bigger house; he lived in the traditional Chechen way, with his two married sons and countless grandchildren under one roof. There was an empty lot across the street from Sasha's that looked big enough. But as he later said in his speech at Sasha's funeral, the main reason he picked that location was the ancient Chechen saying: "Know your neighbor first, build your house next." From the moment they met each other, they became the closest of friends: a mercurial oper and a weathered freedom fighter, the "Chechen Che," as I described him to my friends in America.

———————

April 2, 2003: Russian oligarch Boris Berezovsky, fighting extradition to Russia on fraud charges, is released on £100,000 ($160,000) bail by Judge Timothy Workman, pending hearings scheduled for October. Speaking to reporters outside the Bow Street Magistrates Court in London, Berezovsky dons a satirical mask of President Putin to underscore his claim that the case was a farce.

For those not intimately familiar with international law enforcement, the processes of asylum and extradition may seem like mirror images. In practice, however, they are very different. Of the millions of asylum seekers around the world, the vast majority have never had problems with criminal law; most tend to be victims of discrimination, genocide, or political persecution who are seeking a safe haven. The granting of asylum is an administrative process carried out in secrecy by immigration authorities. In the United States, applicants are seeking a green card; in the United Kingdom, a residence permit.

Those who are subject to extradition, on the other hand, rarely seek asylum. They are fugitives from justice who usually hide from authorities, often using false identities. Because of various multilateral and bilateral treaties, states are obligated to catch them and deport them to face criminal charges in foreign lands. If, like Zakayev and Boris, the targets believe the extradition charges are false, they can seek exemption from deportation in a court of law, in an open hearing. Those hearings are very different from criminal trials; the court does not decide on the question of guilt or innocence. In effect, the burden of proof rests with the defendant: he has to demonstrate that the request to give him up is without merit or politically motivated, or that he would face an unfair trial, torture, or death if extradited. In other words, defendants face a presumption of guilt, not innocence.

Extradition and asylum are thus conflicting concepts, not mirror images. An asylum request would not be considered if there is an extradition case pending, and the court, as a rule, would not hear an extradition case against someone who has been granted asylum from the same country.

The extradition request for Zakayev came before he even considered seeking asylum, so there was no conflict. But with Boris, by April 2002, an asylum request had been pending for eighteen months. The British government surely knew that if it was granted, Boris's asylum would make the Kremlin go berserk. The Russian government's new request to extradite him, therefore, was something of a relief for the Brits. The home secretary wrote to Boris that his asylum plea had been turned down because of the extradition charges. Boris's fate was no longer in the hands of the executive branch. Instead, Judge Timothy Workman would decide it.

Zakayev's and Boris's extradition hearings—the two intertwined cases that tested the reach of the Kremlin and proved far more difficult than the average political assassination—lasted from April to November 2003. They were so beset with bizarre twists, unexpected developments, and odd coincidences that they eventually convinced me to believe in Sasha's constant stream of conspiracy theories. They unfolded in parallel with our investigation of the Moscow bombings and growing suspicions about the theater siege. The improbable in one reinforced the unbelievable in the other, until I felt as if my life had turned into a made-for-television espionage thriller.

The most bizarre of all was an incident with a man I'll call Pavel. At a bail hearing for Boris on April 2, his security guards, a squad of French Foreign Legion veterans, spotted a tall, skinny man with a wrinkled face, perhaps age fifty, in a gray suit. They had also noticed him earlier that day skulking around Boris at the Russian Economic Forum. They kept an eye on him. Then Sasha noticed him talking to a Russian by the name of Nikita, who was part of Boris's retinue. The man came up to Nikita outside of the courthouse to introduce himself. He was a small businessman from Kazakhstan, living in London. The chat with Nikita did not last long and did not get much beyond the introduction.

Pavel appeared again at Boris's next court hearing, on May 13. As soon as he could, Sasha converged on him like a tornado.

"Confess!" he blustered. "Who sent you to spy on us?"

Remarkably, Pavel *did* confess. He was moonlighting for the Russian Embassy, he said, entrapped by the FSB. He wanted to switch sides and work with us. Several days later Sasha brought him to meet me in a Starbucks café on Leicester Square.

Pavel said that he had been recruited by the KGB while working as a Kremlin driver in the Brezhnev era. When the Soviet Union collapsed, he thought his relationship with Kontora was over. He started a business but came into conflict with some gangsters and had to flee for his life to Kazakhstan. From there he somehow got to London in 1999, where he applied for asylum and started a small trading company. His asylum was still pending, but in 2002 he was approached in a London park by two Russian diplomats who called out his old KGB code name.

"They said that I should work for them, otherwise they would report my past to the immigration authorities, and I'd be deported. Of course I had not mentioned the KGB in my asylum application. I had no choice," he claimed.

"So what kind of work have you been doing?"

"Going places, writing reports. Russian events, for example. Or, say, details of parking, service elevators, and emergency exits in a department store. With Berezovsky, I was supposed to get friendly with one of you and report whatever I heard, that sort of thing."

"So what do you want from us?"

"I don't know. Can you help me with my asylum somehow?"

"I doubt it," I said. "Perhaps you should write your report to your embassy friends and hope for the best." He was quite possibly genuine, but we had enough of our own problems.

Pavel reappeared a few weeks later, at yet more hearings, this time for Zakayev's case. Sasha brought him to a sushi restaurant in Soho. He had a new assignment, he reported. His embassy contacts told him to buy a fountain pen, a particular model, and see whether he could get it through a metal detector in the Bow Street court. He also had to figure out where in the courthouse people were allowed to smoke: in the lavatory, in the stairwell, and so on.

Sasha became extremely excited.

"That's binary!" he whispered, leaning toward us across the table. "They are setting up a binary attack. There are such binary poisons: you squirt some liquid on a person, say, using a pen, and it is harmless, but then you expose him to smoke, which is also harmless for everyone around, except the one who had that liquid on him. The man drops dead of heart failure. This is what it is!"

It sounded unreal.

"Look, Pavel," I said, "this may be nothing, or it may be something. If you are telling the truth, and Sasha is right, then you may be part of a murder plot. If someone gets murdered, you'll be in big trouble. We will have to report our conversation to the police. If I were you, I'd go to the police, too."

He agreed. Would we help him find a lawyer?

We called George Menzies, Sasha's solicitor, and asked him to meet us urgently in his office. It was almost midnight. Pavel repeated his story while Menzies took notes; he agreed to come in early the next week to review a formal statement for the police that Menzies would draft.

But he never showed up. On the day of their scheduled meeting, he called Menzies to say that he had suddenly been invited to the Immigration Office to discuss his asylum request. Sasha had already submitted his own statement about our Leicester Square conversation to the Special Branch of Scotland Yard.

In early September, Judge Workman told Boris's lawyers that the extradition hearings would be moved from Bow Street to the Belmarsh court, where high-security cases are usually heard, thanks to a request by the Metropolitan Police. They believed that there was a credible threat to Boris's life. Then suddenly, on September 11, the Home Office granted Boris asylum without any explanation. The next day, Judge Workman threw out the extradition request, noting that it was now "quite pointless."

We were stunned, and confused. Could it be that the police, alerted by Sasha and me, had checked out Pavel and corroborated his bizarre story?

"Can you believe it, that they would attack me with a chemical weapon?" marveled Boris. "Can you imagine the lunacy? Say I am Putin; I am trying to get me by legal means. I believe that I will succeed, otherwise why start? And at the same time, I am sending a hit squad into the court. Volodya must be really insane."

"Boris," I replied, "my wife is a psychologist. She says that it is wrong to forecast the other guy's behavior by imagining yourself in his place. What sounds crazy to you may be pretty reasonable to him. He is KGB and you are not. That's why we are here."

"True. That's why Sasha is so valuable. He looks at the world with their eyes. If he can imagine a plot, they could be planning it for real. I wonder what the Brits are thinking?"

I still didn't know what to think. Yet ten days later, on September 21, the *Sunday Times* reported that there indeed was a plot. Citing "highly placed sources," the paper said that "an SVR agent . . . planned to fill a pen with [poisonous] liquid and then stab Berezovsky in the arm when passing by." The *Times* quoted an unnamed Whitehall official who confirmed that "MI5 had been approached by a man claiming he had been sent to Britain to murder the tycoon and they had referred the matter to the police." The rival *Guardian*, however, was skeptical; it quoted another intelligence source: "Across the agencies, the take has been that this would mark a significant escalation of Russian activity in London above [Kontora's] current capabilities."

Athens: On August 21, 2003, Vladimir Gusinsky is arrested upon his arrival from a holiday in Israel, based on an Interpol warrant on charges of fraud and money laundering. He is released on bail but ordered to remain in the country. On October 14, a Greek court rejects Moscow's request to extradite him. At a hearing lasting only a few minutes, the three judges decide that the charges against Gusinsky do not amount to a crime under Greek law.

If Pavel was the FSB turncoat who unexpectedly helped Boris win asylum, a man named Duk-Vakha Dushuyev, a Chechen whose story was no less bizarre, proved to be the reason Zakayev defeated Russia's attempt at extradition. Sasha was once again the go-between, and once again triumphant.

The Russian charges against Zakayev were severe: according to them, he was a torturer and a mass murderer. He was said to have led a Chechen gang in the 1999 war and to bear the responsibility for killing at least three hundred Russian officers. The indictment went on to claim that Zakayev had personally tortured a suspected Russian informer, Ivan Solovyov.

"When Solovyov refused to 'confess' to co-operating with the Russian Federal Security Service, Zakayev produced a gun which he threatened Solovyov with," the indictment stated. "He then pressed the barrel of the gun against Solovyov's little finger on his right hand and pulled the trigger, shooting the finger off. He did the same thing to the left hand, shooting two fingers off."

Zakayev was also alleged to have kidnapped and tortured two Russian Orthodox priests. Presiding over the hearings was Judge Workman.

There was no presumption of innocence here: the defense had to prove that the charges were false, not the other way around. Zakayev's lawyer pointed out that all of the opposing witnesses and victims had signed their statements in November 2002, when Zakayev was already in a Danish jail, suggesting that the case had been hastily concocted. But it wasn't much of a defense. On the morning of July 24, the defense announced a surprise witness, a man whose particularly damaging sworn testimony against Zakayev had been introduced by the Russian side. It was Duk-Vakha Dushuyev, a Chechen who, in his signed statement, had claimed that he personally saw Zakayev give the orders to kidnap and torture the priests. How he got out of Chechnya and into England was a mystery.

Duk-Vakha Dushuyev was a short, balding man. There was a frozen, odd grin on his face, possibly the result of the ordeal he now unveiled to the court. On November 27, 2002, he said, he was detained by the FSB in Grozny and brought to a Russian army base, where he was thrown into a filthy pit half-filled with water and covered by a metal grid. The pit was so narrow that he could not sit, and so shallow that he could not stand up. He spent six days there, bent over, handcuffed, and with a sack over his head. He was taken out for interrogations, during which he was beaten for hours, tortured with electric shocks, and threatened with having his throat slit unless he agreed to give testimony against Zakayev. On the sixth day he agreed to testify that as a fighter under Zakayev's direct command in 1997 he overheard him giving the orders to kidnap the priests.

He was brought to an investigator's office in Grozny to sign a statement, the one submitted by Russia to the London court, only with Dushuyev's name blacked out. Then he was put in front of a TV camera operated by men in military uniform, where he repeated his allegations. On December 15 his "interview" was shown on NTV as a report by "special correspondents" from Chechnya. Two months later he was tried for belonging to an "illegal armed formation" and given a suspended sentence. He was released on January 29.

Judge Workman stated the obvious: that this turn of events was "dramatic." He demanded from the prosecutor the full, unredacted testimony of Dushuyev and an explanation for why the original testimony did not mention that it was obtained while in custody, as the law required.

Sitting next to me in the crammed, spellbound courtroom, Sasha beamed. It had been he, a.k.a. Edwin Redwald Carter, who had arranged for Dushuyev's safe delivery into the hands of British lawyers.

The other charge against Zakayev, that he had shot off the fingers of Ivan Solovyov, also fell away. This time it wasn't Sasha who helped undermine the witness, but Anna Politkovskaya, in a story in *Novaya Gazeta*, which emerged after Solovyov testified. She wrote that Ivan Solovyov was actually well-known in Zakayev's hometown in Chechnya. People had seen him with fingers missing— apparently lost to frostbite—back in 1992, six years before the alleged shooting episode. The story also said that according to one of his drinking buddies, before departing for London, he had bragged about making a deal with the FSB to testify against Zakayev in exchange for "plenty of booze."

Zakayev's lawyer completely destroyed Solovyov on the witness stand. On November 13, 2003, Judge Workman ruled for Zakayev.

The Kremlin lost both bids to extract its London enemies through the legal system.

Moscow, January 2004: The campaign for Russia's presidential elections, scheduled for March 14, is in full swing. In the aftermath of a scandal concerning a conscript's death from abuse, President Putin pledges to work for the abolition of the draft. The Union of Committees of Soldiers' Mothers claims that 3,500 con-

scripts die every year from hazing, malnutrition, and disease, among the 1.1 million-member Russian army.

To an outside observer, there was never much of a chance that Ivan Rybkin could defeat Putin's bid for reelection. With the Kremlin's control of the media and the Russian people's traditional love of a powerful leader, Putin should not have had to bother thinking about Rybkin beating him at the polls. But insiders knew that Rybkin's campaign was a major concern for the Kremlin. Putin knew that he owed his popularity to the absence of alternative voices, not the success of his policies. There was great popular discontent at the grass-roots level. Moreover, as a KGB veteran, he knew better than anyone that regimes that come into power by trickery are often dissolved by trickery. Central to any plot is a credible, often unexpected pretender. After all, Putin himself came to power by emerging from total obscurity within a few short months. The apartment bombings were his trump card. They could easily become his Achilles' heel. A national campaign by someone like Rybkin, who would not hesitate to revive the bombing story, was something that he could not discount easily.

Backed by ample cash from Boris and the network of Liberal Russia branches around the country, Rybkin was planning to pick up where Yushenkov had left off. He wooed the protest electorate, particularly the antiwar and antidraft voters. Through his campaign he was aiming at establishing himself as the embodiment of anti-Putin sentiments, with an eye, perhaps, not at winning this election but setting himself up for the succession struggle of 2008. Rybkin's strategy was to renew his peacemaking mission and attempt once again to paint Putin as a man who was wasting innocent Russian lives in a useless war with an enemy who desired peace, a war that had been started on a controversial pretext. What Rybkin did not realize was the extent to which his opponents were prepared to play dirty.

At the end of January he was approached by an intermediary who, he knew from his time as NSC chief, had contacts with the rebel Chechen president Aslan Maskhadov. The man conveyed

Maskhadov's suggestion to set up a meeting similar to the one Rybkin had in Zurich with Zakayev in 2002. This, of course, would have been a coup for Rybkin's campaign. He agreed. The preparations would be handled under the utmost secrecy and the meeting would take place "in or around Chechnya" on terms set by the Chechen side.

According to the plan, Rybkin was supposed to slip out of FSB surveillance and go to Kiev, where he would meet a Maskhadov representative who would take him to the rendezvous.

Rybkin went to London to consult with the London group. All of us liked the idea, but Zakayev said that he was surprised he didn't know about it. He would need a few days to communicate with Maskhadov to double-check the intermediary's credentials. Rybkin went back to Moscow, where he got the word from his contact that everything was ready. There was no time to waste. He decided to go ahead without waiting for Zakayev's confirmation. That was his big mistake. As Zakayev learned later, the invitation to meet with Maskhadov was bogus.

Rybkin's stopover in Kiev, the capital of Ukraine, was supposed to be handled by Boris's local contacts. By then Boris was heavily financing the Orange opposition to the dictatorial regime of Ukrainian President Leonid Kuchma and had extensive contacts there.

As Rybkin told me later, on the evening of February 4, as a precaution to make sure he wasn't followed, he drove some one hundred miles to the town of Kaluga, the first stop on the Moscow–Kiev railway, to catch up with the overnight express, which arrived in the Ukrainian capital the next morning. And then he vanished.

He was reported missing by his campaign staff on Saturday, February 7. It was the day after the Central Election Commission had formally registered him as a presidential candidate, with his submission of 2 million signatures, as required by the rules.

Rybkin's disappearance became a sensation. Headlines around the world blared the news: "Russian Presidential Candidate Missing." Police launched a search. Soon, reports claimed that a "well-informed source" in the FSB had hinted that Rybkin had been spotted relaxing in a sanatorium near Moscow.

Rybkin resurfaced, in Kiev, on February 10. In his first interviews he seemed inconsistent, indeed, incoherent.

"I have a right to devote two or three days to myself," Rybkin told the Interfax news agency. "I came to Kiev to visit my friends. I switched off my mobile phone and never watched television," he said, explaining why he was unaware of the media frenzy. When he arrived in Moscow later that day he was more cryptic: "I am back as if from a round of difficult talks in Chechnya, and I am glad to be back." Asked if he had been detained, the grim-faced candidate said, "It is hard to detain me, but there are good people in Kiev, and I am very grateful to them." We in London were at a total loss to explain what was going on and were afraid to make inquiries over the phone, fearing to make things even worse.

Sasha immediately came up with a perfectly logical conspiracy theory. But he was hardly the only observer to jump to conclusions. "I think that he came under pressure and was intimidated," charged the leader of the Democratic Union, Valeria Novodvorskaya. "I believe that as an alternative, they threatened to kill him. I think that Rybkin gave up. Moreover, they offered him a way out. He may have arrived from Kiev but it was the FSB that had bought him a return ticket."

"He was drugged," said former KGB general Oleg Kalugin in an interview from Washington. "There are psychotropic substances and not only did the Russian special services not give up using them, but they have developed them further over the last few years."

"They gave him SP-117," Sasha argued. "Once you get SP-117, they can do whatever they want with you, drive you around, put you in bed with girls or boys, tape you, and so on. Then you get one pill of antidote and you are normal again and don't remember what happened."

"On a tape it would look like a very drunk man having fun," said Kalugin. "Or he would confess that he works for twenty different foreign intelligence services. Then they would tell him to stop his presidential campaign, all public activity, or they will give the material to the media."

On February 12 I went to meet Rybkin as he arrived from Moscow at London's Heathrow Airport. He looked pale and exhausted and sported a resigned smile. His story essentially fit Sasha's and Kalugin's scenario. The next day he repeated it at a press conference at the Kempinski Hotel.

His Ukrainian contacts, he said, had taken him to a flat in Kiev. He was offered some tea and sandwiches and felt drowsy. He did not know what happened next. He woke up four days later in a different apartment, where he was shown a compromising video of himself. As he spoke about it, he seemed close to tears. It was made by "horrible perverts . . . I don't know who did it," except that they spoke Russian. "I know who benefited from this," he added.

Following the press conference we urged Rybkin to undergo toxicology tests. They detected nothing unusual. His presidential race and political career were over.

On the day of Rybkin's press conference, Zelimkhan Yandarbiyev, Chechnya's exiled former president, was assassinated in Doha, Qatar, when a bomb blew apart his car as he left a mosque with his teenage son. Russia's security services denied any involvement in the attack.

Doha, Qatar, July 1, 2004: Two Russian secret agents, Anatoly Belashkov and Vasily Bogachyov, are convicted of murder and sentenced to twenty-five years in prison for the assassination of Zelimkhan Yandarbiyev. "The Russian leadership issued an order to assassinate the former Chechen leader," states the judge at the trial. He adds that the plot had been discussed and set in motion after a meeting at Russian intelligence headquarters in Moscow in August 2003.

The attack on human rights organizations came in the president's annual state of the nation address to Parliament, on May 27, 2004. Putin lashed out at "some" nongovernmental organizations, which, instead of representing "the real interests of the people," are serving "dubious group and commercial interests." The NGOs, he said, are only interested in securing funds from "foreign bodies and influential Russians." This is happening "amid a global competitive (economic) war" against Russia, in which "political, economic and media resources are being used. . . . Not everyone in the world wants to deal with an independent, strong, and confident Russia."

"Our calls to end the war in Chechnya have annoyed the Kremlin," commented Lev Ponomarev, whose group, For Human Rights, had been accused by a Justice Ministry official of inciting prison riots using funding from Berezovsky's foundation.

In response to Putin's speech, Boris pledged additional funds to the IFCL. I set out to organize a trip to Washington for the national chairperson of the Committees of Soldiers' Mothers and the head of one of their regional committees; they would take with them a strong antiwar message. The Kremlin's policy in the Caucasus only breeds terrorism, they argued. They spoke before Congress, urging the United States to increase funding for democracy in Russia, which had been dramatically reduced in the years of the Bush administration. Then they went to see Tom Graham at the White House. But he told them the same thing that he'd said to Sergei Kovalyov more than a year earlier: We sympathize with you, but the United States is not prepared to confront Putin over Chechnya.

Beslan, North Osetia, September 1, 2004: A group of Muslim rebels take nearly twelve hundred children and adults hostage in a school, wiring it with explosives. On the third day of the siege gunfire breaks out and the building is stormed by Russian special forces: 344 civilians, including 186 children, die in the ensuing explosions and shooting. The Maskhadov government condemns the attack. Warlord Shamil Basayev claims responsibility.

The horrific news from Beslan—of terrorists rounding up innocent schoolchildren in a gymnasium and hanging explosives on a rope over their heads, suspended from two basketball hoops—riveted the world. The aftermath of the raid, and the carnage, raised new questions about Russian law enforcement tactics, but there was universal outrage at the hostage-takers. Yet to newly reelected President Putin, much of the commentary coming from the West must have been maddening. It looked as if some Westerners held him partly responsible for the attack on the school. Every expression of outrage was qualified by a suggestion that he needed to learn his lesson and negotiate with Maskhadov.

When Putin took to the airwaves himself to address the nation in the aftermath of the disaster, he lashed out. The blame for the attack rests with Russia's international enemies, he declared. "Some would like to tear off a 'juicy piece' from us," he said. "Others help them. They help because they believe that Russia, as one of the major nuclear powers, is still a threat to them—a threat that should thus be removed. And terrorism is, of course, a mere instrument to achieve such aims."

Two days later he spoke to a group of foreign academics and journalists. "Why don't you meet Osama bin Laden, invite him to Brussels or to the White House, engage in talks, ask him what he wants and give it to him so he leaves you in peace? You find it possible to set some limits in your dealings with these bastards, so why should we talk to people who are child killers?"

Soon Foreign Minister Sergei Lavrov added, "We are cooperating with the USA and our European partners in the fight against terrorism. However, the USA giving asylum to Ilyas Akhmadov and Great Britain doing the same for Akhmed Zakayev cannot fail to make one think of double standards. . . . Those who provide shelter to terrorists are directly responsible for the tragedy of the Chechen people."

"Russia has the right to carry out pre-emptive strikes on militant bases abroad," added Defense Minister Sergei Ivanov. These "pre-emptive strikes may involve anything, except nuclear weapons," he added.

"You know who they mean when they say 'terrorist bases abroad'?" asked Sasha. "They mean us, Zakayev and Boris and I."

Moscow and London, October 2004–March 2005: In the aftermath of Beslan, the Union of Committees of Soldiers' Mothers, the largest Russian NGO, defies the Kremlin by starting "people's negotiations" with Chechen separatists. The Kremlin accuses CSM of being paid agents of foreign interests. However, opinion polls show 66 percent support for the CSM initiative. Under diplomatic pressure from Russia, the Belgian government refuses to let the CSM delegation into the country for a meeting with Akhmed Zakayev in the European Parliament in Brussels. On February 2, 2005, Aslan Maskhadov orders a unilateral cease-fire as a gesture in response to the CSM appeal. The radical warlord Shamil Basayev says that he too will observe the cease-fire. The Russian forces ignore the truce. On February 24, 2005, Soldiers' Mothers meet with Zakayev in London in the presence of several European parliamentarians, issuing a "Peace Memorandum." Two weeks later Aslan Maskhadov is killed in a Russian commando raid.

With the death of Maskhadov the Kremlin contention that the Chechen separatist government is nothing more than a bunch of terrorists moved one step closer to becoming a self-fulfilling prophecy. The new Chechen president was a moderate Muslim scholar named Abdul-Halim Sadulayev, virtually unknown in the West, who was a compromise figure acceptable to various field commanders, perhaps precisely because of his weakness. He lacked the legitimacy of Maskhadov, who had been elected in an internationally recognized democratic vote. He did not have Maskhadov's inclination to seek accommodation with Russia. At the same time, the realization that both the West and the Islamic world outdid each other in appeasing the Kremlin—a total sellout of Chechnya—strengthened the defiant suicidal streak of the field fighters. The influence of the radical wing increased dramatically. One of the first things the new Chechen president did was bring Shamil Basayev, the terrorist warlord, into his government.

"Basayev is a terrorist," I said to Akhmed Zakayev. "I don't see how you can stay in the same government with him."

"You are becoming just like the Bush administration," retorted Akhmed. "What do you want from us? For ten years the Russians have been killing us—40 percent of our population is dead—and no one said a word. Now everyone is outraged about Basayev. I did not invite him to join the government, and I wouldn't have if it were up to me. I fought with him all my political life. And now you want me to quit and leave him in control? So, okay, I quit. There will be no one left to stand up to the radicals. And what about those who think the way I do? We are still people, with a young generation growing up, both at home and all over Europe. They will say, Zakayev quit? Basayev is our leader? This would only mean Basayev had won, with Russian and Western help. No, I will stay and keep fighting."

In the weeks following Maskhadov's death, a fiery debate erupted between the two principal ideologues of Chechen independence: Zakayev, who argued for a Western-style democratic state, and Movladi Udugov, who hoped for a strict Islamic republic. Just as in occupied Europe during World War II, listeners in Chechen towns and villages and in the mountain rebel encampments tuned in to the broadcasts of Radio Liberty to hear the émigré politicians talking about the time "after the victory." Zakayev's and Udugov's visions clashed across the pages of their respective Web sites, Chechen-Press.info and KavkazCenter.com, each with thousands of attentive readers in the Russian and Western European Chechen diasporas.

Sasha Litvinenko took the sellout of the Chechens very close to his heart. He became a frequent contributor to the ChechenPress Web site. Zakayev eagerly provided him with as much space as he wanted. ChechenPress became Sasha's tribune; in 2005–2006 he authored more than a hundred opinion columns there, with titles like "Kremlin Werewolves," "The Heroism of Mikhail Trepashkin," and "Politkovskaya Killers Cover Their Tracks."

He took his mission to reach out to the Chechens very seriously, as an obligation. He once told me that he saw himself as "one of those Germans who were helping Jews."

"When the war ends, I will be the only remaining Russian whom the Chechens will still call a friend," he said, "and Akhmed, perhaps, the only Chechen who will be willing to talk to the Russians. So the two of us will negotiate the next peace treaty."

At one point he told Marina, "Akhmed and I are like brothers. They should bury us next to each other. Not in London. In Chechnya."

CHAPTER 14

THE "TINY NUCLEAR BOMB"

Moscow, June 8, 2006: The State Duma adopts legislation giving the FSB authority to send commandos to assassinate "terrorist groups" abroad. "The amendments provide for special operation units of the FSB to be used at the discretion of the President against terrorists and bases that are located outside the Russian Federation for the purpose of interdicting threats to the Russian Federation," says Mikhail Grishankov, deputy chairman of the Duma Security Committee.

As Putin's presidency settled into its second term, the security services roamed freely in the corridors of power. Over 70 percent of top government appointments were taken by former FSB officers. With virtually all television broadcasting under Kremlin control, regional leaders subdued, and no opposition in the Duma, the political process ground to a halt. In the aftermath of the destruction of Liberal Russia and the abortive presidential bid of Ivan Rybkin, our London group of dissidents realized that the FSB could never be chased from the Kremlin by constitutional means. But we did not despair: the events in neighboring Ukraine suggested another way.

The nonviolent overthrow of Ukraine's Moscow-backed authoritarian regime in late 2004 and early 2005, thanks to the crowds camping on Independence Square in Kiev, was a major setback for Putin. It quashed his drive to reinvent the Soviet Union by installing puppet administrations in the satellite states. But there was more to it: the Orange Revolution provided a blueprint for regime change in Russia itself. The ingredients included massive nonviolent street protests fomented by a network of civic organizations, at a moment of instability, such as a transition of power. (The Orange Revolution began as a protest against a vote count that had apparently been rigged.) The knowledge that Boris Berezovsky was heavily involved in the Ukrainian events only added insult to injury for the Kremlin.

Since early 2004 Ukraine had become the principal focus of Boris's, Sasha's, and my activities. In the period immediately preceding the standoff in Kiev, Boris quietly channeled more than $40 million to the Orange camp, making it possible to sustain the street protests for nearly two months. When Viktor Yuschenko, the democratic opponent of the Moscow-backed candidate, Viktor Yanukovich, was felled by a mysterious poisoning in September 2004, we despaired. Not only the Ukrainian future, but the fate of freedom in the entire post-Soviet bloc seemed to hang in the balance. Thankfully, Yuschenko survived to win the presidency in a second, carefully monitored runoff election. In the aftermath of the Orange victory, the IFCL established an office in Kiev with an eye toward using it as a bridgehead for a similar peaceful revolution in Russia.

In the period prior to the Orange Revolution, Sasha, Felshtinsky, and I expended a major effort on trying to solve a mystery that was the Achilles' heel of the authoritarian regime of Ukrainian president Leonid Kuchma: the murder of a Kiev journalist, Georgy Gongadze, in September 2000. Most people believed that the critical journalist had been eliminated on Kuchma's orders. Gongadze's murder fueled a conspiracy theory that galvanized Ukrainian society and became the rallying cry of the Orange camp. After the revolution, Sasha, Felshtinsky, and I testified to the Ukrainian prosecutors investigating the Gongadze case, which, like Yuschenko's poisoning, remains unsolved to this day.

When Anna Politkovskaya was gunned down by an assassin in Moscow on October 7, 2006, the parallels with Ukraine were striking. She was perhaps the most outspoken critic of Putin in Russia. Could Anna play the same martyr's role that Gongadze had performed for

Ukraine? Could her murder be a spark that would lead to the down-fall of the FSB regime during the presidential election in 2008?

Both sides realized the far-reaching political implications of Anna's death and blamed it on each other. Speaking at a press conference during a visit to Germany on October 10, President Putin blamed Anna's assassination on unnamed opponents aiming to destabilize his regime. "We have information, and it is reliable, that many people hiding from Russian justice have long been nurturing the idea of sac-rificing somebody in order to create a wave of anti-Russia feeling in the world," Putin said. The following week, speaking at the Frontline Club in London at a Politkovskaya commemoration, Sasha Litvi-nenko accused Putin of ordering her murder.

The mood in October 2006 was a reciprocity of paranoia. The Kremlin and the London group accused each other of murder, and nursed conspiracy theories that were mirror images of each other. Each accused the other side of killing people with the aim of blaming it on them. It set the stage for the climax of Sasha's story. Three weeks after Anna was shot as she carried a bag of groceries in the elevator of her apartment house in Moscow, and a year before Putin would have to step down after serving two terms as president of Russia, Sasha was murdered by a mysterious poison.

The call from Radio Echo Moscow came on Saturday, November 11, 2006: "Can you confirm that Alexander Litvinenko has been poisoned?"

I was in Paris en route to London, and I didn't know anything about it so I went on the Internet to check. The initial source of the report was Akhmed Zakayev's Web site, ChechenPress.info, which announced that on November 1, Sasha had been poisoned, allegedly by the FSB.

I reached Sasha on his cell phone. He was in a small community hospital in North London, not far from his home. He sounded vig-orous.

"I was throwing up for three days before they took me to the hos-pital. The doctors think I ate bad sushi, but it's not that, I know."

"What about the Italian guy?" I asked. According to Zakayev's Web site, Sasha became ill after eating sushi with Mario Scaramella, of whom I had never heard before.

"Well, we were in the sushi bar together, so he could have slipped something into my soup."

My initial reaction was that this was just too much. An Italian lacing his miso soup with poison? Surely it was just a case of bad sushi, I thought.

I called Marina. She said doctors had found a bacterium in his system, which she "could not even begin to pronounce. They gave him some antibiotics."

"Okay, then. I will be in London tomorrow."

It sounded so innocuous. I did not see Sasha until Wednesday, November 15. He was still feeling lousy, and I began to be slightly worried: two weeks is just a bit long for food poisoning.

What I saw when I arrived at Barnet Hospital did not make me feel better. They kept Sasha in an infection-safe environment. I had to put on plastic gloves and an apron before entering the ward, and refrain from touching him, to protect him from accidentally catching a bug from outside.

"He is neutropenic," the doctor said, meaning that his white blood cell count was down. This happens when the bone marrow stops producing cells needed to fight off infection. No food poisoning would cause such a symptom.

"Why?" I asked.

"We don't know. Theoretically it may be a virus, something like AIDS, or an unknown reaction to the antibiotic he received initially, or a large dose of some chemotherapeutic drug, or heavy irradiation. But he was not near any radiation source and has not received chemotherapy. And he is HIV-negative. Frankly, we are at a loss."

"We suspect foul play," I said. "Have you notified the police?"

"At this point the cause can be benign or sinister. We can't contact them until we are sure. We're waiting for a toxicology report."

Sasha looked thin and gray. He had not eaten for two weeks, subsisting on IV transfusions. But he was moving around the room, and he was in a fighting mood.

"The way it started, I thought I'd die," he reported. "But I imme-diately drank a gallon of water and made myself throw up, to clean the stomach. These morons, they didn't listen to me. When I told them I was poisoned by the KGB, they wanted to call a psychiatrist. You have to get it into the British press."

"I already called a couple of journalists. But no one will touch it without police or hospital confirmation. When toxicology arrives, we'll know for sure what's wrong with you."

By now, thanks to Sasha and Boris, I was an expert in publicizing unbelievable explanations of incredible events, and this one was the most incredible yet. On the other hand, a very ill man was in front of my eyes, and there was no better theory than poison.

"Tell me about the Italian."

"The Italian has nothing to do with it. I named him on purpose, as a trick. The real man is Andrei Lugovoy, but please keep it secret. I am trying to lure him back to London."

True to himself, Sasha was playing out another gambit. He was sure that Lugovoy, Boris's former head of ORT security, had poi-soned him. After his illness was reported in Russia, Lugovoy called him from Moscow to wish him a swift recovery.

"I told Lugovoy that I suspect the Italian, to make him feel it's safe to come again, to finish me off," he smiled wryly.

Just about a year earlier, at a grand party Boris threw on his six-tieth birthday in a rented castle outside of London, we had shared a table: Sasha, Marina, Andrei Lugovoy, and I. At the time he barely registered in my memory; he was a shadow from the Russian past, one of two hundred guests. But as Sasha told me at the hospital, that party was the beginning of a surprisingly intense interaction between them. Back in Moscow they had never been close.

After having served fourteen months in prison in connection with Glushkov's attempted escape, Lugovoy went into business and became immensely successful, benefiting from the new Russian pros-perity caused by skyrocketing oil prices. His core enterprise was his security agency, which provided bodyguards to hundreds of nouveau riche Muscovites. He bragged to Sasha about his multimillion-dollar investments in the food and services industries. He suggested that they work together; Sasha could be his man in London. Surely there must be British security companies interested in the Russian market.

Sasha produced impressive references from the security companies he had been working with. Over the year they met two or three times. No real business had come of it, but the prospects seemed great. His last meeting with Lugovoy was on November 1, in the Pine Bar at the Millennium Hotel on Piccadilly, two hours after he went out with Mario Scaramella. Lugovoy was with another Russian, Sasha said, whom Sasha had not met before. "He had the eyes of a killer," he said. He knew the type.

The next morning, I went to the hospital with Boris, who like myself had initially discounted Sasha's illness as a stomach bug. Sasha was visibly worse. His hair had started falling out; he pulled a pinchful to demonstrate. He was suffering tremendously from an apparent inflammation of his gastrointestinal tract, all the way from his mouth, which was so painful he could barely talk or swallow, to his bowels. It was as if his insides had been burned by an unknown irritant. The doctors had started him on painkillers. They still did not know the cause of it all.

I contacted Prof. John Henry, the renowned toxicologist at St. Mary's Hospital, who had gained considerable fame, in the Russian universe at least, in 2004 when he diagnosed the poisoning of Viktor Yuschenko simply by looking at his face on TV. It was the substance called dioxin, he said, and indeed, some time later, lab analyses confirmed it.

I described the symptoms to Professor Henry over the telephone.

"Hair loss is a hallmark of thallium," he said. "But bone marrow malfunction sounds strange. Does he have muscle weakness?"

Thallium, a heavy metal, had been banned in the United Kingdom but was readily available as a rat poison in grocery stores throughout the Middle East. It acts by slowly destroying the outer shield of nerve cells. Survivors may have long-term neurological problems. A nurse in Qatar made headlines in the 1970s when, after reading Agatha Christie's novel *The Pale Horse,* she recognized a case of thallium poisoning that had baffled doctors. Thallium poisoning was the basis of a conspiracy theory swirling around the death of Yasir Arafat. Some say the CIA planned to embarrass Fidel Castro by sneaking thallium into his shoes, hoping it would cause his beard, eyebrows, and pubic hair to fall out.

On the strength of these stories and Professor Henry's guess, I finally persuaded a reporter, David Leppard from the *Sunday Times,* to see Sasha at the hospital. Leppard had been willing to listen to out-landish theories in the past; he was the one who broke the story of Pavel, the fountain-pen man. He realized, of course, that without objective confirmation of poison there was no story, but he came just in case the toxicology report proved foul play; then, by press time, he would have an exclusive for the Sunday paper. He interviewed Sasha in Barnet Hospital on Thursday evening.

Moscow, November 15: Speaking at the Duma, Russian Prosecutor General Yuri Chaika announces a cooperation agreement with the British Crown Prosecution Service. He indicates that investigators probing the assassination of Anna Politkovskaya will explore the theory that the journalist's killers might be linked with certain persons in London.

On Thursday, November 16, we had a strategy meeting with Boris and Lord Tim Bell, his media adviser. By then Boris and I were both convinced that Sasha had been poisoned. We were not sure about the *why,* but there was no doubt regarding the *who*: Who else other than Kontora would want to harm Sasha? We wanted to alert the media.

Tim Bell was extremely concerned.

"Boris," he said, "you have cast yourself as the archenemy of Putin: politically, personally, and ideologically. Reasonable people believe that you are on the good side in this crusade, even though they may question your motives. For the public at large, this is all pretty irrelevant because it's all about politics in a faraway land. But this time, the situation is very different. A crime has been committed on

British soil, an attempted murder. The story will reach many people, who will react intuitively. The problem is, most people will not *want* to believe it was Putin. People are instinctively averse to the idea of governments or presidents ordering murders. The more it seems obvious, the deeper they will go into denial. You will be going against the tide, and you are the anti-Putin. If people don't want to think it was Putin, then they'll think it must be you. The louder you say it was him, the more this will happen."

By the end of the day on Friday the 17th the toxicology report came in. It was official: Sasha had been poisoned with thallium, Marina told me on the phone from the hospital. She sounded relieved, in one sense. At least they knew what it was. They were starting him on an antidote.

At that point, all hell broke loose. An armed police squad arrived at Barnet just as Sasha was being readied for transfer to the University College Hospital (UCH) in Euston, the top medical facility in Britain. Before he was discharged, Marina had the good sense to get a medical summary of Sasha's case written up by the attending physician. I had it sent by messenger to Boris's office, where we were holding council, and we immediately faxed it to New York. By then our émigré network in America was helping us seek the world's leading authority on thallium poisoning.

In the meantime, another police squad converged on the house of Akhmed Zakayev in Muswell Hill.

"They took Tolik away," Zakayev reported on the phone. While Marina was at the hospital, Tolik stayed with the Zakayevs after school.

"You won't believe it," he said. "Eight cops in three cars said they had orders to take him. They terrified my grandchildren. 'Why did they arrest Tolik?' they asked."

I rushed to UCH only to discover that the ambulance, escorted by police, had beaten me there. The doors on Sasha's floor were locked. Through a window I could see two policemen at the end of a corridor. As I gestured to attract their attention, two solemn-looking gentlemen in suits emerged from the elevator. They were obviously there to visit the same patient.

"May I inquire who you are?" one of them asked.

"And who are you?"

He gave me his card and wrote down my numbers. He and his companion were from the Scotland Yard antiterrorist unit. They asked me to give them a day to question Sasha. I tried to call Marina, but she was nowhere to be found. There was nothing more I could do. I went out for a drink.

As I settled in at a nearby pub, Zakayev called: "They are holding Marina."

"What?"

"She called me from a hospital phone. They have taken her cell phone away, and would not let her see Sasha, or leave. Tolik's cell phone is off, too. When the police took him, they told me they were bringing him to Marina, but they didn't follow through. I am on my way to the hospital," he said.

We got to Sasha's floor at about the same time. A uniformed officer appeared.

"We want to see Mrs. Litvinenko."

"She can't see you right now."

"Is she in custody?"

"No, she is not, but she can't see you."

Cops are cops everywhere, I thought. There is only one way of dealing with them.

"Well, if she is not here in five minutes, we are calling the press to say that you have arrested her."

"Please wait while I call my superior."

Two minutes later, the antiterrorist detective appeared, the one I had met earlier. He was obviously the boss around here.

"Look, I'm sorry," he said. "They've overdone it a bit. They're the local police and they don't know what's going on. They were told to secure the witnesses."

"Why are you holding the kid?"

"He was at a police station, and they are bringing him back to Mr. Zakayev's house right now. I apologize again."

A moment later they brought Marina. "Thank you for rescuing me, boys," she said. "They just returned my phone." She was shaken, but trying to smile. It was past midnight. Zakayev drove her home.

On Saturday morning I picked up Professor Henry on my way to UCH. Thallium, he explained as we drove, "is tasteless, colorless, odorless. It takes about a gram to kill you. For the first ten days or so it looks like a typical case of food poisoning. Hair begins to fall out only after two weeks, which gives the assailant ample time to get away. It's a poisoner's ideal weapon," he said.

In the hospital he gave the young doctor a lecture about thallium: "The body tries to get rid of it by excreting it into the gut, but it is quickly reabsorbed. The antidote works by capturing it in the intestines."

They were giving Sasha dark blue pills of "Prussian Blue," an antidote dye. The large pills were extremely painful to swallow given the state of his mouth. But he was a brave soldier. He immediately appreciated Henry's authority. "I know you'll get me out of this, Professor," he said.

"You are doing well," Henry said, cheering him up. "Let me see how strong you are. Squeeze my hand. Oh, you are strong!"

"I could still do push-ups if not for these tubes," Sasha said, pleased.

But when we left the room, Henry looked perplexed.

"It looks very strange. They are treating him for thallium, but with thallium he should've lost his muscle strength, and he has not."

I showed him the toxicology report from Barnet Hospital.

"See," he said, "it says here that the level of thallium is elevated, but only 'three times over the norm.' This is too low to account for his symptoms."

On Sunday the papers broke the story: "Russian Spy Poisoned in London. Anti-terrorist Police Investigate."

"Sasha is not a spy," protested Marina. "He never spied. Why do they call him a spy?"

"This is the least of our concerns right now," I said.

We were sitting in the UCH cafeteria downstairs. Sasha had just been transferred to intensive care "as a precaution," the doctors explained. They were now giving him a fifty-fifty chance of survival.

Marina was wearing dark glasses. There was a crowd of reporters outside, but they could not get to her. The hospital had deployed extra security to keep them at a distance. Ever since the *Sunday Times* hit the stands, the press had been chasing her, forcing her to use the back entrance to the hospital. Reporters were seeking out her address at Muswell Hill. Scotland Yard assigned two officers to her, who hung around just in case of a problem.

She did not want to speak to the press yet. "You know me," she said to Zakayev and me. "This is your game. I want to stay out of this as long as possible."

In truth, I was just getting to know Marina. I would remember our conversation later, after Sasha's death, when she decided she was ready to face the media. She did it with force and grace, in spite of her aversion to the limelight, as an obligation to Sasha, like a settler's wife who puts aside her laundry and picks up her fallen man's rifle to defend her home.

While he was at the hospital, however, Marina managed the disaster quietly, maintaining the household routine, keeping Tolik's schedule, holding her emotions at bay, with only the redness of her eyes betraying her lonely anguish. I saw her several times a day, but she never showed any sign of despair nor gave any cause for worry.

Later, she explained to me how she managed to live through those weeks.

"The truth is, I never believed that he would die. Not when they said fifty-fifty, not later, even up to the very end. If I had admitted that he could die, I would have broken down. But I kept telling myself it was just another crisis, the third in our marriage. The first was when he was in prison, the second when we were running away in Turkey. I used the coping skills that I had learned before. It was like being caught in a stream: you swim along hoping for the best and doing what you minimally have to do. You keep your head above water."

———

Upstairs on the ICU floor, armed police were standing guard. Besides Marina, only Zakayev, Boris, and I were allowed into Sasha's room. We had to clear any other visitors he wanted to see. But we did not see much of him. Most of his time was taken up by the antiterrorist detectives; by late Sunday they had spent probably twenty hours with him. They were obviously rushing against time to get as much out of him as possible.

On Monday morning, Professor Henry visited again. When he emerged from a conference with the attending physician his expression was dark.

"This is not thallium," he said. "His bone marrow function is totally gone, while his muscles are strong—if it were thallium it would have been just the opposite. They now handle him as if he had an overdose of a chemotherapeutic drug, even though he didn't. The point is, at this stage the cause does not really matter. They are more concerned with the effects, such as sudden organ failure. He is getting weaker."

"But they found thallium at Barnet."

"That's the mystery. He has definitely gotten a little bit of thallium, *plus* something else . . ." Suddenly he interrupted himself. "Or, wait a minute. Perhaps it was radioactive thallium."

You had to be a scientist to follow Professor Henry's train of thought. A small amount of a highly radioactive variety of thallium, that is, an isotope, would not cause any *chemical* damage to Sasha's body, such as muscle weakness. However, it would create heavy *radiation* damage, such as bone marrow destruction and hair loss. This was exactly what happened to a KGB defector by the name of Nikolai Khokhlov in 1957, whose tea was laced with radioactive thallium by Soviet agents.

"But they have checked Sasha for radioactivity and found nothing, haven't they?"

"They did. Twice. But hospitals are geared to deal only with gamma radiation. If it was alpha radiation they wouldn't pick it up. And I must confess that I do not remember my physics: whether thallium emits alpha or gamma rays."

There are two kinds of radiation: high-energy, penetrating radiation called gamma rays, and low-energy radiation, such as alpha emission, which does not penetrate even a sheet of paper, not to mention human skin. In medical school they teach only about gamma radiation: people get exposed to it in places like Hiroshima or Chernobyl. Doctors also use gamma rays in isotope diagnostics when they inject a small amount of a gamma-emitter into a patient, and then register the emissions in a scanning chamber to detect cancer cells. But there is no place for alpha radiation in medicine, and no equipment to detect it in hospitals. Even if Sasha were packed with an alpha emitter, no common medical device would notice it.

But his body would. Alpha radiation in the environment is harmless; it cannot get past skin. If an alpha-emitting substance is ingested, however—that is, swallowed or inhaled—it spreads quickly throughout the body, to all organs and tissues, gets inside every cell, and attacks from within. The low energy of alpha radiation, like a short-range weapon, is more than sufficient to cause havoc inside the living cell. It attacks the DNA in the nucleus, shredding it into fragments. The cell dies. Particularly vulnerable are rapidly dividing cells, such as in the lining of the intestines, in the bone marrow, and those in the hair roots; hence Sasha's symptoms.

On Monday Professor Henry called me: "I checked my books. Thallium is a gamma-emitter. They would have detected it in the hospital. But they should keep looking for alpha-emitters. I will have to talk to Scotland Yard."

The first question Sasha asked me on Monday morning was about the press. Had they finally understood? Did they get it right—that he was poisoned by Kontora? He was still fighting his war, and he wanted to make the most of it.

"Sasha, there are ten TV cameras and fifty reporters outside. But as you know, one look is worth ten thousand words. To get the most impact I need a picture of you, the way you look," I said apologetically.

Marina shot me an angry glance.

"Give me a mirror," Sasha said.

She went out to look for a mirror.

"What are my chances?" he asked, using the moment alone.

"They give you fifty-fifty, but you are a strong—"

"I know, I know," he interrupted. "Look, I want to write a statement, in case I don't make it. Name the bastard. Anya [Politkovskaya] did not do it, so I will, for both of us. You put it in good English, and I will sign. And you'll keep it, just in case."

"Okay, I will, but we will tear it up together when you get out of here."

"Sure we will."

He had trouble speaking. Still, as he was dictating his statement I could sense something very new in his tone. For the first time, I was receiving instructions from him, and in a manner that left no room for discussion. Through our whole relationship there had been a certain boyishness in him. He had assigned me the role of a grown-up, from whom he expected to get approval. Now he had grown up, sure of himself, talking while I took notes. It was as if the venom that aged him twenty years in three weeks had also made him wise and confident. Later, when Marina told me about the "other Sasha" who had revealed his hard edge to her only rarely, I recognized this side of him.

Marina returned with the mirror. For a minute he studied himself. He was satisfied—he looked terrible.

The next day, his image, a compression of suffering and defiance, flashed on millions of TV screens around the world. Meanwhile his would-be posthumous *J'accuse,* signed in the presence of Marina and another witness, lay sealed in an envelope in my hotel safe.

I brought him the newspapers. His photo was on every front page.

"Good," he said. "Now he won't get away."

Those were his last words to me.

Moscow, November 21: Several Duma deputies allege that Boris Berezovsky and Akhmed Zakayev are behind the Litvinenko poisoning. "Berezovsky's close links to Chechen terrorists [suggest] they could have organized both the murder of Politkovskaya and the poi-

soning of Litvinenko," says the former FSB chief Nikolai Kovalev. The next day, Tom Parfitt, the Moscow correspondent of the Guardian *writes, "The idea that the Kremlin gave an order to eliminate Mr Litvinenko seems highly unlikely. He just wasn't worth it . . . [but] Berezovsky's position is looking increasingly shaky—along with the positions of other individuals whose extradition Russia is demanding. . . . They need evidence to back up their claims that they'll face retribution if they're sent back to Russia. The death of a liberal journalist and the poisoning of an 'enemy of the FSB' ought to satisfy Judge Timothy Workman."*

For the next twenty-four hours, Sasha was heavily sedated, and he slipped in and out of consciousness. Most of the day on Wednesday, November 22, I was dealing with the press in an endless succession of interviews in the propaganda war with the Kremlin that was now in full swing. I finally came to the hospital in the afternoon. I looked at him through the glass from an adjoining cubicle. He had aged more in the past day; he now looked like a seventy-year-old man, bald, gaunt, skin over bones. He had not eaten for twenty-two days. He had had several visitors: George Menzies, his solicitor; Andrei Nekrasov, the filmmaker; Akhmed Zakayev's entire family; Boris with Lena. Valter Litvinenko, his father, had flown in from Russia, and he and Marina alternated holding vigil at his bedside: he at night, she in the daytime.

Before Marina left for the night on Wednesday, Sasha suddenly woke up and looked at her. "I am going home, darling," she said. "I will be back in the morning."

"Marina, I love you so much." They were his last words to her.

That night he went into cardiac arrest and was put on a respirator. He never regained consciousness, dying at 9:21 p.m. the next day, Thursday, November 23. His father was at his bedside. The staff at the hospital phoned Marina just as she returned home from her day shift. She picked up Tolik and they went back to the hospital.

London, November 24, 2006: Sasha's statement is released to reporters outside University College Hospital:

> *I would like to thank many people. My doctors, nurses and hospital staff for doing all they can for me. The British police who are pursuing my case with vigour and professionalism and are watching over me and my family.*
>
> *I would like to thank the British government for taking me under their care. I am honoured to be a British citizen. I would like to thank the British public for their messages of support and for the interest they have shown in my plight.*
>
> *I thank my wife, Marina, who has stood by me. My love for her and for our son knows no bounds.*
>
> *But as I lie here, I can distinctly hear the beatings of wings of the angel of death. I may be able to give him the slip, but I have to say my legs do not run as fast as I would like.*
>
> *I think, therefore, that this may be the time to say one or two things to the person responsible for my present illness.*
>
> *You may succeed in silencing me, but that silence comes at a price. You have shown yourself to be as barbaric and ruthless as your most hostile critics have claimed. You have shown yourself to have no respect for life, liberty or any civilised value. You have shown yourself to be unworthy of your office, to be unworthy of the trust of civilised men and women.*
>
> *You may succeed in silencing one man. But a howl of protest from around the world will reverberate, Mr Putin, in your ears for the rest of your life.*
>
> *May God forgive you for what you have done, not only to me, but to beloved Russia and its people.*

Perhaps they listened to Professor Henry and brought an alpha-radioactivity detector to the hospital. Or perhaps they took Sasha's blood samples to where his case was eventually scrutinized, the Atomic Weapons Establishment in Aldermaston, Berkshire, Britain's nuclear lab. One way or another, moments after his death the authorities discovered what had killed Sasha: it was the obscure radioactive isotope Polonium-210, an alpha-emitter.

I learned about it from Zakayev, who called at three o'clock in the morning to report that police wearing radioactivity-protection gear had converged on Muswell Hill less than an hour after Marina and Tolik had returned from the hospital. They told them to take only the most necessary things and leave immediately because their lives were in danger. For the rest of the night they stayed at Zakayev's. People wearing bright yellow suits, rubber boots, gloves, and gas masks worked at Sasha's home through the rest of the night, sealing the house, covering the porch and the front lawn with plastic. A heavy police guard surrounded the place.

The detectives from Scotland Yard asked us not to tell anyone about the radioactivity. They first had to assess the public health hazard and make sure that the news of radioactive attack did not create panic in the city. But in the morning, a grief-stricken Valter Litvinenko nearly let it slip when he spoke to reporters in front of the hospital.

"A tiny nuclear bomb killed my son," he said, sobbing.

In the afternoon, Home Secretary John Reid announced that Sasha was killed by radioactivity. A statement from the Health Protection Agency (HPA) added that it was a "major dose." Pandemonium broke out in London. Squads of HPA officials and police, brandishing military alpha counters, roamed the city, retracing Sasha's steps, their every move followed closely by TV news crews. Hundreds of members of the public called the HPA hotline. The British government's emergency planning committee, which last gathered during the subway bombings, met to discuss the situation. News producers scrambled to find experts in nuclear physics for special-report newscasts. Within hours, millions of Britons became experts in polonium, Russian politics, and Boris Berezovsky's conspiracy theories. The entire world learned Sasha's name as the first-ever victim of a nuclear terrorist attack.

It took two weeks before the authorities gave the clearance for Sasha's funeral. His body presented a major environmental hazard; immediately after he died, it was removed to some secret facility and the hospital space was decontaminated. Pathologists attending his postmortem wore radioactivity-protection gear. Finally we were told that the body would be released to us in a special sealed casket, provided by the HPA. Should the family wish to cremate him, they would have to wait for twenty-eight years, until the radioactivity decays to safe levels—nearly eighty half-lives of Polonium-210.

Before the funeral, our closely knit circle was nearly torn apart by another controversy, Sasha's last surprise. As we were discussing the arrangements, Akhmed Zakayev declared that Sasha should be buried in a Muslim cemetery because he had converted to Islam the day before he died. It turned out that on November 22, just before Sasha lost consciousness, Akhmed brought a mullah to the hospital who said an appropriate prayer. As far as Akhmed was concerned, Sasha died a Muslim.

I did not know about the mullah, and I was furious with Akhmed. Sasha had never been in any way religious; in fact, he told me that he did not understand those who were. His only passion was to win his battles and to make his point. True, he often said, "I am a Chechen," but I said that too. That did not make me a Muslim. That was a statement of solidarity, not at all an expression of faith. Not to mention that on the last day he surely was not thinking clearly.

"I know why he did it, Akhmed," I said. "He felt guilty for what Russia had done to the Chechens and wanted to make a gesture. Like a German would want to become a Jew after the Holocaust. But it was a mistake. This will not help your cause. With what's going on in the world, let's face it, Russian propaganda will do everything to shift focus from the murder to the conversion. You are playing into their hands."

"I am not playing," said Akhmed. "Everything was done properly, so he is a Muslim."

Akhmed was a stubborn man. Yet that stubbornness is why the Russians will not win the Chechen war unless they kill off the entire stubborn population.

"I am not an expert in conversions," I said, "but I am an expert in biochemistry. With the amount of sedation he got on that day, I can't be sure he was rational."

"Acts of faith are not rational," said Akhmed.

The matter was deferred to Marina.

"Let everyone believe about Sasha whatever he wants," said Marina wisely. "You can have your service in a mosque and we will have ours in a chapel." Marina ruled that Sasha would be buried in nondenominational grounds.

On December 8, in the pouring rain, as the police kept the media off-limits, Sasha was laid to rest in Highgate Cemetery in London, his grave surrounded by the tombs of famous Victorians and a few atheists, including Karl Marx and the physicist Michael Faraday.

Death surrounds life like a frame around a painting: it signifies completion and bestows definition. A life recently concluded is a freshly painted picture framed for an exhibition, no longer subject to change, additions, or redactions, no second takes, not even final touches. The life is complete, and signed. Yet this frozen set of forms and colors is forever at the mercy of its viewers—hanging on a wall, it is subject to debate and to criticism.

Sasha's life, as soon as it had ended, became more meaningful, more awash with significance than it had been before November 1, 2006.

As I was coming to grips with his death, I realized that in Sasha I witnessed a miracle of transformation, of the kind when black turns white, right and wrong change places, death and salvation reverse punishment and reward. Within six short years from the time he fled Russia, a scared and confused member of a corrupt and murderous clique, he became a crusader, and then died a torturous death for it. In a different type of witness, his conversion would perhaps evoke ecclesiastical reference. I can simply say that Sasha turned out to be a greater man than most.

For Marina, there was no framing. "He was so superreal, he charged me so much, that I just continue running on that energy as if we are still wired to each other. I don't think it will ever stop."

CHAPTER 15

THE HALL OF MIRRORS

Moscow, February 1, 2007: Speaking at a Kremlin press conference, President Putin indicates that the Russian secret services considered Litvinenko an insignificant target, and would not, therefore, have bothered to murder him. "He didn't know any secrets," says Putin. "Before being fired from the FSB Litvinenko served in the convoy troops and had no access to state secrets." On the same day, Scotland Yard announces that it has completed its investigation and sent the Litvinenko file to the Crown Prosecution Service to determine whether anyone should be charged with a crime. The content of the file has not been disclosed.

"When Watergate was first reported, the White House brushed it aside as a 'third-rate burglary.' Then layers of revelations began peeling away, one after another, and the walls around Nixon came tumbling down," said George Menzies over lunch, some time after Sasha's death. "Sasha's case will become Putin's 'third-rate poisoning.' I have a hunch that this murder will be solved."

George was reacting to my lecture about Polonium-210 as a murder weapon. In the annals of forensic science, I explained, Sasha's murder will stand out for its ultimate irony: polonium is simultaneously the best and the worst murder weapon ever devised.

Whoever chose polonium to kill Sasha did so because the chances of its ever being discovered were close to zero. It could not be easily identified chemically: the toxicology lab found only low levels of thallium, a minor contaminant of polonium production. Polonium was unlikely to be detected by its radioactivity, since common Geiger counters were not designed to detect alpha rays. Polonium is perhaps the most toxic substance on earth: a tiny speck is a highly lethal dose, and one gram is enough to kill half a million people. But it is absolutely harmless to a handler unless it is inhaled or swallowed. Most important, polonium had never been used to murder anyone before, so practically no one in the expert community—toxicologists, police, or terrorism experts—would have been looking for it or expecting it. It was sheer luck, plus Sasha's phenomenal endurance, that it was found. He had received a huge dose. Had he died in Barnet Hospital within the first two weeks, his death would have been attributed to thallium, meaning that anyone could have given it to him.

The irony is that once it *was* detected, polonium became a smoking gun. No amateur killer—even one awash with money—could have used it.

For a freelance killer, polonium in the amounts involved in the attack on Sasha would be impossible to obtain. Polonium is a highly controlled substance made in nuclear labs for use in devices eliminating static electricity, in which it is contained in tiny amounts. According to Dr. John Harrison of the Health Protection Agency, Sasha had received a dose of at least 3 gigabecquerels of radioactivity, which is equal to about a hundred lethal doses. To obtain this amount of polonium from the end product available on the market, one would have to purchase hundreds of recently manufactured static-electricity devices and develop a technology for extracting, concentrating, and handling polonium, which would be virtually impossible for an amateur freelancer.

Any perpetrator who came up with the idea of employing polonium for a sinister purpose would necessarily have to have a high level of sophistication and knowledge of physics, medicine, and radioactive surveillance procedures, not to mention an understanding of polonium's production and distribution. All in all, it would have required a touch of genius, combined with tremendous resources—

and access to polonium in the first place—to develop a murder plan of this sort on an ad hoc basis. Only an established organization with expertise in the area of science-based poisoning could have perpetrated this crime.

Ninety-seven percent of the known production of polonium, about 85 grams annually, takes place in Russia. Some is exported for industrial use, primarily to the United States. The Russian nuclear reactor that produces polonium is subject to International Atomic Energy Agency (IAEA) safeguards, such that each production cycle is supposed to be logged and recorded, although the IAEA does not register polonium per se.

In a story on December 18, 2006, the Russian Web site Gazeta.ru quoted Ekaterina Shugaeva, press secretary of Techsnabexport, the only Russian company officially licensed to transport and export Polonium-210. "Polonium is extremely complex in production and handling," she said. "This capability exists only at Sarov [a nuclear facility at an old Soviet weapons lab, near the city of Samara]. No one else has the expertise to produce it." According to Shugaeva, the production cycle starts with the neutron bombardment of bismuth (a metal) at the Ozersk nuclear reactor, near the city of Chelyabinsk. From there, the half-product is transferred to the Sarov facility. There, the polonium is purified from the bulk of bismuth, enriched, and packed. Polonium-210 is produced in a monthly cycle and is dispensed in capsules, which are placed into sealed containers. The containers are then exported to customers in the United States via an air cargo terminal in St. Petersburg. One hundredth-of-a-gram capsule of freshly produced polonium contains five thousand lethal doses.

When Polonium-210 decays—its half-life is 138 days, meaning that half of any given amount decays in the first 138 days, followed by a fourth in the next 138 days, and so on—it turns into lead, a nonradioactive metal. As the amount of polonium decreases, the amount of lead increases. By measuring the proportion of lead in a sample of polonium, an investigator can figure out how old the sample is and establish the precise date it was produced. Moreover, the production process leaves characteristic isotope impurities in every batch. By comparing the lead content and the impurities present in two samples of polonium, an investigator should be able to say whether they came from the same batch, produced in the same laboratory on the same day.

Samples of Russian polonium have presumably been available to British law enforcement from American sources. The Polonium-210 found in Sasha's body has by now undoubtedly been checked against the Polonium-210 exported to the United States. From the level of lead and the isotope composition, the investigators should have been able to unequivocally establish the batch and production date of the poison—unless, of course, it originated from an illicit reactor, which is not subject to the IAEA safeguards.

By early spring 2007, the British authorities had not yet released any information related to the polonium source. But there is little doubt that physicists in the British nuclear facilities, working with spies in the British secret services, know exactly where and when the exotic nuclear poison that killed Sasha was produced.

———

Polonium, once it has been identified, is a detective's dream. Like an invisible dye it marks everything it touches, and it cannot be washed off. Once the right equipment is used, traces of polonium are detectable in a dilution as unimaginably weak as a millionth-of-a-millionth part. If someone, say, turns on a light in a hotel room with a contaminated hand, the light switch will be radioactive for months. From the amount and distribution of radioactivity on an armchair, an investigator can tell whether it was the right or the left hand that left the trace, and whether the hand was contaminated from the outside or the radioactivity came from the tiny droplets of sweat of someone who ingested the poison. In other words, traces left by a perpetrator and a victim are distinguishable from each other.

The Scotland Yard detectives uncovered several polonium trails in and out of London. Again, no official information has been released as this book goes to press. However, enough has been leaked from reliable sources to London newspapers to reconstruct a more or less complete picture, and the investigators essentially confirmed these leaks to Marina.

Within hours of Sasha's death, HPA radioactivity hunters identified and closed off several contaminated sites in London, including Itsu, the sushi restaurant on Piccadilly where Sasha met Mario Scaramella, and the bar in the Millennium Hotel where he had tea with the Russians. As the investigation progressed, they added dozens of other places to the polonium map; the eventual list included offices, restaurants, hotel rooms, homes, cars, and airplanes in several countries. Hundreds of people all over Europe showed varying degrees of polonium contamination, spreading from the epicenter of the "tiny nuclear bomb" exploded in London. When the dust settled, the investigators had a pretty complete understanding of how to read the map. As the Scotland Yard liaison officer told Marina, "We know exactly who did it, where, and how."

One of the polonium trails uncovered was left by Sasha. On the morning of November 1, 2006, he was clean. Detectives discovered a ticket in his pocket that led them to the bus that he took to Central London that day. No traces of polonium were found on the bus.

At about 6 p.m. Akhmed Zakayev picked him up from Boris's Mayfair office to bring him home to Muswell Hill. After that trip, Zakayev's Mercedes was rendered unusable by the tremendous amount of radioactivity Sasha left on the front seat.

Apparently the poisoning occurred in the Millennium Hotel bar, at around 5 p.m. Investigators found the teapot that was laced with the poison, which in turn contaminated the kitchen, including the dishwashing machine. The concentration of polonium at the hotel bar was apparently the highest of all, and it was airborne—indicating that the powder had been slipped into the pot of tea—because seven workers in the bar and several patrons tested positive for polonium.

Between the Millennium bar and the time Zakayev picked him up, Sasha stopped at Boris's office, where he used the fax machine. Accordingly, some radioactivity was found on the machine.

Everything that he touched after returning home was heavily contaminated. The amount of radioactivity shed during the first three days of his illness—that is, before he was taken to the hospital—was enormous. According to an early estimate, it would cost more than £100,000 ($200,000) to clean the house to make it safe to reinhabit. Six months later, Marina and Tolik were still unable to return home.

Of all the people who were in contact with Sasha, Marina was the most exposed, since she cared for him and cleaned up during the three days of extensive vomiting. She tested positive for ingesting polonium—thankfully, not enough to cause an immediate health hazard. Remarkably, her levels were not even high enough to leave their own secondary trail. This is significant because it suggests that anyone who did leave a radioactive polonium trail did not pick up the poison from Sasha. Most likely, such a person was in direct contact with polonium himself. Tolik, who stayed in the same house for three days but had much less physical contact with his father, has not been contaminated at all.

Apart from Sasha, only two people left polonium trails: Andrei Lugovoy and his associate, Dmitry Kovtun, Lugovoy's school friend and army buddy and a veteran of GRU army intelligence in his own right. Kovtun accompanied Lugovoy to two meetings with Sasha, on October 16 and November 1.

The levels and spread of radioactivity they left behind suggest that they handled polonium directly, rather than ingesting it, because there were significant traces of radioactivity. The body dilutes polonium before excreting it in sweat; the amounts that would have had to be ingested to produce traces equal to those of Lugovoy and Kovtun would almost certainly be lethal.

When Scotland Yard releases its computer-aided simulations of radioactivity spread, it will be possible to say exactly where and how the poison was handled before it ended in Sasha's teapot. What can be said at this point is that Lugovoy and Kovtun were shedding radioactivity *before* Sasha was exposed on November 1. For example, Lugovoy contaminated the leather sofa in Boris's study when he visited him on October 31. On his way to London on October 28–31, Kovtun left a trail of polonium in Hamburg, Germany, in the apartment of his ex-wife, where he stayed, and in the car that drove him to the airport.

Both men left behind a trail of polonium on their previous visit to London, on October 16–17: in hotel rooms, offices, restaurants, and on the British Airways plane that took them back to Moscow. It was during that visit that they contaminated the Itsu sushi restaurant on Piccadilly, the one that Sasha and Mario Scaramella also visited on the day of his poisoning. That coincidence was the source of much initial confusion until it was established that on November 1 Sasha and Scaramella sat at a different table than the one occupied by Lugovoy, Kovtun, and Sasha two weeks earlier.

What Lugovoy and Kovtun were doing with polonium in London during the October 16 visit is a mystery. One hypothesis is that there were two attempts to put polonium into Sasha's meal; the first one, possibly at Itsu, did not work out, so the assassins came back for a second attempt, which succeeded. Another hypothesis is that the October 16 meeting was a dress rehearsal.

For me, there is yet another possibility: that Lugovoy and Kovtun botched the operation on October 16, missed their target, yet contaminated themselves; in short, they screwed up. So for the second attempt, their handlers sent a professional killer, "the third man." The two hapless agents served only to bring the hit man into contact with the target. This third-man theory has been promoted in the press by the ex-spy Oleg Gordievsky, who quotes his own anonymous sources. There was a "tall man with Asian features" who accompanied Dmitry Kovtun on the flight from Hamburg on October 31. He was captured by airport surveillance cameras and then vanished without a trace. The passport he used to enter Britain was from a European country, but the investigators were unable to trace him to any hotel or to any flight leaving the country.

The police never gave Marina any hint in support of the third-man theory, but they have not disputed it, either. It is consistent with what Sasha told me and others: Lugovoy brought along a man whom Sasha had never seen before and who had "the eyes of a killer."

Finally, there was yet another man, Vladislav Sokolenko, who was hanging around with Lugovoy and Kovtun on November 1. His role is unclear, although he apparently was not contaminated by polonium.

There is no doubt that many questions will be answered in court—*if* the perpetrators are brought to trial. If the Crown Prosecution Service concludes that the perpetrators cannot be realistically apprehended, the police may still release the file. Then we would see not only the detailed

polonium maps, but also the record of the minute-by-minute movements of Sasha, Lugovoy, and Kovtun through the streets of Central
London, which are fully covered by CCTV surveillance cameras.

The story would be incomplete without considering a few alternative
murder theories, which have been discounted after the polonium
trails told their tales.

First, there was Mario Scaramella, a hapless political consultant
who happened to be in the wrong place at the wrong time. His relation to Sasha had to do with a squabble in Italian politics about some
old and unproven allegations that the Italian prime minister Romano
Prodi had been a KGB spy since the cold war. Back in 2004 Sasha
told the Italian parliamentary commission investigating those rumors
that once he had overheard his mentor General Trofimov referring to
Prodi as "our man." The conversation with Trofimov, however, took
place in 2000, after the Prodi-KGB scandal broke out in Italy in October 1999. So Trofimov could have been only repeating hearsay. In any
case, it is unlikely that someone would deploy polonium in 2006 to
kill Sasha for an inconsequential statement he made in 2004.
Scaramella tested positive for polonium, but only in minute amounts.

Then there was Yulia Svetlichnaya, a Russian graduate student in
Britain who briefly made headlines by claiming that Sasha had
planned to blackmail a "Russian oligarch," not Berezovsky, who
"had a connection with the Kremlin, a connection with Putin."
Svetlichnaya had met Sasha while doing research for her book and he
had corresponded with her.

There were numerous suggestions that Sasha's former colleagues
in the URPO or some other rogue elements among present or former
FSB officers had a motive for killing him. This theory became particularly popular when it was reported that a Russian Spetsnaz commando unit was using Sasha's image for target practice.

There was also a report by Yuri Shvets, another former KGB
officer living in Washington, that Sasha had been compiling a file on
a "prominent Kremlin figure" as part of a due diligence research for
a commercial client.

All these theories suffer from two faults: they fail to explain access to polonium and the involvement of Andrei Lugovoy.

To my mind, no midlevel rogue officer, no hired hand, no hastily assembled hit squad could possibly get unauthorized access to the material, which, after all, is as suitable for a massive terror attack as any weapon of mass destruction: Polonium-210 is more toxic than anthrax and as good for making a dirty bomb as plutonium. Only the top levels of the Russian government should have access to it. And I am convinced that in the Russian government, all matters related to the London dissident group are personally controlled by the president. The London operation simply could not have been authorized without his knowledge.

Likewise, only a very persuasive argument could have brought Andrei Lugovoy into the project. After all, he is not a poor man, but worth somewhere around $20 to $25 million; he would not have done it for money. He did not have any motive to kill Sasha. Only a very powerful interest could have convinced him to get involved.

Why would anyone go to such lengths to kill a man living in a rented house in Muswell Hill? Here I agree with Putin: whatever Sasha had done or would do was not worth the trouble. He was not the ultimate target; his death was a means to an end. A very important end that justified the awesome means. There is only one credible murder motive—the one that Lord Tim Bell named even before Polonium-210 and Andrei Lugovoy became part of the equation: to pin a murder on the other side in the unending contest of wills between Putin and Berezovsky.

Regardless of Scotland Yard's confidence that they know "who did it, where, and how," they are unlikely to ever see their suspects in court. Lugovoy and Kovtun will never talk because they will never be extradited. That much, Russia's prosecutors have already told the British. Instead of assisting the British investigation, the Russian government has been pursuing its own.

The Russian probe is designed as a mirror image of the British: there are detectives, witnesses, suspects, and a working theory, which balance everything that the Brits have to offer. Every British finding has a Russian counterfinding, every statement a counterstatement. Even the rhetoric is reciprocal. The Russians are using classic disinformation tactics, which are as reminiscent of the old KGB style as is the murder itself. The Kremlin-controlled press blasts the Western media for a cold war–style propaganda campaign.

As was outlined in a *New York Times* interview of Kovtun and Lugovoy published on March 18, 2007, the Russian countertheory regards them, not as perpetrators, but as "an injured party," the victims of a murder attempt with polonium that occurred during their first visit to London on October 16. After being contaminated, they claimed, they carried traces of polonium back to Moscow, and then again to London on their second visit. In the Russian frame of reference, the reciprocal pair of suspects are Zakayev and Berezovsky.

In April 2007 Russian investigators flew to London to question Boris and Akhmed, balancing Scotland Yard's visit to Moscow to interview Lugovoy and Kovtun in December 2006. If and when the Brits indict the two Russians in Sasha's murder, the Russians are likely to retaliate by charging Boris and Zakayev with an attempt on Kovtun. Because the case will never go to court, the question of who killed Sasha will never be officially resolved. The press will keep presenting a "balanced" view. Without a judicial conclusion, Sasha's murder will turn into a zero-sum game between two conflicting conspiracy theories, each the mirror image of the other. On the two ends of the hall of mirrors—with Sasha's body in the center—are the two main protagonists of this story, Boris and Putin, one the nemesis of the other. One of them did it. The choice is in the eye of the beholder.

A friend of mine who lives in Moscow said, "For you it's Putin, which is understandable because you work for Boris and live in the West. But I live in Moscow and Putin is my president. Not just a president, but someone who, rightly or wrongly, is adored and revered by most of the people. He restored our national pride and self-confidence. He is like the queen of England. If I imagined for a moment that he is the murderer, I couldn't live in this country. So it simply must be Boris, regardless of what evidence you produce. Boris is *supposed* to be vile."

My friend represents a better part of Russia, its conscientious class. He wants to believe it was Boris. The majority, I am sure, are the opposite: they want to believe it was Putin—and they are proud of him for it. Litvinenko, in their view, was a traitor, and the president got him. With polonium. Serves him right. That's what *vlast* should be: awesome.

———

A remarkable case in point illustrates the depth of the self-delusion of the Russian educated class with regard to their *vlast*. Yegor Gaidar is the former prime minister who, along with Chubais, was the architect of the economic reforms in Russia early in Yeltsin's presidency. Gaidar, an internationally respected figure, is presently a director of an economic think-tank in Moscow. He happened to be in Ireland at the time of Sasha's death, attending a conference at the National University of Ireland in Maynooth. In what was perhaps the most bizarre, albeit underreported, twist of the Litvinenko affair, on the morning of November 24, Gaidar was poisoned too.

Here is how he described what happened to him in a December 7, 2006, letter to the *Financial Times*, entitled "How I was poisoned and why Russia's political enemies were surely behind it."

"After I crossed the threshold of the conference hall, I collapsed in the university hallway," Gaidar wrote. "I can remember very little about the events of the following several hours. Those who tended to me as I lay on the floor found me bleeding from the nose, with blood and vomit flowing from my mouth. I was pale, unconscious. It appeared as though I was dying."

After spending a night in an Irish hospital, Gaidar insisted on returning to Moscow, where he underwent a thorough checkup. His "doctor was unable to explain such large-scale and systemic changes in the body [by] illnesses known to medicine, nor any of their most exotic combinations." Gaidar is sure that he was poisoned, and that he would have died had he collapsed fifteen minutes earlier, when he was alone in his hotel room.

"Who of the Russian political circle needed my death on the 24th of November 2006, in Dublin?" he wrote. "I rejected the idea of complicity of the Russian leadership almost immediately. After the death of Alexander Litvinenko on November 23 in London, another violent death of a famous Russian on the following day is the last thing that the Russian authorities would want. . . . Most likely that means that some obvious or hidden adversaries of the Russian authorities stand behind the scenes of this event, those who are interested in further radical deterioration of relations between Russia and the West."

In his letter Gaidar stopped short of naming the "adversaries of the Russian authorities." But later, several Russian Web sites published a facsimile of a letter sent by Gaidar to none other than George Soros, apparently in response to his get-well wishes. The "Dear George" fax was dated November 29, 2006. It named Boris Berezovsky as a suspect behind Gaidar's poisoning. Gaidar asks Soros to "remind [Western] public opinion" about "who we are dealing with" in Boris.

"His main goal today is to make trouble for V. V. Putin, to undermine his regime," wrote Gaidar. "His means [to that end] is harming Russia's relations with the West.

"As someone who is not much of a friend with the Kremlin," argued Gaidar, Soros would be "particularly effective" in smearing Boris. He suggested that in doing so Soros should allege Boris's "cooperation with international terrorism."

The publication of the leaked letter to Soros caused a storm in the liberal camp. Most commentaries urged Gaidar to disavow it as a fabrication. But Gaidar remained silent. Eventually Soros's office in New York confirmed to a reporter, without comment, the receipt of the letter.

In early April 2007, in the departure hall of Berlin Airport, I bumped into Katya Genieva, a prominent liberal figure in Moscow who had accompanied Gaidar to the Dublin conference. I was curious to learn more. Is it possible that Gaidar had simply had a stomach bug and made a fool of himself over nothing?

"Good Lord, Alex! How could you say that?" responded Katya in horror. "He nearly died. I was poisoned too."

It turned out that she was having breakfast with Gaidar that morning. Apparently she got a much lower dose, and her symptoms were milder, but she was very ill for four months and her own doctors believe that she had been poisoned by an unknown substance. She had no doubt it was an attempted assassination. She also confirmed the authenticity of the Soros letter.

"Is it possible that Gaidar was blackmailed by the Kremlin into smearing Boris?" I wondered.

"Of course not," said Katya. "Yegor Timurovich really believes Berezovsky is behind it."

———————

I agree with Gaidar on one thing. His poisoning was related to Sasha's and was meant to reinforce its public effect. There are only two theories worthy of consideration explaining these events, and two principal suspects. If one of them is not the murderer, the other is. The problem is, as far as I am concerned, only one theory stands up to scrutiny of the facts.

———————

Moscow April 16–17, 2007: Thousands of protesters battle riot police in the streets of Moscow and St. Petersburg in two days of anti-Putin demonstrations. The White House calls the Russian authorities' reaction "heavy-handed." Observers note that the disturbances may be a prelude to a bloodless revolution of the kind that toppled governments in Ukraine and Georgia. "Previously, the CIA would channel money to opposition forces in the countries. . . . Now opposition forces are being financed through a system of various institutions and foundations. This probably explains why such organizations have been mushrooming in this country," observes ex-Soviet leader Mikhail Gorbachev.

———————

London, April 19, 2007: In a letter to Home Secretary John Reid, Yuri Fedotov, the Russian ambassador to the United Kingdom, urges the British government to take immediate action over Boris Berezovsky's recent comments calling for the overthrow of the Putin regime. "The absence of a reaction would have some impact on bilateral relations," the letter warns. A copy of a warrant for Bere-zovsky's arrest, signed by the Russian prosecutor general Yuri Chaika, is also enclosed.

Writing about death, it's impossible not to think about one's own mortal self. Sasha died before my eyes the most horrible death imaginable, long, torturous, and inescapable. Visions of atomic annihilation—from the mushroom cloud of Hiroshima to the fallout of Chernobyl, which haunted my generation, turning millions into neurotics—came back to me as I watched him fading away. He had no chance from the instant he swallowed that tea: the doctors said that he received a dose equivalent to being in the epicenter of the Chernobyl catastrophe *twice*. All of those who were there *once* died within two weeks. His case will make medical history as the only instance of exposure to such a high dose of radiation from within: the initial gastric and intestinal symptoms; then a latent period of comparative well-being, referred to as the "walking ghost" phase, when the body's cells, devoid of functioning DNA, continue running by inertia, until all organs and systems start failing one by one. The worst possible way to die.

And yet, for all I know, it is hard to imagine a more meaningful and "rewarding" end, if one can apply these notions to death at all. Sasha, an oper par excellence, solved his murder by naming the perpetrators and the man who sent them on the job, even before the critical evidence arrived or the murder weapon was recovered. A consummate conspiracy theorist, not only did he offer one of the most incredible theories of all, but in his death he managed to offer the most compelling proof. By doing so he gave credence to all his previous theories, delivering justice for the tenants of the bombed apartment blocks, the Moscow theater-goers, Yushenkov, Schekochihin, and Anna Politkovskaya, and the half-exterminated nation of Chechnya, exposing their killers for the whole world to see.

ACKNOWLEDGMENTS

This book would not have been possible without the enthusiasm, acumen, and diligent help of Bruce Nichols of Free Press, who gave his heart and wisdom to our frenzied endeavor and nursed it chapter by chapter, making it a truly collaborative effort. Others at Simon & Schuster on both sides of the Atlantic, particularly Judith Hoover, our liaison with the English language, and everyone else on the production team have done their utmost to bring this project to completion against a deadline that many said was impossible to meet. Our agent and steward in the unfamiliar undertaking of authorship, the magnificent Ed Victor, proved every bit true to his reputation as a legend in the industry. There are several sources and friends who opted for not being mentioned by name, for obvious reasons. We are indebted to them all and, of course, to all those who provided information and are quoted in the book.

We are blessed with wonderful friends—the Zakayev and Berezovsky families, George Menzies and Jane, Olga Konskaya and Andrei Nekrasov, Nikolai Glushkov and Yuli Dubov, Lord Tim Bell and Jennifer Morgan—who stood by Sasha in his final fight and who helped and looked after Marina during these arduous times. Oleg Gordievsky and Vladimir Bukovsky deserve special praise for their friendship and insight.

Valter and Zinaida were there for Marina when she needed them most, and Valentina was her true friend in need. Alex would not have survived these months if not for shelter and amenities provided by Anukampa and Timosha.

ACKNOWLEDGMENTS

Marina is especially thankful to Jay and Colin of the Metropolitan Police and Giacomo Croci for being her guardian angels.

Most of all we are grateful to Svetlana, who was there all the way from Antalya to Highgate, and to Tolik, for being his mother's source of comfort, strength, and hope.

INDEX

INDEX

INDEX

INDEX

INDEX

ABOUT THE AUTHORS

ALEX GOLDFARB, PH.D., was a dissident scientist who left Russia in the 1970s, joining the faculty of Columbia University. After the Soviet Union collapsed in 1991, he went to work for U.S. philanthropist George Soros directing charitable initiatives in Russia. He befriended Alexander Litvinenko in the 1990s. They became close when Goldfarb accompanied the ex-spy and his family in their dramatic escape to freedom in 2000. Goldfarb later helped Litvinenko work on his memoirs and supported his efforts to expose the abuses of the newly ascendant FSB. Goldfarb is currently the executive director of the International Foundation for Civil Liberties, set up by Boris Berezovsky as an umbrella group for human-rights activists.

MARINA LITVINENKO first met Alexander at her thirty-first birthday party, in 1993, when he was a young officer in the FSB. They married and she gave birth to a son soon thereafter. In 2000, the three of them sought asylum in the United Kingdom, and she continues to live in London with her twelve-year-old son.